10.93

Essay Index

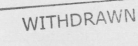

Brave Ships
of
England and America

By
Joseph Leeming

Illustrated by
Grattan Condon

Essay Index

Essay Index Reprint Series

BOOKS FOR LIBRARIES PRESS
FREEPORT, NEW YORK

STANDARD BOOK NUMBER:
8369-0024-3

LIBRARY OF CONGRESS CATALOG CARD NUMBER:
68-58801

PRINTED IN THE UNITED STATES OF AMERICA

"As concerning ships, it is that which everyone knoweth and can say, they are our weapons, they are our ornaments, they are our strength, they are our pleasures, they are our defense, they are our profit; the subject by them is made rich, the Kingdom through them, strong; the Prince in them is mighty; in a word, by them, in a manner, we live, the Kingdom is, the King reigneth."

To Nell and Paul Curtis

Who made each voyage and fought each battle.

Contents

vii

Contents

1

The Thomas

King Edward III's Flagship at the Battle of Sluys

ALFRED the Great, who built a fleet of small ships to guard the English coast against the Norse and Danish pirates, is known as the founder of the British navy. Some centuries later in the reign of King John, another navy, composed of merchant ships from Dover and the south-eastern ports, was assembled and used to good purpose against the French. Under William Longsword, the king's half-brother, this fleet in the year 1213 destroyed a French fleet that had been assembled on the coast of the Netherlands to carry an invading army to England. Four years later Hubert de Burgh, Governor of Dover Castle, defeated another attack on England by hastily improvising a fleet and driving off the French squadron that was attempting to gain the English coast-line.

It was Edward III, however, who used the navy to such good purpose that his quarrel with France was fought out, not on English soil, but on the continent, and through this shrewd and skilful use of sea-power became the real founder of the naval might and tradition of England.

The battle of Sluys has been called the sea-fight that inaugurated the long and victorious career of the British navy. It was, in truth, the greatest naval battle in which the English had up to that time engaged; and it was a magnificent victory, not only because it overwhelmed the enemy, but in its more far-reaching results. By giving King Edward undisputed command of the channel, it made possible his successful invasion of France and secured for England the possession of Calais. With both Dover and Calais in their control, the English were the masters of the narrow strait of Dover through which all the sea-borne trade between northern Europe and the rest of the world had to pass. Whenever they wished, they could halt the stream of merchant ships and in this way bring pressure to bear on any of the powers that showed signs of unfriendliness, whether the German cities of the Hanseatic League, the wealthy merchants of the Low Countries, or the traders of Genoa, Spain and Venice. It was largely as a result of this dominant position on the straits that the King of England was the "Sovereign of the Seas," and that every foreign vessel was obliged to lower her topsails and salute any "King's ship" she met passing through the English Channel.

All these powers and advantages were the outcome of the battle of Sluys and the good work done on that day by the King's ship *Thomas* and her supporters. To the English, this battle was one of the first real lessons in the strength and invincibility that spring from mastery of the seas.

It was in 1340 that King Edward III claimed the title of King of France and prepared to attain his kingship by conquest. There was at that time no Royal navy, so when Edward declared war he was obliged to assemble a fleet. First, there were a few "King's ships," and during times of peace the king hired them out to merchants. When he

2

called them back to serve in the navy, he took the crews into his pay, and filled the ships with knights and fighting men. Other ships were obtained from the merchants of London and other ports, and a third group of vessels came from the famous Cinque Ports. Under their charters they were granted certain valuable privileges in return for which they were obliged to provide the king, whenever he called upon them, with fifty-seven ships and twelve hundred men and boys for fifteen days free of all cost. At the end of this period, if the king still required the ships, he was free to use them by paying the customary rate of hire.

Edward's own ship, which carried him to victory at Sluys, was the *Thomas*. She was a cog, a type of vessel which came into extensive use at about the time that the French wars began. The largest cogs were about 250 tons burden, and it is probable that this was the size of the *Thomas*. Generally they carried two masts, a single square sail on each.

In all probability, the *Thomas* was decked over amidships to

3

provide a platform for the archers and fighting-men, while at the bow and stern there were small raised platforms for the knights. No cannon were mounted, for these were not as yet in use. The method of attack was to lie alongside the enemy, throw out grappling irons to hold the two ships together, and then board and engage in hand-to-hand fighting on deck.

King Edward's efforts to assemble a fleet made slow progress at the start and by April he had only forty ships ready and fully equipped. Gradually other ships responded to the summons and came to join the king's forces, some from the northeast coast, some from the Thames, others from Southampton and the Cinque Ports and some from as far away as Bristol. Many of the ships were very small, little more than oversized rowboats with a mast and a single sail, and for these the voyage to the rendezvous was a slow affair, since they were obliged to hug the coast and run for shelter whenever the wind freshened and the waves ran high.

By the beginning of June, King Edward's navy was assembled and ready to set out for the Low Countries where the French fleet was reported to be assembled in the harbor of Sluys, a small fishing village, northeast of Bruges. All told, the English fleet numbered two hundred ships, ranging from big cogs like the *Thomas* down to small open sailing boats. The king's army now went on board the ships, many of the barons taking their heavy war horses, to be used if a landing were made and the French army offered opposition. Every ship was crowded to the gunwales with a closely-packed mass of men, knights and nobles in shining armor and plumed helmets, yeomen, archers and billmen in stout leather jerkins and close-fitting steel caps, armed with the English long-bow or with a "bill," a wicked weapon, which was a combined pike and battle-axe.

At the mastheads of the ships floated the brightly colored banners of the knights and barons who commanded their complements, and on the *Thomas* and the ships of the principal commanders there were trumpeters whose loud blasts were to give the signal for battle.

Spread far and wide over the sea like a great flock of sea-birds, with their multitudinous white sails gleaming in the sunshine, the two hundred ships sailed away to the southward, keeping close to the land and anchoring as darkness fell each night. After reaching the North Foreland and allowing the stragglers to come up, the fleet struck eastward toward the Flemish coast, arriving off Blankenberghe during the forenoon of June 23rd. Here they were joined by a further fifty English ships under the command of Admiral Sir Robert Morly. When the ships had anchored, Edward sent three of his knights ashore with their horses. Riding to the eastward over the sand dunes, they reached a point where, unobserved, they could get a good view of the enemy's fleet. Upon their return, they reported that the French were still at Sluys, six or seven miles away, and that they appeared to have about three hundred ships, several of exceptional size.

From fishermen Edward obtained further information as to the strength and disposition of the French vessels. The fleet was commanded by two knights, the Sieur de Kiret and the Sieur de Bahuchet, who, in addition to their own ships, had a squadron of Genoese vessels commanded by Barbavera, an experienced admiral and a veteran of many Mediterranean sea-fights. The French commanders, made confident by the superior number of their ships and men, were plan-

5

ning to fight on the defensive, according to the reports received by King Edward on board the *Thomas*. They had anchored their ships in a long line close to the shore, bows pointing seaward, and had grouped them in three divisions—the left, center, and right, the latter being Genoese vessels. The ships of each division were lashed together side to side with heavy chains to prevent the English from getting in between the ships and boarding them at the waist where they were low. The French commanders believed that the only way the English could board their ships would be by climbing over the lofty bows, a difficult undertaking with all the advantage on the defenders' side. To make it even more impossible, the French had built stout barricades across the forecastle decks. Archers and Genoese cross-bowmen were stationed behind these barriers; others were in the fighting-tops on the masts, from where they could shoot down a deadly fire upon attacking soldiers below them.

The ship on the extreme left of the long French line was the *Great Christopher,* a large English vessel, captured in the Channel by the French two years before. The English were determined to get her back. Possibly her position in the line had something to do with the plan of battle King Edward prepared as soon as his knights returned and told him what they had seen. It is more likely the king detected at once the inherent weakness of the French formation, and planned his attack so as to take full advantage of it.

Led by the *Thomas,* the English great ships were to close in and concentrate upon the ships at the left of the French line. While this assault was being carried out, the French would be unable to send reinforcements because their ships were held in place by the heavy chain lashings. The very factor which the French considered their greatest strength—the forming of their fleet into an almost solid floating fortress—was thus turned into a fatal weakness. According to King Edward's plan, one ship after another, starting with the *Great Christopher,* would be overwhelmed by superior English forces. While this attack was being carried forward, the smaller English ships were to cruise back and forth in front of the French line and behind it, thus enabling their long-bowmen to pour arrows into the anchored Frenchmen, weakening them so that resistance to the oncoming ship-to-ship assault would be materially lessened.

Edward told his commanders of his plan and on the following morning he led his fleet to sea and, having arrived off the harbor of Sluys, arranged the English ships for the attack. The fleet, with its two hundred and fifty ships, was an imposing sight. Banners were flying from every masthead, and on the raised platforms at the bows and sterns of the *Thomas* and the other large ships, barons and knights with their attendant men-at-arms stood close together arrayed in complete armor, naked swords and long-handled bills gleaming in their hands. Along the bulwarks and in the fighting-tops the archers were ready with their stout long-bows and plentiful supplies of cloth-yard shafts.

Shortly before noon, when the tide started to move swiftly toward the shore, the trumpeters on the *Thomas* sounded the signal for attack. As their clarions blared out over the sea, the ships pointed toward the shore, the sailors sheeted home the bulging square sails and the fleet rushed down before the wind to fall upon the enemy.

In the van the *Thomas* and the other ships crashed down against the *Great Christopher*. Even before the ships closed and threw out their grappling irons, the English archers were at work, commencing their deadly fire when their ships came within about sixty yards of the enemy. Many aboard the French vessels at the left of the line fell mortally wounded by the English arrows which seemed to fill the air as the remaining distance between the two fleets was rapidly narrowed. The French ships' cross-bowmen replied, sending their heavy bolts whizzing through the air, but as they could not shoot as rapidly as the English, their effort did little to stop the onward charge of the *Thomas* and her sisters.

Now the leading English vessels crashed against the *Great Christopher,* and threw out their grappling irons, while the other ships of the English van swarmed about the bows of the French ships next in line, pouring in clouds of arrows at close range and trying to board. While a thousand voices shouted, "St. George for England!" knights and men-at-arms swept over the *Great Christopher's* bulwarks, hacking their way through the crowded ranks of the defenders. At the same time, King Edward drove the bow of the *Thomas* between two of the French vessels and, sword in hand, vaulted aboard one of them and commenced to lay about him like a lion. The air was filled with the vast uproar of the battle, the crashing of broadswords on helmet and breast-plate, the rallying cries of the French, and the great bull-like roaring of the English, "St. George for England!" They drove the enemy before them, first from the decks of the *Great Christopher,* then from the ships next in the line.

While the English knights and fighting-men battled slowly forward along the bridge of boats, scores of the smaller English ships sailed in behind and attacked the enemy from the rear, while the main body of the fleet still cruised along the front of the French line, pouring in arrows or driving in between the ships and engaging in hand-to-hand fighting. Soon the English archers had cleared the enemy tops of their cross-bowmen, and then from their own tops shot one flight of arrows after another into the densely packed masses of fighting men on the enemy's decks.

It was a savage struggle, for the French defended their ships with the utmost courage, ship after ship fighting to the last man to stem the progress of the English knights. At each stage of the battle, however, the English had the advantage, for each French ship was surrounded and stormed by the combined forces of several English vessels. No quarter was asked or given.

Late in the afternoon all the ships of the left and center squadrons commanded by de Kiret and de Bahuchet were captured and their crews slain or driven overboard. Then the English drove on against the great Genoese vessels of the right, commanded by Barbavera. Many of these were taken, too, but as the tide commenced to turn, King Edward gave the order to break off the attack, fearing that his large ships might go aground and be at the mercy of the enemy. The weary knights and fighting men clambered over the bulwarks of the English ships, and the fleet withdrew into deeper water. With them the English took some of the best of the captured ships, including the *Great Christopher*. Others of the French ships were set afire and as darkness descended the flames from the burning hulks illuminated the scene of the battle and the nearby low-lying coast.

During the night, Barbavera managed to slip out to sea with the ships which had not been captured or destroyed. Thankful to escape, he made his way down channel and returned to Genoa. The French fleet was utterly destroyed. Considering the savagery of the battle, the superior forces arrayed against them and the overwhelming nature of the victory, the English losses were incredibly small, amounting to about four thousand men.

The battle of Sluys, the first great victory of the British navy, gave England dominion of the seas for many years. In the long wars with France that followed, the freedom of English ships to go and come unhindered across the channel carrying troops and supplies to France was of inestimable importance to the English army. This undisputed position of mistress of the seas was won for England by the *Thomas* and the other gallant ships that carried the day at Sluys.

2

The Matthew

The First European Ship to Reach North America

SPRING was in the air and along the waterfront of Bristol, in the west of England, all was activity and bustle. Shipwrights were at work on scores of vessels, setting new rigging, fitting new spars, bending sails, caulking decks, and in all respects making the ships of the Bristol trading fleet ready for sea. Bearded mariners stalked through the streets, bringing stores aboard or intent on other business for their ships, while merchants and ship owners watched the lading of cargo and discussed the voyages in prospect and the profits they hoped to make.

One ship in particular seemed to excite the greatest interest on the part of the townspeople gathered on the quays to watch the work on the fleet. This was the *Matthew,* a caravel with high stern-castle and high-bulwarked forecastle, owned by John Cabot, the greatest Bristol merchant adventurer of the day.

Cabot himself, venerable and dignified, with white locks and long pointed white beard, was even now standing near his ship in earnest conversation with a group of his friends and fellow merchants.

"You think then, Master Cabot, you will find a shorter way to

11

the Indies than that discovered by this Italian, Columbus?" asked one of the group.

"I am sure of it, my friend," Cabot explained. "The more northerly the course followed, the shorter must be the sea-passage. The continent of Europe is much broader toward the north than toward the south, and I reason that the Asian continent is similarly shaped. It follows then, does it not, that the northern portions of the two are closer together by many hundreds of leagues. Columbus sailed to the south, where they are far apart. From Bristol I will sail to the west and north, and will come the sooner to the other shore."

"But how came you by this knowledge?" asked another.

"Many years ago, when trading with the spice merchants of Arabia, I queried them on all matters having to do with the Indies and the continent that lay to the east. From what they then told me, I came to the conclusion, long before this Columbus made his first voyage, that the spice islands of the east could be reached by sailing to the west, and that the continents were closer together at the north."

John Cabot had been much put out when word was brought to England four years before, in 1493, that Columbus had found the Indies by sailing across the Atlantic. He was a Genoese by birth, and had spent many years trading between that city and the countries bordering the eastern shores of the Mediterranean. His talks with the eastern traders, together with a careful study of the writings of Marco Polo and the theories of Ptolemy, an astronomer who lived at Alexandria in the second century A.D., had convinced him that the world was "round" and that a short route to the far east could be found by sailing westward. In short, Cabot had followed the same

reasoning as Columbus, and, at about the same time, had come to the same conclusions.

He had come to Bristol in 1489 and, from the year 1490 on, he sent out one or more expeditions each year to try to reach the continent that lay on the other side of the Atlantic Ocean. Cabot himself led several of these ventures and in 1494 he may actually have sighted the North American coast. Thus, although it is not widely known, Cabot was actively trying to find the short ocean route to the Indies at the very time Columbus was embarking on his famous first voyage. It was little wonder, then, that Cabot was annoyed when he discovered that his rival had succeeded where he had failed.

When word of the voyage of Columbus was brought to England, Cabot went to London and asked King Henry VII to give royal support to another expedition. The king quite readily gave his consent, for he did not want the Spaniards laying claim to all the newly-discovered lands with their untold resources of gold and silver, precious stones, and exotic tropic foodstuffs and spices.

Word of what' was going on came to the ears of de Puebla, the Spanish ambassador to England, and he hastily reported Cabot's plans to his masters at Madrid. On receiving Puebla's despatch, the Spanish authorities immediately sent a protest to England, pointing out that the expedition would be a violation of the papal bull of 1494, by which the Pope had divided the world to the west of Europe between Spain and Portugal.

But this message arrived too late. King Henry had already issued letters patent, authorizing his "well-beloved John Cabot" and his three sons, Lewis, Sebastian, and Sancius, "to sail to all places, countrys, and seas of the East, of the West, and of the North . . . to seek out, discover, and find whatsoever isles, countrys, regions, or provinces of the heathen and infidels, which before this time have been unknown to all Christians."

In accordance with the terms of his letters patent, Cabot had fitted out the good ship *Matthew*, and early in the year 1497, he was ready to leave on his great adventure. The *Matthew*, though a splendid ship for her day, would indeed seem small to us, for, in addition to Cabot and his son Sebastian, she carried but eighteen mariners aboard.

On a morning of early May, 1497, the *Matthew* sailed down Bristol Channel on her way to the sea. How long her voyage would be, or what would be found at the end of it, no member of the crew could tell. These sailors of old Bristol knew only that Columbus had sailed from Spain and kept on until he had come to islands never before seen by men of Europe. This, they understood, was what their commander, Master Cabot, intended to do, and, like true British sailors, they were ready to follow him loyally.

The *Matthew*

It is probable that Cabot sailed the *Matthew* across to Ireland and, after having obtained his bearings on its southwestern extremity, sailed thence along a certain degree of latitude, after the manner of the navigators of his time. With their astrolabes they could determine their latitude with a very fair degree of correctness; but longitude was another and far more difficult matter.

Westward into the unknown the little craft made its way. The weather was bright and fair, and no gales beat upon the *Matthew*. This was fortunate for it is doubtful if she could have survived a really savage north Atlantic storm. Other ships sent to the west on earlier expeditions had been sunk or driven home, shattered by the overwhelming fury of the Atlantic's mighty waves.

According to Sebastian Cabot, the voyagers "sailed happily" as, day after day, they beat steadily further toward the setting sun. A month went by; May ended; the first half of June went by; still there was no sight of land. We do not know whether Cabot's sailors, like those of Columbus, had thoughts of mutiny bred by fear that they would sail over the edge of the world. It is probable, however, that they were confident in their leader and were of good cheer and stout of heart.

At last the great day came—the look-out man saw the dim outlines of the land. John Cabot's feelings of triumph and elation may easily be imagined. His reasoning had been correct, and there before him through the ocean mists rose the mountain peaks of the fabulous land of Cathay, the richness and splendor described by Marco Polo.

As the *Matthew* drew in toward the shore, it soon became evident that the land was of a far more stern and forbidding nature than the smiling countryside of Cathay, with its palaces and temples and fair sunlit vistas. Steep and menacing mountains rose toward a lowering northern sky, and the land that lay ahead seemed made of rock and iron. It was the island now known as Newfoundland.

A landing was made, and the men probably went ashore to explore and stretch their limbs. No detailed record has been left of what happened, but it is known that they found the island inhabited by savages clad in skins, for they captured three and took them home to England as a gift for the king, their patron. Polar bears may have been seen and possibly the great auks, birds which at one time nested in great numbers on Newfoundland's cliffs.

What John Cabot thought of his newly-discovered land, no one can say. He was convinced, however, that he had reached some part of the continent of Asia, previously visited by Marco Polo. There was one source of wealth and commerce, which may well have brought him abundant satisfaction. This was the Newfoundland fisheries.

"The sea is full of fish," wrote an Italian contemporary who talked with the Cabots after their return to England, "which are taken not only with a net but also with a basket in which a stone is put, so that the basket may plunge into the water. . . . The Englishmen, his partners, say that they can bring so many fish that the kingdom [of England] will have no more business with Islande [Iceland]."

The enormous value of these fisheries was soon proved and—what few people today realize—they yielded more wealth to England than Spain reaped from all her plunder of the gold and silver mines of the South. From 1501 onward, fleets from the southwestern ports— Bristol, Barnstaple, and Bideford, Fowey, Dartmouth, and Plymouth—

sailed regularly to Newfoundland, and year by year the product of the fisheries increased. In 1615, it was sold in England for £200,000. By 1640 its value had risen to £700,000; and by 1670 to £800,000. Spain's annual haul of treasure never reached these latter figures. For the year 1521 it was estimated at £52,000, and for the year 1545 at £630,000. That was the peak. By 1575 it had fallen to £440,000, and by the end of the century to £280,000. Thereafter the value declined rapidly, while the Newfoundland fisheries, year after year, yielded a handsome return.

Leaving Newfoundland, Cabot set the *Matthew* on a northerly course and sailed for many days along the coast of Labrador. During this part of the voyage the days grew longer and longer until a latitude was reached where there was continual daylight. Never before had the English sailors seen so weird and awesome a happening as this. Night was banished, but the dim, eerie light struck terror into their bones. Perhaps they had sailed clear out of the world they knew, and had entered some strange domain lorded over by an evil wizard? Who could tell how soon he might send his legions of demons shrieking down upon them to rend them limb from limb?

And across the sky, coming without warning, spread ghostly, lurid flames—green, red and yellow—long fringes of light spreading and blazing with an unearthly glow. At times, when these fierce devil-flames were at their highest pitch, there came a crackling, rending sound that terrified even the stoutest hearts among the crew. Was it the sinister laughter of those vast beings into whose power they had cast themselves?

Then, too, might they not sail over the northern rim of the world and drop, spinning and turning, with sickening swiftness, through endless regions of space—down, down, down—never to come to rest until they reached the very bottom of the abysmal universe.

Fear spread among the men and paralyzed their wills. Soon, floating majestically down from the north, came monstrous and glittering castles and palaces of ice, with towers and battlements of diamonds glinting like blue-white flames under the glancing rays of the sun. Were these the wizard's castles or vast engines of destruction loosed like fire ships to break their fragile craft?

Before long, the men had had enough. Terror of the unknown took possession of them. In a body they demanded that Master Cabot turn about and make sail for home. Home—in England—where there were both day and night, and warmth, and green fields, and cities and towns filled with men and women and creature comforts. Home —where they would be safe from the unknown horrors of the ice-king's wrath.

Cabot had no choice but to turn back. Southeast by south, the *Matthew* turned away and bounded down to warmer latitudes and bluer seas. Then, with sails filled by the westerly wind, she set a true course for England and the sights of home. Toward the end of July, after an absence of only three months, the *Matthew* sailed up the Bristol channel and came to anchor off the well-known foreshore of her own home port.

What an ovation the good people of Bristol gave to John Cabot, Sebastian, his son, and the stout ship *Matthew* of their port! The *Matthew's* voyage meant that Spain no longer was the only country to have a claim upon the riches of that other western world. Now

England, too, was great upon the seas and mistress of new and fabulous territories. Honors were heaped upon John Cabot; he was called Grand Admiral. "He is dressed in silk," wrote one observer, "and the English run after him like madmen."

Cabot believed he had discovered the country of Kublai Khan which, nearly two centuries before, had been visited by Marco Polo. A report of his voyage made soon after his return stated that Cabot "reports he has discovered, seven hundred leagues off, the mainland of the country of the Gran Cam [or the Grand Khan, for whom, also, Columbus was searching], and that he coasted along it for three hundred leagues, and landed, but did not see any person. But he has brought here to the King certain snares spread to take game, and a needle for making nets, and he found some notched trees, from which he judged that there were inhabitants. . . . The discoverer of these things has planted a large cross in the ground, with a banner of England."

It was not until 1498 that Columbus, on his third voyage, reached the South American mainland at the mouth of the Orinoco River. Thus, though the credit of discovering the New World belongs to Columbus and Spain, the Cross of St. George was the flag first to be unfurled on the mainland of the continent.

An even greater consequence of the *Matthew's* voyage was the planting of the flag of England on the shores of the New World. From this event came England's interest in the region discovered by Cabot, its settlement and further exploration by the English, and the whole future history of North America.

3

The Edward Bonaventure

The Ship that Opened up the Russian Trade for England

SEBASTIAN CABOT, recently appointed "Grand Pilot of England," strode restlessly up and down the long room of his London chambers, speaking forcefully and now and again striking one fist resoundingly upon the other to emphasize his words. His companions, Sir Hugh Willoughby and Captain Richard Chancellor, seated in one of the deep windows overlooking the Thames, were listening attentively and, from time to time, when Cabot made some special point, nodded their heads in agreement.

"Look you now, Sir Hugh," said Cabot, "the Spaniards guard the southern route westward to the Indies, and, as you well know, England has not sufficient strength on the seas to wrest it from them. To the south and east, around the Cape of Good Hope to India, the Portingales block our path."

"But have you given up hope entirely of finding the northwest passage to the Spice Islands?" asked Sir Hugh.

"Nay, friend, not altogether," Cabot replied. "But my voyages in that direction with my father convinced me that the difficulties would be enormous. The cold, the icebergs, the bleakness of the coast."

He halted in his pacing, and, looking squarely at his two listeners, said, "Mark my words, Sir Hugh, and you as well, Captain, there is a shorter and easier sea route to the east. And it is my intention that it shall belong to England."

Willoughby and Chancellor leaned forward eagerly, their faces lighted with surprise and interest.

"What say you, Master Cabot?" asked Chancellor. "A shorter route, and one that may belong to England? Where is this route? What shall we do to mark it out?"

"Hah! that is good!" Cabot exclaimed. "I had great hopes that it would be of concern to you. The route is there; of that I am certain. But we need men of courage to explore it and make the way for others to follow. Sir Hugh, I am wondering if you would be the leader. And, Captain Chancellor, I wish you to be pilot-major."

Both men rose to their feet, and Sir Hugh grasped Cabot by the hand.

"I know not where your route may be, good Master Cabot, or what dangers may attend it. But this I do know—that I and Chancellor would be honored to go wherever you may say."

"Good! Good! This is what I had hoped," said Cabot. "I had little fear that you would not accept, but the seas are perilous, and many a man, even of stoutest heart, fears to voyage into unknown parts."

Now Cabot explained his new route to the Indies to them.

"It is north about, mark you, but to the northeast. The ships will sail along the northern coast of Muscovy, and so come to Cathay."

All his reasons for believing this to be a shorter and easier way to

the east than the passage to the northwest were then gone into.
Following his voyages to Newfoundland and Labrador in company
with his father, Sebastian Cabot had served for thirty years as pilot-
major of Spain. During this period he had been able to learn all
that the Spaniards had discovered on their voyages to the New World,
and also what the Portuguese knew of the route to India by way of
the Cape of Good Hope, opened up in 1498 by Vasco da Gama. From
many talks with mariners, merchants and travelers who had visited
the east, he had become convinced that the northern oceans would
furnish a way thither, as well as the broader oceans of the south.

With the consent of Willoughby and Chancellor to lead the expedition, he went ahead rapidly with plans for the first voyage to the
northeast. Three ships were fitted out in the spring of 1553, the
Bona Esperanza, 120 tons, the *Edward Bonaventure,* 160 tons, and the
Bona Confidentia, 90 tons. Commanded respectively by Sir Hugh
Willoughby, Captain Richard Chancellor and Captain Cornelius Dur-
foorth, they carried crews of thirty-five, fifty, and twenty-two men. Of
the three, only the *Edward Bonaventure* survived the perils of the
northern seas and returned to England.

Cabot, the veteran mariner, supervised the fitting out of the
vessels, and, due to his wide experience, the fleet was better equipped
than any that had yet sailed from England. Particular efforts were
made to make the three ships "staunch and firm." According to a
contemporary account of the voyage: "In certain parts of the ocean a
kind of worm is bred, which many times pierceth and eateth through
the stoutest oak that is. Therefore, that the mariners, and the rest
to be employed in this voyage, might be free and safe from this danger,

they (the shipwrights) cover a piece of the keel of the ships with thin sheets of lead." Lead-sheathing had been in use in Spain for half a century, but the *Edward Bonaventure* and her consorts were the first English vessels to be so treated.

While Sir Hugh Willoughby was the leader of the expedition, Richard Chancellor, as pilot-major, held a post of very nearly equal importance. Like Martin Frobisher, Humphrey Gilbert and other well-known navigators of that period, he was a protégé of Sir Henry Sidney, father of the famous Sir Philip. The esteem in which Chancellor was held is indicated by the speech of Sir Henry to the merchants financing the expedition.

"My very worshipful friends, I cannot but greatly commend your present Godly and virtuous intention," Sir Henry declared. "But principally I rejoice in myself that I have nourished and maintained that wight (Chancellor) which is like, by some means and in some measure, to profit and stead you in this worthy action.

". . . And you are also to remember into how many perils for your sakes, and for his country's love, he is now to run. . . . We commit a little money to the chance and hazard of Fortune. He commits his life (a thing to a man of all things most dear) to the raging sea, and to the uncertainties of many dangers. . . . We shall keep our own coasts and country. He shall seek strange and unknown kingdoms. He shall commit his safety to barbarous and cruel people, and shall hazard his life amongst the monstrous and terrible beasts of the sea."

Everything was in readiness early in May, 1553, and on the twentieth of that month the three ships weighed anchor, spread their sails to the breeze and stood bravely down the Thames. As they approached Greenwich, where the Court was then staying, "the courtiers came running out, and the common people flocked together, standing very thick upon the shore. The privy council, they looked out at the windows of the Court, and the rest ran up to the tops of the towers. The ships thereupon discharged their ordinance and shot off their pieces, after the manner of war, insomuch that the tops of the hills sounded therewith, the valleys and the waters gave an echo; and the mariners, they shouted in such sort that the sky rang again with the noise thereof."

So the three ships sailed down the stream and over the horizon toward the dread unknown. Word was brought back by fishermen that they had seen them skirting the coast of Norway. Then no more was heard for many months. The story of their voyage was not received in England until Chancellor beat his way back across the North Sea late in the following year.

The vessels enjoyed a fair passage to Norway, Chancellor recounted, and, after following its coast-line, rounded the northern extremity of Europe, the North Cape, and entered the Arctic Ocean without mishap. This was in early September, four months after the departure from England. Eastward they sailed, beneath the pale gray northern skies, until a violent gale sprang up which drove the ships apart. As the tempest swept down on the little flotilla, Willoughby, "with his loudest voice," cried out to Chancellor, earnestly requesting him to stay near at hand. But the pilot-major could not comply. High seas dashed over all the ships and the wind, screaming down from the west, drove the *Bona Esperanza* far ahead of the *Edward Bonaventure*. Soon Willoughby's ship was swept "quite out of sight, and the third ship also."

The *Bona Confidentia* was never seen again. Sir Hugh, however, eventually came to a broad and protected harbor on the coast of Russian Lapland, at the mouth of the River Arzina, and, the stormy wintry season being at hand, decided to shelter there till spring. Of their fate we know nothing more than that, during the course of the winter, every man of the sixty-two died, probably of the terrible cold and the scurvy.

Few documents are more moving than the journal kept by Sir Hugh, which was found beside his frozen body by Russian fishermen who came to the harbor in the spring. Beginning with brave confidence, Willoughby wrote: "The voyage intended for the discoverie of Cathay and divers other regions unknown, set forth by the right worshipful master Sebastian Cabot." Then, after recounting the incidents of the voyage and telling of the storm and the finding of the harbor, Sir Hugh set down the words: "We sent out three men south-southwest, to search if they could find people, who went three days' journey, but could find none. After that we sent other three men westward, which returned likewise. Then sent we three men southeast three dayes journey, who in sort returned without finding of people, or any similitude of habitations."

Very different was the fate of Richard Chancellor. It was his good fortune to make a voyage which opened a new era of commerce for the English. Following the great storm, the *Edward Bonaventure* sighted land and came to anchor off a settlement which proved to be Vardo, a community of fishermen on the northeast coast of Norway. After waiting here a week, in the hope that the other two ships might arrive, Chancellor set out again, resolved "either to bring that to passe which was intended, or else to die the death."

There speaks the true British character. The daring, resolution and dauntless courage are magnificent beyond words.

Some among Chancellor's crew tried to dissuade him from pursuing the voyage. Fears beset them and they dreaded what unknown perils might lie ahead of them. But in spite of all their entreaties, they could not bend the iron will of their leader. He ordered the anchor to be weighed and the sails spread, and then resolutely "held on his course towards that unknown part of the world, and sailed so farre that hee came at last to the place where hee found no night at all, but a continuall lighte and brightnesse of the sunne shining clearly upon the huge and mighty sea."

In time the *Edward Bonaventure* entered the bleak White Sea and reached the mouth of the River Dwina, near the place where Archangel now stands. Chancellor landed and, to his immense relief, was greeted in friendly fashion by the natives, who immediately sent a courier to the Czar to notify him of the extraordinary event, the arrival of a ship from western Europe. Upon receiving the message, Ivan the Terrible at once sent a messenger inviting Chancellor to visit his court at Moscow. This was before St. Petersburg was founded, and at that time the interior of Russia was virtually unknown to Englishmen and other Europeans. To Chancellor it may well have seemed that he was reenacting some of the adventures of Marco Polo, when he entered the wilds of the vast and mysterious empire of Russia.

He has left us a vivid and entertaining account of his journey by sledge from the White Sea to Moscow, of the lavish entertainment proffered him by the Czar, and of the life at the semi-barbarous Russian court. He was very much impressed by the contrast between the squalor and coarseness of the life of the people and the wealth and sumptuousness of the court.

All in all, Russia seemed to Chancellor like "a young horse that knoweth not his strength, whom a little child ruleth and guideth with a bridle."

While Chancellor was in Moscow, the crew of the *Edward Bonaventure* had an experience of cold so terrible that it was beyond their wildest imaginings. "In their going up only from their cabins to the hatches, they had their breath often times so suddenly taken away, that they eftsoones fell down as men very neere dead, so great is the sharpnesse of that cold climate."

Throughout the long, cold winter the ship lay at anchor, swinging with the tides, beneath the Northern Lights. With the coming of spring, Chancellor made his way north from Moscow and, with joy in their hearts, the mariners spread their canvas to the breeze and set sail for England and home.

With what joy Sebastian Cabot received the news of the *Edward Bonaventure's* safe arrival can readily be imagined. Chancellor gave him a full account of the voyage, of his reception at the Russian court and of the possibilities for English trade with Russia that the venture had opened up. He brought with him a letter from Ivan the Terrible, addressed to "the most excellent King Edward VI," in which the Czar stated his willingness to trade with the English.

"If," wrote the Czar, "you will send one of your Majesty's council to treat with us, . . . your country's merchants . . . shall have their free mart with all free liberties through my whole dominions . . . to come and go at their pleasure, without any let, damage, or impediment."

This letter had been hard to obtain, for the German Hansa merchants who traded with Russia by way of the Baltic Sea and had a Russian headquarters at Novgorod had fought against it tooth and nail. For three hundred years the powerful Hanseatic League, composed of the leading merchants of a group of German cities, had enjoyed a monopoly of the rich Russian trade. Special privileges had been given to them as early as the year 1269, and thereafter they had excluded all rival foreign merchants from Novgorod, the center for the great bulk of Russia's foreign trade. Any foreign trader who succeeded in making his way to Novgorod was severely punished by these early German business men, a state of affairs which did little to gain them the good will of their rivals.

Now, Chancellor, though unsuccessful in finding a northeast passage to the Spice Islands, had broken once and for all the tight-fisted monopolistic grip of the Hansa merchants, and every Englishman rejoiced to see their power begin to wane. Russia had not been the only country whose trade the Hansa had attempted to dominate. The English had had difficulty with them in all the Baltic countries, in Scandinavia, the Netherlands, and Italy and France, where they had attempted to control all foreign trade.

Sebastian Cabot and those "certain grave citizens of London" who had financed Chancellor's expedition were quick to take advantage of the golden opportunity now brought to England. They were determined to develop the vast new market that the *Edward Bonaventure's* voyage had made accessible and to do their utmost to drive out the Hansa merchants. To this end, a company of Merchant Adventurers, the famous Muscovy Company, was founded in London for the furtherance of the Russian trade. Within a short time it developed a commerce of great value.

To Russia, the Muscovy Company's ships carried the wool, tin, oxhides, pewter and pottery that were England's staple exports of that time, and also the olive oil and wine of France and Spain, and the silks, cambrics, Turkish carpets, currants, rhubarb and spices that other English vessels had brought in from the Mediterranean and the Levant. On their homeward voyages the vessels brought Russian furs, valuable timber, and tar and pitch needed for building and caulking the ships of England's expanding merchant marine and navy. Two Russian products that the English were especially glad to get were honey and wax, both of these being of great value, as honey was then the only known means of sweetening food and wax was used in great quantities for the candles which were the universal means of illumination.

Wax was one of the most expensive commodities of those times, often costing as much as the equivalent of fifteen or twenty dollars a pound. It was frequently presented to royalty, Edward III having received one hundred pounds of wax, among other gifts, from the City of London.

The exploits of Drake, Sir Walter Raleigh, and some of the other English adventurers are better known, perhaps, than those of Richard Chancellor. The voyage of the *Edward Bonaventure,* however, was the first that brought to England that trade which was to form the basis of her future commercial greatness. It was an adventuresome voyage, but its object was not adventure. Its purpose was to win for England a position comparable to that which Columbus had given to Spain and da Gama to Portugal, and in this it succeeded. The *Edward Bonaventure's* voyage set a precedent, which others in later days were able to use as a guide, and thus win for England her envied place amongst the nations of the world.

4

The Ark Royal

Lord Howard's Flagship at the Defeat of the Armada

THE *Ark Royal* was the flagship of Lord Howard of Effingham, the commander-in-chief of the little English fleet that put to rout the great and "invincible" Spanish Armada. For the prominent part she played in one of the world's decisive battles and in shaping the destinies of England, she belongs beyond question among the famous ships of all time.

The *Ark* was originally built for Sir Walter Raleigh and was christened the *Ark Raleigh*. However, when England learned of the plans for invasion and conquest that were being made by Philip of Spain, the ship was taken over by the Elizabethan navy to serve as a man-of-war, and renamed *Ark Royal*. She was unique among the ships of her time, for she had four masts instead of the customary three.

The *Ark Royal* was a vessel of 800 tons and one of the largest English men-of-war of the period. Her armament is not known, but in all probability it consisted of about thirty-six large guns—demi-cannon, culverins or falcons—and twenty-eight small, quick-firing pieces such as fowlers, port-pieces and bases to be used mainly to repel boarders. For a complement, she carried 425 men.

Lord Howard was pleased with his flagship. Of that there is no doubt, for in a letter written shortly before the battle with the Armada, he wrote, "I protest before God and as my soul shall answer for it, that I think there were never in any place in the world worthier ships than there are for so many. And as few as we are, if the King of Spain's forces be not hundreds, we will make good sport with them. And I pray you tell her Majesty from me, that her money was well given for the *Ark Raleigh,* for I think her the odd ship in the world for all conditions. . . . We can see no sail, great nor small, but how far soever they be we fetch them and speak with them."

Philip's plans to invade England by means of the Invincible or Most Happy Armada were well known many months before the actual attempt took place. English spies, sailors serving in English merchant ships and returning travelers all brought news of the mighty fleet being assembled and of the training of troops.

When the Spanish force was ready for the attack on England—at least in respect to the number of ships and men—it was a truly formidable one. There were 128 ships—sixty-four galleons and galleasses, and eight galleys rowed by three hundred slaves each and carrying fifty guns apiece. These seventy-two vessels constituted the capital ships comparable to our present day battleships. In addition, there were fifty-six smaller vessels of different types, such as pinnaces, zabras and pataches. The officers commanding the soldiers included almost all of the nobles and knights of Spain.

To cope with the Armada, the English had assembled an imposing battle fleet of about one hundred ships—sixty-nine galleons or great ships, and the remainder pinnaces and other vessels of small dimensions. Although the English ships were somewhat smaller than the

Spanish galleons, they were swifter and more easy to handle, and, in addition, they carried much heavier guns than the Spaniards. Speed and striking power—these were the factors that were to decide the issue, even as they determine the outcome of present day naval engagements.

In this connection, it is extremely interesting to learn that the Spanish, at the time of the Armada, placed little reliance in cannon, but still aimed to lay their ships alongside the enemy, send over boarding parties, and attempt to take the vessel by hand-to-hand fighting. "The cannon was held by the Spaniards to be an ignoble arm, well enough for the beginning of the fray and to pass away the time till the moment of engaging hand-to-hand," says a Spanish historian.

The English, on the other hand, had been rapidly learning the value of staying clear of the enemy's grappling hooks and of using the great guns to sink or dismast his ships. Very few among the Spaniards realized that the great gun in the hands of the English was a terrible weapon.

When the Armada sailed from Lisbon on the twenty-eighth of May, 1588, it was a brave sight, of that you may be sure, and one that stirred the deepest emotions in all who witnessed it. The galleons, with their high sides and lofty fore and stern castles, had sails brilliantly embroidered with crosses, coats-of-arms and pictures of the saints. From their mastheads floated the banners of Spanish knights and nobles and the great red and gold standard of Spain. All the other ships were equally gay with pennants and flags, and their decks were crowded with cheering soldiers who, confident of victory, waved light-hearted farewells to those on shore.

In brave array there passed out to sea the great Armada of Portugal, commanded by the Duke of Medina Sidonia; the Armada of Biscay, under the Vice-Admiral of the fleet, Juan Martinez de Recalde; the Armada of the galleons of Castille, the Armada of Guipuzcoa, and the Armada of Andalusia.

Far to the north, under grayer skies, the *Ark Royal* and her consorts waited—grim, silent, and with terrible destructive power—ready for action whenever the time should arrive.

What with bad weather, sickness among the crews and poor navigation, it took the Armada nearly two months to make the voyage to the English Channel. At the very outset a gale and a shortage of food forced many of the ships to take refuge at Corunna. Here they stayed until the rest of the ships, scattered by the gale, put in their appearance. On July the twelfth, they left Corunna and, with a fair wind from the south, fared so well that in four days' time they were at the entrance to the English Channel.

The *Ark Royal*

Then another gale roared down upon them from the west. The high-sided, top-heavy galleons rolled helplessly in the troughs of the enormous seas that swept in from the Atlantic. The open galleys were driven to seek safety on the coast of France.

When the gale subsided the ships managed to gather together again and prepared to sail up channel. Their objective, given to them in instructions from their king, was to join forces with the Duke of Parma, who was in the Low Countries, and enable him to ferry his army across the channel in flat-bottomed boats. The combined armies were then to conquer England, and after that, Ireland.

Filled with confidence by the formidable appearance and great size of their fleet, the Spaniards surged on to the eastward. Moreover, as the day was very foggy, they believed that the English were not aware of their presence.

That night, as they passed along the south of the Cornish coast, they received a rude shock. Beacon fires blazed along the cliff tops and stretched away farther than the eye could reach. They had been discovered! The alarm had been given!

"Night sank upon the dusky beach, and on the purple sea,
Such night in England ne'er had been, nor e'er again shall be,
From Eddystone to Berwick bounds, from Lynn to Milford Bay,
That time of slumber was as bright and busy as the day;
For swift to east and swift to west the ghostly war-flame spread,
High on St. Michael's Mount it shone: it shone on Beachy Head.
Far on the deep the Spaniards saw, along each southern shire,
Cape beyond cape, in endless range, those twinkling points of fire."

Early in the morning, while it was yet dark, the Spaniards met fishing boats from Falmouth, and learned that Howard and Drake had already sailed from Plymouth to intercept the Armada. Thomas Flemyng, in Drake's old and trusted ship, the *Golden Hind,* had brought word of the Armada's arrival to Plymouth where Lord Howard and his officers were playing bowls on the Hoe. As the old story goes, all were eager to leave at once, but Drake imperturbably insisted on finishing the game, saying, "There's time for that and to beat the Spaniards after."

A few hours later the Spaniards found confirmation of the news given them by the fishermen. Shortly after daybreak on the twenty-first of July, they sighted the *Ark Royal* and ten other of the Queen's ships, beating up to westward so as to get the weather-gage. Then, in another few moments, forty ships, led by Drake in the famous *Revenge,* came into view.

Onward sailed the Armada, making no effort to maneuver for position or to stand and make ready to receive the English.

Soon Howard, having reached to windward, turned the *Ark Royal* about and started in pursuit. A glorious sight she must have been as she plunged forward over the white-cap waves before the strong wind that blew from the west. At her fore and bonaventure mizzen floated the flag of St. George of white canvas with a blood-red cross of cloth sewn on; at her mainmast was the royal standard; at her mizzen was the flag of the Tudor rose. Along her gun deck, on either side, the gunners stood ready to put their cannon into play the moment the ship was in position to open fire. Standing on the high poop deck, Howard and his officers conned the great ship and watched with satisfaction the rapidly narrowing stretch of water between them and the enemy.

Soon the English were able to open fire and their heavy guns, which hurled a larger shot a longer distance than those of the Spaniards, battered away with a will at Philip's mighty fleet. Howard, in the van, brought the *Ark Royal* alongside the Spanish flagship and blasted her high and low until he was forced to withdraw by the swarms of Spanish ships that bore up to aid their leader. Meanwhile Drake was hammering the Armada of Biscay, commanded by Recalde.

Surprised and badly frightened by the universal success of the English, the Spaniards were thrown into confusion. Many of their ships collided with each other, and one, the *San Salvador,* was torn apart by the explosion of a powder magazine and had to be abandoned. Many other Spanish ships received terrible punishment, but by stopping up the holes made by the English shot they were still able to maintain their places in the line.

That night Lord Howard appointed Drake to keep in touch with the enemy, guiding the remainder of the fleet by the big poop lantern of the *Revenge.* The *Ark Royal* dropped astern and took up station in the van of the English forces. All went well until Drake, peering through the darkness ahead, saw that one of the enemy's big ships was straggling behind the Armada. The desire to capture her was overwhelming. Not wishing to share his prize with others, he turned to one of the sailors on the quarter-deck.

"Put out the poop lantern," he ordered.

Then he steered the *Revenge* close aboard the Spaniard, taking her completely by surprise, boarded her with pike and musket and took her captive. He put a prize crew aboard and sent her into Dartmouth. Then he hastened to overtake the *Ark Royal*. Lord Howard, while gratified at the capture of so large a vessel, was far from pleased with Drake's conduct, for the extinguishing of the *Revenge's* lantern had caused great confusion among the English ships.

During the next day the two fleets moved slowly on up the channel, keeping in touch but not coming into action. On the following day, however, there was a terrific engagement as the fleets were passing Portland Bill. According to Hakluyt, it was "the most furious and bloodie skirmish of all."

In the night Lord Howard had driven ahead of the other English ships and, when morning broke, the *Ark Royal* was almost alone among the enemy. Nothing daunted by his exposed position, Lord Howard commenced to fire upon the nearest ships, and soon was joined by others of the fleet. With guns blazing to keep the Spaniards at bay, the *Ark Royal* led her consorts toward the Dorset coast in order to drive the Spanish ships toward mid-channel and prevent a possible landing. Coming close to the land and baffled for want of sea room, the English ships were forced to tack and were closed by the enemy in the act of going about.

"We have them! The English dogs! They are trapped!" the Spaniards could be heard shouting exultantly.

On drove the galleons to the kill, their crews cheering and shouting, drums and trumpets sounding above the booming of the guns. With straining sails and plunging bows, the great ships beat the waters aside. A few moments more and they would run down and sink the more lightly built English vessels.

The *Ark Royal*

In this moment the fortunes of England hung in the balance. In this moment the history of the world might have been altered.

Suddenly, when all seemed lost, the fortune of the English changed. The galleons were nearly upon them—and the wind shifted. The great white sails of the English ships filled and tugged at their straining sheets; one by one the *Ark Royal, Revenge, Victory* and the others gathered momentum, and with high-pitched bowsprits pointing seaward, slipped out from under the enemy's bows, pouring in so devastating a fire as they passed that the Spanish ships were forced to turn away.

All through the morning and the long summer afternoon the battle raged furiously to the deafening roar of the great guns' thunder. The fiercest encounter was begun toward mid-afternoon. The *Ark Royal,* with the *Revenge, Lion, Victory, Dreadnought* and *Mary Rose* near at hand, drove into the thick of the Spanish main body and fought more savagely than in any encounter yet waged against the Armada. Within pistol shot of the enemy, the flagship laid about her as though her men had gone berserk. According to those who took part in the battle, the great ship appeared to be everywhere. Now forging ahead through her own gun smoke to plunge into the melée and aid some hard-pressed consort, now ranging up alongside some towering galleon or low many-oared galley and firing salvo after salvo at point-black range, she battered the enemy until the afternoon sun was nearing the horizon. Many a galleon tried to close and board, but all were driven back with splintered bulwarks and shattered side-planking.

The action off Portland was followed by a comparatively quiet day, but another engagement took place off the Isle of Wight on the next day. It began by the English very nearly succeeding in cutting off the Spanish galleasses. Closing in, the English blazed away with ear-splitting broadsides which brought masts and spars cascading down on the Spaniards' decks, and battered many a gaping hole in their wooden sides.

The fight with the galleasses, Lord Howard tells us, "continued a long time and much damaged them, so that one of them was fain to be carried away upon the careen and another by a shot of the *Ark* lost her lantern which came swimming by, and a third his nose. There were many good shots made by the *Ark* and the *Lion*."

Before the action could be completed, however, the main fleet of the Armada crowded around the English, and they were forced to draw away, for they had used up all the ammunition they could spare. There was nothing for them to do but follow and watch the Spaniards, who were anxious to reach their rendezvous with the Duke of Parma. During this lull in the fighting, Lord Howard called a number of his captains and subordinates on board the *Ark Royal*, where he knighted them for the bravery and daring they had shown during the pursuit.

On the evening of the twenty-seventh of July, the Armada anchored off Calais, and the English watch-dogs, following them in, also came to anchor a cannon-shot distant to windward. To add to the uneasiness of the Spaniards, a squadron of thirty ships, which had been watching for Parma off Dover, arrived between seven and eight o'clock in the evening.

On board the ships of the Armada the feeling spread that some great catastrophe was about to come to pass. "We rode there all night at anchor," wrote one of the Duke of Medina Sidonia's officers, "with the enemy half a league from us likewise anchored, being resolved to wait, since there was nothing else to be done, and with a great presentment of evil from that devilish people and their arts."

" 'Tis my thought, gentlemen," Lord Howard told his assembled captains, assembled in a council-of-war, "that now, with the enemy vessels close together and to leeward, the most likely method of attack is by means of fireships. What think you?"

An immediate assent was given, and plans were laid for launching the attack that very night. Eight of the least valuable ships were chosen, hurriedly dismantled and filled with powder, pitch and brimstone. Just after midnight, with both wind and tide setting in the direction of the closely-huddled enemy, the eight ships were set on fire, and, with sails set, bore down upon the Spaniards. With orange-yellow flames rising to their mastheads, the white-hot floating infernos crashed in amongst the Spanish vessels, filling those on board with terror which spread from ship to ship like the all-consuming flames. In a panic, they slipped their anchors or cut the cables, and sought to hoist their sails and stand out to sea. In the midst of the terrible confusion, the screams of the terrified, the giving and countermanding of orders and the fear-inspired haste, many of the ships crashed into others. But by one desperate expedient or another all the ships except one of the big galleasses managed to make good their escape, but when morning broke they were scattered over the sea along the coast off Gravelines and unable, because of the wind, to make their way back to Calais.

The *Ark Royal,* with several other ships, turned aside to capture

41

a galleass which had lost her rudder and gone ashore. Drake, in the *Revenge,* pressed on after the Spaniards. Some fifty of their ships had managed to gather together and against these the English concentrated their fire, surging forward one after another to deliver one broadside from close range, then going about to deliver the other on the opposite tack.

So daringly and relentlessly did the English deliver their heavy blows that it soon appeared they might win a complete and decisive victory. At the end of five hours' fighting, about sixteen of the Spanish galleons had been cut off from the rest of the fleet and were so cruelly battered as to seem on the point of surrender. At this point a terrific rain storm came up which hid the enemy from sight and put an end to the firing. One of the Spanish galleons went down with all on board, and three were driven ashore on the Zealand banks.

Then came the disastrous flight of the Armada with the English pressing at their heels, for the Spaniards preferred to brave the northern seas and make for home by way of the Orkneys than face again the guns and the men of bulldog breed on board the *Ark Royal,* the *Revenge,* and other English men-of-war. The English followed them until they were off the Firth of Forth. Then, running short of powder and provisions, they put back to Harwich.

Storms and fogs were to complete the defeat of the Invincible Armada. Two of the ships were blown to Norway and wrecked. Others were driven to the shores of Scotland and Ireland where many of the Spaniards were drowned, "and divers slaine by the barbarous and wilde Irish." Wreck after wreck crashed onto sharp-fanged rocks or drifted on the waves, and out of all the vast flotilla which had sailed so proudly on its mission of conquest, only fifty-three Spanish vessels ever returned to their home ports.

Spanish sea-power was ended by the defeat of the Armada, and England gained new confidence in her maritime destiny. In this great achievement the *Ark Royal* played a glorious part.

5

The Red Dragon

The Flagship of the East India Company's First Fleet

DRAKE'S voyage around the world in the *Golden Hind*, which was completed in the year 1580, did much to stir the imaginations of the English and to increase their interest in the wonderful possibilities of the eastern trade. This trade, first developed by the Portuguese, was controlled by Spain at the time of Drake's voyage. In the year 1580 the Spanish and Portuguese dominions had become united under the Spanish crown, and the wealth of the Indies had thereby become the possession of England's greatest enemy.

No Englishman realized the magnificent richness of the trade, however, until Sir Francis Drake captured the great carack, *San Felipe,* homeward bound from the East Indies, after his famous raid on the port of Cadiz in the year 1587. The ship and her cargo were found to be worth £114,000 in Elizabethan money, or in modern coinage about a million pounds sterling. But the most valuable of all the things found aboard the carack were her papers, which revealed the long-kept secrets of the Indies trade.

These papers, telling in detail of the rich cargoes that Spain had been bringing from the east, were a revelation to the merchants of London. A few years later their imaginations were stirred again when

44

a Portuguese East Indiaman, *Madre de Dios,* was captured and brought into Dartmouth. Her cargo of Oriental treasures astonished all who saw it. There were jewels and golden silks, damasks, calicoes and carpets, ivory and incense, beautifully wrought quilts and canopies, drugs and a vast store besides of spices—pepper and nutmeg, cloves, cinnamon and ginger.

Talk of the East Indies' trade was now on everybody's lips, and soon a number of London merchants petitioned Queen Elizabeth for permission to send a fleet of well-found vessels to the East. When the Queen delayed in giving her assent, the merchants grew more and more impatient, for a new rival—the Dutch—had now entered the field. Their ships were rounding the Cape in ever-increasing numbers, and they were establishing "factories" or trading posts in many of the richest territories. Finally, on the last day of the year 1600, Elizabeth gave her assent.

The company was composed of two hundred and eighteen merchants, aldermen, knights and esquires, who took as their title, "The Governors and Company of the Merchants Trading unto the East Indies." The regions over whose trade they were given a monopoly were vast and varied, for they embraced all ports, islands and places in Asia, Africa and America between the Cape of Good Hope and the Strait of Magellan. The company's intent, however, was to trade principally with India, and that is how matters worked out.

The East India Company was to be one of the most powerful trading concerns the world has ever seen. It was to be the instrument through which India would become a part of the British Empire. For two and a half centuries its sailing ships were to dominate trade with the east, and carry home millions of pounds' worth of cargo. Like many another venture, however, the Company began in a small way.

Under its charter, the Company was allowed to send "sixe good ships and sixe good pynnaces" and "five hundred mariners, Englishmen, to guide and sayle." Actually, however, only four ships were sent on the first venture, as this was all that the Company could pay for. The merchant adventurers had "joyned together and made a stocke of seventie two thousand pounds, to bee employed in ships and merchandizes." The purchase of the four ships, the expense of fitting them out and furnishing them with men, provisions, stores and munitions for a voyage that would keep them away from England for nearly two years, consumed £45,000 of the original capital. This left £27,000, which was invested partly in merchandise for the vessels' cargoes and partly in Spanish money with which the natives of the east were known to be familiar.

The "Generall of the Fleet" was Captain James Lancaster, and his flagship was to be the *Red Dragon*. This ship of 600 tons had had an adventurous career. She was owned by the Earl of Cumberland, one of the founders of the East India Company, and had been armed by him to rove the seas and capture Spanish and Portuguese vessels returning richly-laden from the eastern and western Indies. During this period of her career she had been known as the *Mare Scourge* or "Terror of the Seas," and had carried out many a foray that entitled her to such a name. She was an ideal vessel for the first voyage of the East India Company, for she was heavily armed and built for fighting and long distance ocean cruising.

Captain Lancaster deserves more than passing·mention, for he was

a remarkable man, gallant in action, utterly loyal to the interests of those he served and of proven courage and endurance in the face of difficulties and obstacles. Moreover, he knew the sea-route to the east, for he had commanded a ship which had made the voyage in 1591.

Every imaginable difficulty and danger was encountered during the voyage: terrific storms, attacks by hostile natives on the Comoro Islands, the death of more than half the crew from scurvy, fierce battles with heavily armed Portuguese ships off the coast of India and a mutiny on the part of his homesick and desperate crew while off Ceylon. Yet Captain Lancaster's mettle stood the test.

The story of this voyage was eventually written by Hakluyt, and made Captain Lancaster's character and ability known to the world at large. When, therefore, the Governors of the East India Company commenced to prepare for the sailing of their first squadron and sought to find the best commanders for their ships, Captain Lancaster stood out as one of the most suitable mariners in all of England for such a voyage.

In addition to the *Red Dragon*, the squadron for the first voyage included the *Hector*, 300 tons and 108 men; the *Ascension*, 260 tons and 82 men; the *Susan*, 240 tons and 88 men; a victualling ship of 130 tons which was called either the *Guift* or the *Guest*. These ships were loaded with such English products as were likely to bring good value in the eastern trade. There were many rolls of good cloth, and the other goods carried consisted chiefly of metals—iron, lead and tin.

Queen Elizabeth gave Captain Lancaster letters of commendation addressed to "divers Princes of India," and presents for the princes were carefully chosen and taken aboard. These included feathered plumes, looking-glasses, beautifully finished pistols, girdles, glass toys, spectacles, drinking glasses and silver plates and spoons.

The ships were loaded and made ready for sea during the winter of 1600-1601, and in February of the latter year they took their departure from Woolwich. Captain Lancaster did not seem to be in a great hurry, for, having reached the mouth of the Thames, he anchored and waited on the Downs so long for a fair wind that it was Easter Day before the ships reached Dartmouth. Here they "spent five or six dayes in taking in their bread and certaine other provisions." Everything was then ready for the main part of the voyage. The ships "hoysed their anchors," beat down Channel to the Bay of Biscay and left England and home far astern, as they ploughed steadily on toward the unknown.

Continuing to the southward and crossing the Equator, all went well until the month of July, when scurvy broke out among the sailors on all the ships except the *Red Dragon*. A contemporary account of the voyage says that the reason why the General's men stood better in health than the men of the other ships was this: "he brought to sea with him certaine Bottles of the Juice of Limons, which hee gave to each one, as long as it would last, three spoonfuls every morning fasting, not suffering them to eate anything after it till noone. . . . By this meanes the Generall cured many of his men, and preserved the rest."

Conditions on the other ships became serious. Even the "merchants tooke their turnes at the Helme, and went into the top to take in the top-sayles, as the common Mariners did." At last, however, on the ninth of September they arrived at Saldanha Bay, now Table Bay, where they anchored and "hoysed out their boats." The crews of the *Hector, Ascension* and *Susan* were so weak that the *Red Dragon's* men had to go aboard them to furl the sails and put the ship's boats over the side.

The squadron stayed at Saldanha Bay for a month and a half to permit the men to rest and recover from the scurvy, but at the end of October they got underway once more and a few days later rounded the Cape of Good Hope, scudding along before a "wind West Northwest, a great gale." Madagascar was reached in December and the ships stayed there until early in March. They next went to the Nicobar Islands, far to the eastward across the entire breadth of the Indian Ocean. These were touched at because Captain Lancaster had visited them on his previous voyage.

With the *Red Dragon* showing the way, the squadron now made for Acheen, at the northwest extremity of Sumatra. Here English trade with the East Indies was actually started. The Dutch were already established there, but they received the English ships with friendliness

49

and presented Captain Lancaster to the native King of Acheen, who granted them freedom of trade and freedom from paying customs duties on any merchandise they wished to land or take on board.

To take advantage of this opening, Captain Lancaster put ashore two of the merchants who had come out in the *Red Dragon* from England. Their instructions were to get together a cargo of pepper for the *Red Dragon* to carry back to England. While they were engaged in this pursuit, the captain set sail to the northward, intent upon a venture of his own.

From his previous voyage he knew that scores of well-laden Portuguese merchant vessels passed through the Straits of Malacca, which connect the Indian Ocean with the China Seas. Now every Elizabethan seaman was eager for a fight at sea, especially against any Portuguese or Spanish ship, and Lancaster was no exception. In addition, he knew of no easier way to obtain a rich cargo for his homeward voyage. Accordingly, he led his squadron to the entrance of the straits and posted double lookouts to scan the sea for any approaching ships.

He had not long to wait, for a day or so after he had reached his cruising grounds, a big Portuguese carack, the *St. Thomé,* came bowling along through the straits, totally unaware that English vessels were in the vicinity. It was late in the afternoon when the *St. Thomé* was sighted, "and being toward night," wrote one of the men on board the *Red Dragon,* "a present direction was given that we should all spread our selves a mile and a halfe one from another, that she might not passe us in the night."

The four English ships spread out across the straits to take their stations for the night, but the *Red Dragon,* nearest to the Portuguese ship, closed in on her before night fell and delivered a rapid fire from her bow guns. The English sailors cheered when they saw the carack's mainyard come crashing to the deck. Lancaster then gave the order to cease firing, for he did not wish to bombard the stranger during the darkness, fearing "lest some unfortunate shot might light betweene wind and water, and so sinke her" with her valuable cargo.

At daybreak the *Red Dragon* attacked again and took the *St. Thomé*. All four English vessels gathered close around her and, so great was her cargo of eastern goods—silks and spices, carpets and calicoes, drugs and hides, ivory and jewels—that six days were required to unload them and put them aboard the smaller English ships.

With the rifling of the *St. Thomé* completed, Lancaster sailed back to Acheen and loaded his cargo of pepper, to which were added some tons of cinnamon and spices.

From Acheen the ships went on to Bantam on the island of Java, and here the *Susan* and *Ascension* completed their cargoes and set out for England. The *Red Dragon* and the *Hector* visited other Javanese ports, sent their merchants ashore to trade with the natives and soon had exchanged their remaining stores of cloth, lead, iron and tin for all the pepper and spices they could carry. Early in the new year of 1603—after an absence of more than two years from England—they took on board stores and made final preparations for the long voyage home.

In late February they left the palm-fringed shores and yellow beaches of the Indies behind. "We went all aboord our ships," says the old account, "shot off our ordnance, and set sayle to the sea toward England, with thankes to God, and glad hearts, for his blessings towards us." For nearly a month there was good weather; strong easterly winds drove the ships across the Indian Ocean. But this good fortune was not to last, for on "the eight and twentieth day we had a very great and furious storme, so that we were forced to take in all our sayles. This storme continued a day and a night, with an exceeding great and raging sea, so that in the reason of man no shippe was able to live in them; but God (in his mercie) ceased the violence thereof, and gave us time to breath, and to repaire all the distresses and harmes we had received, but our ships were so shaken that they were leakie all the voyage after."

Early in May they once again faced a trial of strength, for another "very sore storm" came down upon them, while to the eastward of the Cape of Good Hope, "and the seas did so beate upon the ship's quarter, that it shooke all the iron worke of her rother [rudder], and the next day in the morning, our rother brake cleane from the sterne of our shippe [the *Red Dragon*], and presently sunke into the sea."

Helpless and well-nigh unmanageable after this accident, the *Red Dragon* plunged wildly on before the storm, with all on board fearing she would at any moment broach to, fall sideways into the trough of the waves and be sent foundering to the bottom. As the old account says, she "drave up and downe the sea like a wracke."

When the fury of the wind abated somewhat, Captain Lancaster set to work at once to rig a jury-rudder. He ordered the *Red Dragon's* mizzenmast to be unstepped, and the crew then "put it forth at the sterne port to prove if wee could steere our shippe into some place where we might make another rother to hang it, to serve our turnes home."

52

This plan, though soundly conceived, did not work, for it was soon found that the mizzenmast was too heavy and put too great a strain on the stern of the ship. Lancaster then ordered the ship's carpenter to cut the mast down and, when this was done, it was again put over the stern. For three or four hours all went well, but then "the sea tooke it off againe."

Captain Lancaster was now in a difficult position, for the men had lost heart and wanted to abandon the *Red Dragon* to her fate, while they went aboard the *Hector*. Captain Lancaster thought his ship had little chance of reaching home, but he was determined to spare no effort to bring her rich cargo safe at last to port.

Unknown to the crew, he now went below to his cabin and wrote the following letter, which he intended to give to the captain of the *Hector,* send him home at once, and upon arrival deliver the letter to the directors of the Company. The letter, cherished by all who honor the memory of the Elizabethan sea-dogs, read:

"Right Worshipful—What hath passed in this voyage, and what trades I have settled for this companie, and what other events have befallen us, you shall understand by the bearers hereof, to whom (as occasion hath fallen) I must referre you. I will strive with all diligence to save my ship, and her goods, as you may perceive by the course I take in venturing mine own life, and those that are with mee. I cannot tell where you should looke for mee, if you send out any pinnace to seeke mee; because I live at the devotion of the wind and seas. And thus fare you well, desiring God to send us a merrie meeting in this world, if it be his good will and pleasure.

"The passage to the East India lieth in 62½ degrees, by the North West on the American side.

Your very loving friend,

James Lancaster."

The letter was given to the captain of the *Hector* and he was told to go on his way A start was made, but after drawing ahead a few miles, the *Hector's* master decided that, even at the risk of disobeying his orders, nothing should stop him from standing by his leader and his wounded ship. He turned the *Hector* about and brought her to a course paralleling that of the *Red Dragon,* but far enough distant to prevent Captain Lancaster from ordering him to change his mind.

Matters now commenced to improve. The storm moderated and the sea went down. Captain Lancaster sent men over the side to put a new jury-rudder in place, and, so well was their work done, that the *Red Dragon* was able to spread all her sails to the breeze and plunge boldly forward through the rolling seas.

Sailing close together, the two ships rounded the Cape of Good Hope and set their course to the northward and "the far northern ports of home." The worst of the voyage was now over. True, they spent long weeks drifting aimlessly through the doldrums; but at last, early in September, they made ready for their final landfall. "Wee tooke sounding, judging the Lands end of England to be fortie leagues from us. The eleventh day we came to the Downes, well and safe to an anchor; for the which, thanked be almightie God, who hath delivered us from the infinite perils and dangers, in this long and tedious Navigation."

The *Red Dragon*

Thus the voyage which had commenced in February, 1601, was now brought to its conclusion two and a half years later in September, 1603. In all respects, the directors of the East India Company had cause for deep satisfaction, not only over the profits of the voyage and the establishment of connections for future trading, but also over the courageous conduct of the expedition by the "Generall of the Fleet." In addition to the cargo taken from the *St. Thomé,* the four ships brought home a million pounds of pepper, and when this was sold, the merchant adventurers of the company received the fabulous return of ninety-five per cent on their capital.

This voyage was followed by many others, as all the world knows, and the East India Company became the largest, richest and most powerful trading organization in the entire world. Many famous East Indiaman, such as the *Trade's Increase, Owen Glendower, Bombay Castle* and *Earl Balcarres* were to sail in the wake of the *Red Dragon.* But to her belongs the honor of having led the stately ships to the East.

6

The Discoverie

Henry Hudson's Ship in Which He Discovered Hudson's Bay

SEATED at a London tavern table, heads close together and deep in earnest conversation, Henry Hudson and his friend Captain John Smith of Virginia were poring over a large map. Smith had obtained the map from what source we do not know, and now he was engrossed in explaining it to Hudson.

"Whether this be a true plan or not, I do not know," he was saying, "but this I do know for certain: it is drawn from Michael Lok's planisphere; and Lok had great repute as a geographer. That you know for yourself.

"Aye, that is true," said Hudson, "and I have great confidence he has rightly drawn America. By your leave, Captain, I will show this to the directors of the Muscovy Company. They have ever been eager to find the way to the South Seas. This map may bring them their desire."

The map so prized by the two great explorers would appear curious to us. It showed the American continent to be shaped something like an hour-glass, the very thin part in the center being located at about 40° north latitude, or in the vicinity of present-day New York. Hud-

son and Smith believed there might well be a passage to the China Sea
through the narrow isthmus at the continent's center.

Several previous attempts had been made to find a passage further
to the north. Cabot in 1497, Frobisher in three voyages between 1576
and 1578, Gilbert in 1578 and 1583 and Davis in 1585—all had tried
and failed. Might it be that they had sailed too far north? Certainly,
if Michael Lok's map were correctly drawn, there seemed a better
chance of finding a passage further to the south. Such a voyage
would have the added advantage of being through warmer seas, without the continual menace of icebergs and vast fields of floating pack-ice.

Hudson was in an excellent position to lay the proposition before
the Muscovy Company, for he had already made two voyages for them
and they had good reason to place confidence in him. On his first
voyage made in 1607 on the *Hopewell,* he had attempted to reach the
South Seas by sailing due north from England to the North Pole, passing it by, and then continuing on to the south. He was stopped by the
great Arctic ice barrier, but the Muscovy Company was anxious for
him to try again. Consequently, the next year he again sailed to the
northward.

This time he followed an easterly course, where he believed that,
by passing between the islands of Spitzbergen and Nova Zembla, he
would find an open passage to the Pole. Again, he was unsuccessful,
but his voyage had important results for his employers. Upon his
return, he reported that the waters surrounding Spitzbergen were alive
with whales. The Muscovy Company lost no time in establishing a
whale fishery based on the remote northern island and for many years
derived from it a rich income, large enough to repay them many times

over for the expense of financing Hudson's two northern voyages. Much of the spotless whiteness of the laces and ruffs worn by the men and women of Stuart England was due to the excellent soaps made from the blubber of the Spitzbergen whales.

However, notwithstanding the wealth that Hudson's explorations had brought the Muscovy Company, its directors did not look with favor upon his plan to find a passage to the South Seas through the midriff of the American continent. For the time being, they wished to concentrate their efforts upon the Russian trade opened up half a century before by Chancellor and upon the new and very promising Spitzbergen whale fishery. As a consequence, Hudson sought the support of a rival corporation, the Netherlands East India Company, and in 1609 sailed for them in the *Half Moon* on the voyage which led to the discovery of the Hudson River.

The Muscovy Company then made an about-face and urged him to return to their service. They now asked if he would attempt to find a northwest passage to the Indies, and Hudson accepted their offer without delay. Not only did he wish to promote the interests of his own country, but he felt certain that a way to the China Seas could be found somewhere to the west or northwest. He was tremendously eager to discover if "through any of these inlets which Davis saw, but durst not enter, any passage might be found to the other ocean called the South Sea."

After some difficulty in finding a suitable vessel, the Muscovy Company selected "the bark *Discoverie*" for the intended voyage, and she sailed from London in April, 1610, pushed northward past the coast of Scotland, and thence pursued a course toward Iceland. The second-

in-command of the little bark was Robert Juet, a surly and ill-favored
mariner who had been mate with Hudson on the *Half Moon*.

The story of this voyage has been preserved for us, at least in part,
by means of a fragment of a journal in Hudson's own hand and a
narrative by one of the crew, Abacuk Pricket, which is remarkable for
its vivid style.

As the *Discoverie* neared the coast of Iceland she was enveloped
in a clammy fog. Those on board could hear the roar of the surf breaking on the rocky shore. Hudson anchored the ship until the fog lifted
and then, with a good gale of wind from the southwest, made good
progress along the coast. "But in our course," says Pricket, "we saw
that famous Hill, Mount Hecla, which cast out much fire, a sign of
foule weather to come in short time." A little further on, the *Discoverie*
came to anchor again in a bay, "where on the shoare we found an hot
Bath, and heere all our Englishmen bathed themselves; the water was
so hot that it would scald a Fowle."

On the first of June the ship left Iceland behind. Three days later it reached the desolate ice-ringed coast of Greenland. Here the ice was so thick that the *Discoverie* could not be brought in close to the land. Hudson, accordingly, steered around the southern tip of Greenland until he raised "the Desolations," a mountainous island off the west coast. "Here," says Pricket, "we saw store of whales, and at one time three of them came close by us, so as wee could hardly shunne them; then two passing very neere, and the third going under our ship, wee received no harme by them, prayzed bee God."

As the *Discoverie* pushed on to the westward, huge icebergs, "great islands or mountains of ice," terrifying in their glittering majesty, drove down upon her from the frozen north. The cold air spreading out from them chilled the men to the marrow of their bones, and seemed to clutch their very hearts with its icy fingers. As in "The Rime of the Ancient Mariner":

> And now there came both mist and snow,
> And it grew wondrous cold:
> And ice, mast-high, came floating by,
> As green as emerald.
>
> And through the drifts the snowy clifts
> Did send a dismal sheen:
> Nor shapes of men nor beasts we ken—
> The ice was all between.
>
> The ice was here, the ice was there,
> The ice was all around:
> It crack'd and growl'd and roar'd and howl'd,
> Like noises in a swound!

The *Discoverie*

One day, as the crew stood gazing awestruck at a towering ice-monster, whose glittering summit seemed to pierce the sky, there was a roaring and crashing as of a thousand tortured devils screaming in agony. With an ear-splitting crash, the great berg split in two, swayed gigantically, then turned over. An enormous wave rushed toward the *Discoverie* and threatened to engulf her.

"Some of our men this day fell sicke," said Pricket. "I will not say it was for feare, although I saw small signe of other grief."

Hudson now needed all his skill as a navigator to guide the *Discoverie* through the thickening fields of ice. Even more, he was forced to call upon all his qualities of courage and leadership to keep his frightened crew from mutiny. The carpenter, who, as we shall see later, was brave and loyal, rallied the crew, supported all Hudson's arguments for keeping on and did much to force the malcontents to return to their duty.

In time, the *Discoverie* won through to the mainland of North America, and, to Hudson's great delight, a broad body of water was discovered. Surely it must be the long-sought northwest passage, and the isles of spice were at the other end.

This watery pathway was the strait now called Hudson Strait, which leads into Hudson Bay. Still there were enormous ice fields stretching away as far as the eye could reach.

"On one of the islands of floating ice was a beare," says Pricket, "which from one to another came towards us, till she was readie to come aboard. But when she saw us looke at her, she cast her head between her hinde legges and then dived under the ice; and so from one piece to another, till she was out of our reach."

Next, landing on the shore of Ungava Bay, they "sprung a covey of partridges (ptarmigan) and shot one." A few days later they saw "some deere, a dozen or sixteene in an herd, but could not come nigh them with a musket shot."

Following the strait, which beckoned them on to the westward, they came to the western end of Cape Wolstenholme. At this place, Pricket and some others were sent ashore to explore the country, and found thousands of sea-birds. One day they came upon "some round hills of stone, which at first I took to be the work of some Christian. Being nigh them, I turned off the uppermost stone, and found them hollow within and full of fowles hanged by their neckes." Evidently they had stumbled on a cache left by Eskimos.

When they returned to the ship, they reported their find and the opportunity of obtaining an abundance of fresh birds for food. But Hudson would not consent to stop. Probably he believed that, in a few more days of sailing, he would come out upon the China Seas and realize the discovery which had been his dream for years. The seeds of tragedy lay in his refusal, for it aggravated the growing discontent of the crew.

All the month of July was spent in exploring the eastern shore of the great inland sea now known as Hudson Bay. On one occasion a storm blew up which forced the *Discoverie* to lie at anchor for eight days, "in all which time wee could not get one houre to weigh our anchor." At last, Hudson, in the face of strong opposition and many threatening words from the crew, ordered the anchor to be weighed. As it came a-peak, a heavy sea broke over the ship. The men were hurled across the deck, some of them were hurt, and the angry mutterings grew louder and more menacing.

For three long and arduous months, Hudson sailed on around the shore of the bay, hoping that any day he would find the passage to the westward that would lead him to Cathay, the Spice Islands, and all the warmth and wealth and palm trees of the Golden East. By the end of October, he was disheartened, but not ready to give up his search. It was evident, however, that he could not continue the voyage until the following spring.

Accordingly, a suitable camping place was found and the *Discoverie* laboriously hauled aground. A few days afterwards, the ship was frozen in. The provisions on board were sufficient for six months, but it seemed possible that they might be held by the ice for an even longer period. The men commenced to growl again, for, they argued, Hudson should have laid in ample supplies of sea fowl. A member of the crew died, and this was taken as an omen of misfortune.

The winter was long and bitter, a long drawn out agony of cold, despair and wretchedness, with little comradely feeling to ease the hardships. Most of the crew had their feet frozen, and the darkness of day as well as night overcast all their thoughts with gloom. One good thing alone befell them. By a miracle of Providence, so it seemed, they were amply supplied with food, chiefly the snow-white ptarmigans, of which they killed well over a thousand.

With the approach of spring, the men grew more morose, savage and angry against their leader. Again, it was chiefly the question of food. The ptarmigans left at the end of winter and the birds that remained—wild geese, ducks and swans—were shy and hard to catch.

Hunger gnawed at the men's vitals. Despair and rage filled their hearts. In desperate bands, they tramped across the country looking for anything that might have the least shadow of sustenance. Even the Arctic moss was greedily devoured.

At last, in May, 1611, the *Discoverie* was got out into the open water. Hudson felt renewed in spirit, for he thought that he would soon reach the tropic warmth and richness of the Isles of Spice. But, alas, tragedy was even then preparing to strike.

When, early in June, the *Discoverie* had left her winter quarters and was ready to recommence her voyage, Hudson divided the remaining food equally among the men, giving to each his proper share. Some ate most of their supply at once and were sick; others, seeing how small the store was, began to plot a mutiny.

"Being thus in the ice on Saturday, the one and twentieth of June at night," Pricket relates, "Wilson the boatswayne, and Henry Greene came to mee lying in my Cabbin lame, and told mee that they and the rest of their associates, would shift the Company, and turne the Master and all the sicke men into the Shallop (a small boat), and let them shift for themselves. For there was not fourteen daies victual left for all the Company, at that poore allowance they were at . . . and therefore were resolute, either to mend or end, and what they had begun they would goe through with it, or dye. . . . Henry Greene went his way, and presently came Juet, who because hee was an ancient man, I hoped to have found some reason in him; but hee was worse than Henry Greene, for hee sware plainly that he would justifie this deed when he came home."

During that night the mutineers made their plans, and early next morning took action. Three of the sailors seized Hudson as he came from his cabin and thrust him, with his little son, John, and several loyal followers, into the *Discoverie's* shallop. When the carpenter saw what the mutineers were doing, he upbraided them fiercely and told them that they would certainly be handed for the criminals they were, when they reached England. But the mutineers were obstinate, and the brave fellow then said that he would cast in his lot with those in the boat, rather than have any part in the mutiny.

Before leaving the *Discoverie,* he secured a musket, some powder and shot, an iron pot and a little meal. With this slender supply, Hudson and his companions were set adrift and soon left far astern. What happened to them no one knows, for they were never seen again, and nothing has ever been found that might indicate how the heroic explorer and his companions met their end.

On the voyage back to England, the mutineers experienced dreadful misfortunes and hardships. At Cape Wolstenholme, where they landed to search for food, they were attacked by Indians and several killed. The survivors finally brought the *Discoverie* out into the open ocean, but within a short time their food supply gave out. Candles were then served out and the miserable sailors ate the bones of birds fried in candle-grease, with vinegar for a relish.

"And sure," says Pricket, "our course was so much the longer through our evil steerage, for our men became so weak that they could not stand at the helme, but were fain to sit. Then Robert Juet died for meere want, and all our men were in despaire."

At last, the ship, almost helpless and at the mercy of the winds, sighted the Irish coast and was brought in by fishermen. Eventually the few survivors took the *Discoverie* to London. They were apprehended and thrown into prison for their crime, but when they were brought to trial the jury returned a verdict of "not guilty" and they were given their liberty.

Hudson, though he failed to find a passage to Cathay, brought about more far-reaching results than any other explorer of his day. His first and second voyages led to the establishment of the great whale fishery at Spitzbergen. His third voyage, in the *Half Moon,* was responsible for the Dutch settlements in North America and the founding of the city of New Amsterdam, later named New York. His fourth voyage, in the *Discoverie,* brought about the founding of the Hudson's Bay Company and the immensely valuable Canadian fur trade.

7

The Mayflower

THE *Mayflower*, of all the ships that brought the first settlers from the Old World to the New, holds the most cherished place in the hearts and minds of both Britons and Americans. No other ship links Great Britain and the United States more closely, nor symbolizes more clearly their identical dreams of personal liberty and freedom from oppression. No other ship reminds us so strongly of the Anglo-Saxon heritage of North America and the deep-lying feeling of brotherhood between Great Britain and the United States. A world of deeply-felt emotion was given expression when the arrival of the first American destroyers to help the British in the first World War was hailed as "the return of the *Mayflower*."

To understand the forces which drove the Pilgrims to leave their homeland and embark on the *Mayflower* for the perilous crossing of the Atlantic, a little must be known about the different sects into which the Protestants of England were divided at that time. Many were members of the Church of England, or the Protestant Episcopal Church, as it is known in America. This was the "Established Church" and had the approval and support of the government. A large number of English Protestants, however, were opposed to the Church of England. Some of them desired to remain in the church, but wished to "purify" it, as they said, and as a consequence were

67

called "Puritans." Others looked upon the purification of the Church of England as an impossible task, and were determined to separate themselves from it. These were called "Separatists" or "Independents." The *Mayflower* Pilgrims were a company of the Separatists.

James I, who became king in 1603, was particularly harsh to all who would not worship in the Established Church. "I will make them conform," he declared, "or I will harry them out of the land." He did not succeed in making them join the Church of England, but he did drive thousands of men, women and children, including the Pilgrims, out of England and across the ocean to the rock-bound coasts of New England.

Persecuted and in despair, the Separatists hardly knew which way to turn. Finally, in 1608, some decided to seek religious freedom in Holland, and went to Amsterdam. Later, in Leyden, they found the religious freedom they sought, but they did not find contentment. Their children were learning the Dutch speech and customs and were becoming more like little Hollanders than English children. For this and other reasons, they did not wish to remain in Holland and, as they could not return to England they determined to go to America, where they could worship in their own way and still live as English people.

In pursuit of this plan, they sent two of their number, John Carver and Robert Cushman, from Leyden to London to obtain the consent of the Council for Virginia to settle in the northern part of Virginia near "Hudson's River." At that time Virginia was the name given to a large section of America and was considered by some to include

almost all the North Atlantic coast. Many difficulties were put in the way of the Pilgrims' emissaries, and it was only through the help of some London merchants, anxious to develop the American fisheries, that they were able to obtain two ships to carry those who wished to make the voyage to the New World.

The Pilgrims who were at Leyden sailed from Delfshaven in the *Speedwell;* those who were in England embarked in the *Mayflower* from London. On July the fifteenth, 1620, they sailed down the Thames and later arrived at Southampton. Here they made the ship ready for sea and waited for the *Speedwell.* Of the departure from Holland, William Bradford, the chronicler of the voyage, says: "They lefte the goodly and pleasante citie which had been ther resting-place near twelve years; but they knew that they were pilgrimes . . ."

Little is known of the design or construction of the *Mayflower,* other than that she was larger than the average English merchant ship of the period. If, as was probable, she resembled the other ships of her class, she was broad-beamed and of heavy build, with a high forecastle and poop, having three masts, two square-rigged and the mizzen-mast bearing a triangular lateen sail. She apparently had considerable space available for passengers, and for her Atlantic voyage she was doubtless fitted out with extra, rudely-constructed cabins.

The master of the *Mayflower* was Thomas Jones, an extraordinary character. He had been a pirate in eastern waters, and had then served a prison term in London for misconduct. Upon his release, he had taken a cattle-ship to Virginia, and it was after this voyage that he was given the command of the *Mayflower*. After serving the Pilgrims, Captain Jones turned again to buccaneering and ended his career as he had begun it, a pirate.

Early in August the two ships left Southampton on their great adventure, the *Mayflower* bearing ninety passengers and the *Speedwell* thirty. For three or four days they beat down the Channel, making but little progress against a westerly wind. Then the *Speedwell* was found to be leaking, and both vessels accordingly put into Dartmouth, where the smaller ship was unloaded and repaired. Another start was made, but three days later the *Speedwell* again commenced to leak, and the two vessels were forced to put into Plymouth. Here it was decided to send the ill-found *Speedwell* back to London with eighteen of her passengers, while the others transferred to the *Mayflower*.

Early in September the *Mayflower's* sails were hoisted again and, with a favoring easterly breeze, she drove past Plymouth Hoe and turned her bluff bows toward the west. In fine weather and with a continuing favorable wind, the little ship now ran swiftly. All on board were able to walk the open decks and they looked forward with good cheer to reaching their journey's end without further delays or mishaps.

Even during this fair weather stage of the voyage, however, some were miserable indeed, for, as William Bradford says, "according to the usual manner many were afflicted with the sea-sickness. And," he adds, "I may not omit hear a speciall worke of God's providence. There was a proud and very profane yonge man, one of the sea-men, of a lustie able body, which made him the more hauty. He would allway be contemning the poore people in their sicknes, and cursing them daily with griveous execrations, and did not let to tell them that he hoped to cast halfe of them overboard before they came to their journey's end, and to make merry with what they had. And if he were by any gently reproved, he would curse and swear most bitterly. But it pleased God before they came halfe seas over, to smite this yonge man with a grievous disease, of which he dyed in a desperate manner, and so was him selfe the first that was throwne overboard. Thus his curses light on his owne head; and it was an astonishmente to all his fellows, for they noted it to be the just hand of God upon him."

After a week or so of good weather, the *Mayflower's* fortunes changed abruptly. The delays occasioned by the *Speedwell's* mishaps had brought her to mid-Atlantic at the time of the savage equinoctial gales. The westerly wind rose in its wrath and the great Atlantic rollers swept along the streaming decks of the little ship. Hourly the wind grew more and more violent until a full gale was hurling its demoniacal fury on the struggling *Mayflower*. As the waves struck her, she trembled from stem to stern. Rolling deeply from side to side, she rose to the giddy heights of one wave after the other, only to plunge dizzily down the moving slope into troughs so deep that she disappeared from view completely. For many days she battled for her life.

Life for those aboard the little ship was well nigh unendurable. The hatches were closed, and the Pilgrims crowded together in the stifling air below decks. As the ship rolled and tossed, they were flung about and many were painfully injured. Above the roaring of the wind and waves, they could hear the creaking and groaning of the *Mayflower's* tortured frames and beams. Water seeped into the living quarters and washed to and fro across the tween deck, adding to the misery of the vessel's company.

One day when the Pilgrims were gathered at prayer in the main cabin, they heard a sound that brought their hearts into their mouths. It was a tremendous wrenching noise; it seemed as if the entire ship were being torn apart. A sailor came below and told them that one of the main cross-beams in the midship part of the vessel had been bent and cracked by the force of the storm. This was serious, for it weakened the whole ship's structure and might soon cause other beams to give way.

Captain Jones had no equipment that could be used to straighten out the beam, and there seemed little hope for the ship's survival unless the storm went down.

One of the Pilgrims, carrying a powerful jack-screw, now made his way to the 'tween deck. By a piece of good fortune, he had brought this tool along with him when he left Leyden, and now it was to be the means of saving the entire venture from disaster. The tool was placed under the beam and eager hands manned the lever that turned the screw, causing it to spiral upwards. After an hour's hard work the beam was forced into its original straight position. Then, in order to make it doubly secure, the sailors shored it up with a stout post extending from the deck to the under side of the beam and lashed it in place.

They felt safer now, but their difficulties were not at an end. The storm subsided for a few days, but soon began to rage again. All sails had to be taken in and the *Mayflower* again tossed helplessly at the mercy of the waves. Again and again she shook herself free of the torrents of water that washed along her decks but, whether by good seamanship or the good design of her hull, she managed to stay afloat. It was during this spell of stormy weather that a baby was born. He was a boy, whose mother was the wife of Stephen Hopkins. The Pilgrims baptized him and, because he had been born on the wild Atlantic, they named him Oceanus Hopkins.

One day, shortly after the baptism, one of the Pilgrims, John Howland, by name, went to the deck to fill his lungs with the fresh air and to stretch his legs, cramped from lack of exercise. He waited until the deck was clear of water, then quickly opened the door of the after-deck house, stepped out onto the deck and slammed the door behind him. At that moment an enormous wave bore down on the ship, cascaded over the bow and filled the waist of the ship with a swirling mass of water.

John Howland was swept from his feet as though he were a bit of cork. In another instant he was carried over the ship's side. He saw dimly the tall wooden side of the *Mayflower* plunging past above him, the water pouring in streams over her bulwarks. He struck out toward her, calling for help; but no voice could be heard above the tumult of the storm and the loud droning of the wind through the standing rigging. At that moment a seeming miracle happened. John Howland felt a rope lash across his body. The main topsail halyard had been cast adrift by the waves and one end was trailing over the *Mayflower's* side. He caught at the rope and clung to it for dear life, while the waves first carried him high aloft and then plunged him dizzily down into their green, swift-moving depths.

Some sailors had run to the bulwarks as soon as they could reach them after the great wave had swept Howland overboard. Now, to their astonishment, they saw that he was still alive and whipping about at the end of the halyard. Though each succeeding wave threatened to sweep them overboard, they hauled on the halyard and took in on it inch by inch, drawing John Howland at last to the level of the deck—and to safety. It was an experience he never forgot, and, as William Bradford says, "though he was something ill with it, yet he lived many years after, and became a profitable member both in church and commone wealthe."

Nearly nine weeks had now gone by since the *Mayflower* had sailed from Plymouth. Day after weary day the Pilgrims had been confined in the close, evil-smelling tween decks, their clothes and bedding sodden wet, and their bodies and minds wracked by the never-ending pitching and rolling. Most of them had become very weak; all were weary of the sea.

But now the storm winds abated and the tired men and women, together with the children, were able to go out on deck into warm sunshine and clean air brought them new strength and some degree

74

of comfort. Three days passed in this way and then, to their great joy, the lookout sang out "Land ho!" They ran to the forecastle and gazed eagerly to the westward. There, a sight for sore eyes, was the land, the low, thickly-forested shore of New England.

There was some disappointment among the leaders of the Pilgrims when Captain Jones told them that the land they had sighted was the eastern side of Cape Cod. They had hoped to land much farther to the south, near the Hudson River. After some deliberation, it was decided to take the *Mayflower* further south and she set out, sailing easily along the coast before a gentle breeze. But after she had sailed for about half a day, she entered an area of dangerous shoals "and roring breakers," and was in danger of being driven aground at any moment. Swift currents swept through the narrow channels between the shoals, and it was only with the greatest difficulty that Captain Jones finally worked his ship out into deeper water.

Clear of the shoals at last, the Pilgrims decided to return once more to Cape Cod, rather than risk disaster when within sight of the land they had struggled so long to reach. Accordingly, the *Mayflower* was turned about and sailed around the "crook-handle" end of Cape Cod. When safely sheltered inside the cape, the anchor was dropped, and the Pilgrims gave heartfelt thanks to God for having brought them safely over the vast waste of waters and through the storms. They had been sixty-five days crossing the Atlantic Ocean. It was the evening of November nineteenth, 1620, when the *Mayflower* came to rest. While the Pilgrims rested and talked over their plans for the future, their leaders discussed the form of government which they would establish. It was decided that it must be a government in which

75

all would join together and in which each would have his or her part.

These are the words of the "Mayflower compact" to which they signed their names:

"In the name of God, Amen. We whose names are underwriten, the loyall subjects of our dread Soveraigne Lord King James by the grace of God, of great Britaine, France, and Ireland king, defender of the faith, etc. Having undertaken, for the glorie of God, and advancemente of the christian faith and honour of our king and countrie a voyage to plant the first colonie in the Northerne parts of Virginia, Doe by these presents solemnly and mutually in the presence of God, and one of another, covenant and combine ourselves togeather into a civill body politick; for our better ordering and preservation and furtherance of the ends aforesaid; and by virtue hereof to enacte, constitute, and frame such just and equall lawes, ordinances, Acts, constitutions, and offices, from time to time, as shall be thought most meete and convenient for the generall good of the Colonie. Unto which we promise all due submission and obedience. In witnes whereof we have hereunder subscribed our names at Cap Codd the 11 of November in the year of the raigne of our soveraigne Lord King James of England, France and Ireland the eighteenth and of Scotland the fiftie fourth Anno Domini 1620."

On the same day that the compact was signed, a party of men was sent ashore to see if the land looked suitable for establishing the permanent settlement. The report was not satisfactory, and other expeditions then were sent out to go farther afield. On Monday,

December eleventh, one such group landed on the mainland at Plymouth. After studying the shore-line, the harbor and the surrounding country, they agreed that this was the best place for their settlement. The *Mayflower* was sailed to the spot, and in her log for December fourteenth, it is written: "The colonists have determined to make settlement at the harbor they visited, and which is apparently, by Captain John Smith's chart of 1616, no other than the place he calls 'Plimoth' thereon."

The mission of the *Mayflower* had now been accomplished. Her colonists had been brought safely to the land they sought, and the good ship was free to return to England and the routine voyages of commerce. During the winter she sheltered in the harbor, but on April fifth she spread her sails to the wind, "set colors and gave Planters a parting salute with the ensign and ordnance," and laid a course for England.

"Hail to thee, poor little ship *May-Flower*," wrote Thomas Carlyle, "poor, common-looking ship, hired by common charter-party for coined dollars,—caulked with mere oakum and tar,—provisioned with vulgarest biscuit and bacon,—yet what ship Argo or miraculous epic ship, built by the sea gods, was other than a foolish bum-barge in comparison!"

8

The Ships of Colonial America

THE colonists who settled America early in the seventeenth century took to the sea almost immediately after their arrival. This was natural, for they were Britons and members of the greatest seafaring nation of the day, and many of them were experienced shipbuilders and sailors. To this inherited and acquired familiarity with ships and the sea were added two other factors which strongly influenced them. One was that they were separated from their homeland and from their nearby markets by open water. The other was that the colonists needed the fish that abounded in the waters off the coast.

Thus, as soon as they had taken care of their first pressing need— that of a roof over their heads—they took their axes to the forests, cut down the necessary trees and set to work to build small vessels. While the landsmen harnessed their oxen, furrowed the earth with plows and planted the first seeds, their seafaring brothers hoisted the sails of their diminutive boats and took to the "wet plowing" of the sea.

Even before the establishment of the American colonies, the great fisheries of the Newfoundland Banks had been known in Europe. When the Pilgrims decided to leave England and asked for a royal charter to authorize their undertaking, King James asked how they proposed to support themselves. "By fishing," was the reply. Where- upon, according to Edward Winslow's narrative, the King declared,

"So, God have my soul, 'tis an honest trade; 'twas the apostles' own calling."

Again, it is told of Captain John Smith that when he was making his way from Virginia to New England, he dropped a fish line over the side when the vessel was over what is now known as George's bank. His hook was taken at once, and again and again, until the deck about his feet was piled high with fish. The enterprising captain immediately saw how profitable fishing could be in these waters and wrote a friend in London: "Truly, it is a pleasant thing to drop a line and pull up six pence as fast as one may haul in." Before many years the annual catch of the New England fishermen had a greater value than the combined produce of the colony of Massachusetts Bay and the two plantations of Providence and Rhode Island.

It was not long before the New Englanders ventured further afield than the longshore fisheries. The horizon beckoned to them and they soon answered its call to see what lay beyond.

The first oversea voyage made by a New England ship of which we have any record is that of the *Virginia,* "a faire pinnace of 30 tons." She was built in 1607, more than a decade before the Pilgrims landed, by a group of colonists who had settled on the Kennebec River. The hardships of the climate proved too much for them, however, and the *Virginia* was built to carry them back across the Atlantic to their homeland with its familiar scenes and comforts. That she was stoutly built is proved by the fact that she carried the colonists safely home and made several more trans-Atlantic voyages without mishap.

A few years after the launching of the *Virginia,* we have a record of another vessel built by the colonists, the *Onrust* of sixteen tons which was completed at Manhattan in 1614. She was first used to explore the coast of New England to the north and Delaware Bay to the south. Then she was loaded with a cargo of furs and despatched across the Atlantic to Holland. Although we have no record of the *Onrust's* dimensions, it is safe to say that with her tonnage she was no more than thirty feet in length; in other words, no longer than one of the lifeboats on a modern liner.

While numerous other small vessels for fishing and the coastwise trade were undoubtedly built during the years immediately following the launching of the *Onrust,* the next vessel of which there is any record was the *Blessing of the Bay,* a barque of thirty tons, built in 1631 at Boston by order of Governor Winthrop of the Massachusetts Bay Colony. She was constructed to provide the Massachusetts colonists with a dependable means of communicating with the settlers of New Amsterdam (now New York) without traveling the weary miles on foot through the forests which separated the two isolated groups of lonely people.

"So we see," it has been said, "that shipbuilding was begun in America under the pressure of necessity and it was fostered by the conditions of life in the new country."

Ten years after the launching of the *Blessing of the Bay,* the good people of Salem, who seemed to have possessed from the earliest times a superiority in all things pertaining to shipping, launched a real ocean-going ship, far larger than any that had hitherto been built in America. This was the *Desire,* of 300 tons, a bigger craft than the *Mayflower* and larger by far than most of the ships in the British merchant marine. The *Desire* was not built for fishing or coastwise voyaging but for

trading with distant ports. As soon as she was ready for sea, she was loaded with fish and timber and despatched to the West Indies from which she returned with cotton, tobacco, negroes taken aboard at the Bahamas and salt loaded at Tortugas. Soon afterwards she set sail for England and made the voyage in twenty-three days, or quite as fast as the first packet-ships which came upon the scene a hundred and fifty years later.

Boston was rapidly becoming an active shipbuilding center, also, and here, in 1643, the first Yankee full-rigged ship was launched, the *Trial,* which went to Malaga and brought back, according to an early chronicler, "wine, fruit, oil, linen and wool, which was a great advantage to the country, and gave encouragement to trade." Another vessel was sent to London at this time "with many passengers, men of chief rank in the country, and great store of beaver."

Within a few years after the establishment of the first settlements, the New England shipbuilding industry was founded and took its place as one of the country's leading enterprises. While there was some shipbuilding in the other colonies to the south, it was New England which took and kept the lead for many years. This was natural, for the forests were filled with great pine trees from which to make masts and yards and sturdy oaks for the vessels' frames and planking.

The different types of craft built in these early days are no longer seen on the high seas and even their names require explanation today. The snow was very popular and was practically a brig, but with a fore-and-aft sail on the mainmast. The ketch was a two-masted vessel, usually with a square rigged foremast and a mainmast carrying a fore-and-aft sail and a square topsail. The pink was schooner-rigged but had no bowsprit or jib. Shallops, bug-eyes, sharpies and smacks were all variations of these types and were all in common use.

But the most outstanding of all early ship types, and the one which had the greatest effect upon marine architecture, was "that incomparable craft," the New England schooner. "The origin of this distinctively Yankee type," says Marvin, "is one of the cherished traditions of New England."

In the year 1713 or 1714 Captain Andrew Robinson, of Gloucester, built a vessel of two masts, bearing on each a fore-and-aft sail set from a gaff and boom, with a jib forward. The model was sharp; the vessel was designed, as Gloucester craft ever have been, for speed as well as for seaworthiness. As the unique two-master was launched, she glided so swiftly and gracefully over the water that an enthusiastic spectator cried, "See how she scoons!" ("Scoon" in the eighteenth century was a word popularly used to describe the skipping of a flat stone over the water when thrown by a strong and skillful hand.)

Captain Robinson, who had been puzzled to find a name for his odd craft, instantly replied, "A schooner let her be!" This word, which had reference at the outset only to the peculiar qualities of Captain Robinson's hull-model, came by natural transfer to characterize the two-masted fore-and-aft rig, destined to stand for a century and a half as the favorite and distinctive rig of American waters.

These Yankee ships were soon faring abroad in great numbers, taking cargoes first to the ports of the West Indies, and then to Europe and the Mediterranean. There is little record of their ventures or the names of the ships; yet there is enough to show us that they were carrying on an active commerce with all the islands and countries bordering the Atlantic, and that while doing so they were fighting against many difficulties. Every voyage they made was fraught with danger; French privateers hovered close around the American coast and throughout the West Indies; when the diminutive Yankee vessels approached the coast of Europe or the Mediterranean, they were almost certain to be intercepted by the Barbary pirates.

There are scores of records such as the following:

(1690) "The ketch *Fellowship*, Captain Robert Glanville, via the Vineyard for Berwick on the Tweed, was taken by two French privateers and taken to Dunkirk."

(1695) "The ship *Essex* of Salem, Captain John Beal, from Bilboa in Spain, had a battle at sea and losed John Samson, boatswain. This man and Thomas Rhodes, the gunner, had previously contracted that whoever of the two survived the other should have all the property of the deceased."

The Barbary pirates or "Sallee rovers" whose headquarters were in Algiers, but whose operations extended from the Mediterranean through the Bay of Biscay and as far north as the English Channel, also captured many Salem ships. As early as 1661, it was recorded that "for a long time previous the commerce of Massachusetts was much annoyed by Barbary Corsairs and that many of her seamen were held in bondage." Indeed, battles with these fierce sea-rovers occurred on nearly every voyage to the coasts of Europe.

Even before 1700, American ships had established themselves upon the principal trade routes. Scores of vessels had been sent across the Atlantic and through the Caribbean. The hardihood and daring of these early mariners was extraordinary, for their tiny sloops and ketches were cockleshells ranging in size from forty to sixty tons and measuring no more than fifty or sixty feet in length. Few sailors of today would care to risk the hazards of such an ocean crossing.

Yet so active were these little Yankee vessels that in 1668, Sir Joshua Childs, once chairman of the East India Company, declared in a Discourse on Trade that:

"Of all the American plantations His Majesty has none so apt for the building of ships as New England, nor comparably so qualified for the breeding of seamen, not only by reason of the natural industry of the people, but principally by reason of their cod and mackerel fisheries, and in my opinion there is nothing more prejudicial and in prospect more dangerous to any mother kingdom than the increase of shipping in her colonies, plantations or provinces."

Indeed, there was some justification for Sir Joshua's alarm, for American ships were not only competing for cargoes with those of England, but the Yankee shipbuilders were competing with established British shipyards in the construction of vessels for sale abroad. In the forty years between 1674 and 1714, just following Sir Joshua's warning, there were 1332 vessels built in New England, and of these 239 were built for or sold to merchants and ship owners in other countries. The reason for the popularity of American vessels over those constructed in England or Europe was chiefly because they could be built more cheaply, owing to the abundant supply of suitable timber. They were also known to be well built and, even in these early days, they had established a reputation for speed and handiness.

The colonial sailors who navigated these tiny craft over the ocean courses contended with so many dangers unknown to modern seamen that the success with which they prosecuted their voyages was astonishing. Their navigating instruments were of the crudest description; their charts were inaccurate; and when after a long voyage they fell in with the land, there were no lighthouses or other marks to guide them or tell them their location. Privateers of all the great European powers—England, France, Spain and Holland—regarded them as fair game practically all the time, and pirates and freebooters abounded.

Even the Indians took to the sea to harass the Yankee blue-water men. The records of the First Church of Salem, for example, contain the following entry under date of July, 1677: "The Lord having given a Commission to the Indians to take no less than 13 of the Fishing Ketches of Salem and Captivate the men . . . it struck a great consternation into all the people here. The Pastor moved on the Lord's

85

Day, which was accordingly done . . . The Lord was pleased to send in some Ketches on the Fast Day which was looked on as a gracious smile of Providence. Also there had been 19 wounded men sent into Salem a little while before; also a Ketch sent out from Salem as a man-of-war to recover the rest of the Ketches. The Lord give them Good Success."

Pirates abounded along the New England coast in the early days, though they were frequently but mean and skulking gentry with little stomach for a fight and resembled not in the least the swashbuckling type of freebooter regarded as typical. One of the best of them seems to have been a certain Thomas Pounds who preyed on Boston shipping until, in 1689, the citizens of that town sent the sloop *Mary* out to capture him. He was found cruising about the waters of Vineyard Sound and was at once attacked by the *Mary*. Pounds refused to surrender and gave as good as he received. Captain Samuel Pease of the *Mary* was mortally wounded. His mate ordered the pirate vessel to strike its colors, but Pounds, brandishing his sword, shouted defiantly: "Come on board, ye dogs, and I will strike you presently." The men of Boston took him at his word and tumbled aboard, smiting right and left until they laid hands on Pounds whom they carried back to Boston for a proper hanging.

Another pirate who came to the same end was John Quelch. In 1703 he hoisted a pirate flag which he called the "Old Roger" on a small brigantine called the *Charles*. The flag was a weird one, bearing the figure of a skeleton holding an hour-glass in one hand and "a dart in the heart with three drops of blood proceeding from it in the other." Quelch came into possession of his ship by leading a mutiny and throwing the lawful skipper to the sharks. He then squared away for Brazil, and during his pirate cruise captured and looted a number of merchantmen. He then sailed into Marblehead with a plausible yarn to explain the loss of the captain and the acquisition of his exceptionally rich cargo. His men talked too much over their rum, however, and the bold pirates were summarily marched off to the gallows.

The people of Salem seemed to have a particular aptitude for shipbuilding and trading and, as a consequence, Salem ships and merchants became better known than those of the other seaboard cities at a very early date. The first of the great merchant princes of Salem was Philip English who came to America from the Isle of Jersey in 1670. At first he sailed as master of his own vessels, but soon he entrusted his ships to others and established himself ashore as a merchant and trader. By 1692, he was considered the wealthiest man in New England and owned twenty-one ships which traded coastwise and carried on an extensive trade with Barbados and St. Christopher in the West Indies, Bilboa in Spain, the Isle of Jersey in the English Channel and all the coastal towns of France.

The cargoes carried by his vessels are tersely described in an old document written by another Salem merchant of the time: "Dry merchantable codfish for the markets of Spain and Portugal and the Straits (of Gibraltar). Refuse fish, lumber, horses and provisions for the West Indies. Our own produce, a considerable quantity of whale and fish oil, whale-bone, furs, deer, elk and bear skins are annually sent to England."

In the coastal trade with Virginia and "Merriland," the Salem vessels carried "Molasses, Rum, Salt, Cider, Mackerel, Wooden Bowls,

Platters, Pails, Kegs, Muscavado, Sugar, and Codfish, and brought back to Salem Wheat, Pork, Tobacco, Furs, Hides, old Pewter, Old Iron, Brass, Copper, Indian Corn and English Goods."

Philip English, like the other New Englanders of his day, was a devout man and careful to send his cargoes forward under the protection of the Almighty. A typical bill of lading for one of his ships reads: "Twenty hogheads of rum, shipped by the Grace of God in the Good Ketch called the *Speedwell* . . . and by God's Grace bound to Virginia and Merriland."

The same piety no doubt abided in the breasts of early New England merchants who sent their vessels to the coast of Guinea to barter for negro slaves' to sell in the West Indies. The infamous slave trade, fostered by the Puritan New Englanders who apparently saw no harm in it, flourished practically from the beginning of ocean commerce in America. The colonies' first large ship, the *Desire,* had brought slaves north from the Bahamas, and hundreds of other vessels followed in her wake.

Most of the slaves went to the southern states and, as Virginia and the Carolinas were developed and one large plantation after the other was established, the New England ship owners profited vastly by supplying them with "rum and niggers." Writing home from Guinea, the master of one of the Rhode Island slavers described the difficulties he was having owing to the great number of Yankee vessels competing against each other for cargoes: "For never was there so much Rum on the Coast at one time before. Not ye like of ye French ships was never seen before, for ye whole coast is full of them. For my part I can give no guess when I shall get away, for I purchast but 27 slaves since I have been here, for slaves is very scarce. We have had nineteen Sail of us at one time in ye Road, so that ships used to carry pryme slaves off is now forced to take any that comes. Here is seven sail of us Rum men that are ready to devour one another, for our case is desprit."

Following shortly after Philip English came Richard Derby, the father of Elias Hasket Derby. After the Revolution, Derby developed the trade of Salem so greatly that the name of this little New England town became far more widely known in Canton, Bombay, Rangoon and Calcutta than that of the much larger cities of New York and Boston.

Richard Derby was born in 1712 and, like many another New England lad, went to sea at an early age. He became a master before he was twenty and remained at sea in this capacity until 1757. During this period he built up a fleet of vessels, ranging from fifty to one hundred tons burden, which he freighted with fish, provisions and lumber for the West Indies from whence they returned with sugar, cotton, rum and molasses. Failing these cargoes, they called in at the Carolinas for rice or naval stores. Mixed cargoes of these goods were then loaded on other vessels of the fleet and despatched to Madeira and Spain where they were exchanged for the products of those countries— fruit, oil, wine, salt, lead or embroidered handkerchiefs and other linen goods.

During the French War from 1756 to 1763, Richard Derby's vessels, like those of every other American ship owner, had many an encounter with French privateers. The Derby ships always went armed, some of them quite heavily. An old letter describes them as having from eight to twelve cannon, "with four cannons below decks for close quarters."

In addition to the French privateers, there were other sea brigands almost beyond number, it being officially reported early in the 1700's that there were fifteen hundred pirates frequenting the American coast, their principal headquarters being at Cape Fear, and in the Bahama Islands. Despite many excursions against them, pirates abounded along the Atlantic coast and throughout the Spanish Main for over a hundred years and caused no end of trouble for the captains and men of the law-abiding merchant vessels.

At the same time, American vessels were plagued almost beyond endurance by the numberless regulations concerning tonnage, customs dues and neutrality imposed upon them by the Mother Country, England. The first of the British Navigation Acts was passed in 1651, and stipulated that all goods grown or manufactured in Asia, Africa or America should be transported to England in English vessels only. Other acts followed forbidding certain "enumerated" articles—tobacco, sugar, cotton, wool and others—to be shipped from the colonies to any country except England. Had it been possible to enforce these laws strictly, the effect on the colonies that produced the "enumerated" articles would have been disastrous, for they enjoyed a flourishing trade in these goods with countries other than England.

All these obstacles were ever present in the minds of the people of the New England coastal towns, particularly because the labor and expense of building many of the vessels was shared on a cooperative basis. An entire community would often stake its combined futures upon the success of a single ship.

"Such a vessel," says an old report, "would represent very little actual money but a great deal of hard toil and stern self-denial. The failure of the enterprise might mean penury, if not actual ruin for the whole community. There were the risks of the sea, the uncharted southern reefs, the fog, the hurricane, and most of all the ferocious pirates who were the plague of the Spanish Main in the eighteenth century. The lucky vessel that escaped all these perils had still another deadly enemy in the cruiser and customs officer of the king, and many a weather-beaten craft returning deep laden was seized in her home harbor and carried off before the eyes of her poor cooperative owners who could only stand by in helpless grief and fury at this wasting of their hard labor of the year."

The efforts of the English Government to suppress American shipping met with relatively little success, although they stirred up a hatred which had much to do with the colonists' desire to become independent. The New England merchants felt themselves quite justified in evading the unjust regulations in any manner that seemed best. One of the ways is indicated in the following letter addressed to Captain Richard Derby when he was about to leave for a voyage to the West Indies in the schooner *Volante:*

"If you should go among the French, endeavor to get salt at St. Martins, but if you should fall so low as Statia, and any Frenchman should make you a good offer with good security, or by making your vessel a Dutch bottom, or by any other means practicable in order to your getting among ye Frenchmen, embrace it. Among whom if you should ever arrive, be sure to give strict orders amongst your men not to sell the least trifle unto them on any terms, lest they should make your vessel liable to a seizure. Also secure a permit so as for you to trade there next voyage, which you may undoubtedly do through your factor or by a 'little greasing' some others."

In short, Captain Derby was instructed to secure a Dutch registry for the *Volante* and thus free her from the liability of seizure as an American vessel under the British Navigation Acts. This was a common practice of the day and by a "little greasing" in the proper quarters any Yankee ship could be temporarily converted into one of Dutch, Spanish or French registry.

By this means and others, American vessels continued to outwit the British, and shipbuilding continued to flourish as one of the young country's most important industries. The records show, for example, that in the year 1769, there were launched on the Atlantic seaboard a total of three hundred and eighty-nine vessels. They slipped into the water at the rate of more than one for every day in the year. Of this fleet, one hundred and thirty-seven were built in Massachusetts; fifty in Connecticut; forty-five in New Hampshire; twenty-two in Pennsylvania; and nineteen in New York.

America took to the sea naturally, enthusiastically and successfully. During the first years of American settlement, before the colonies broke loose from the rule of England, one of the predominant interests of the people was the business of building ships and sending them to far ports on trading voyages.

9

The Triumph

Admiral Blake's Flagship at the Three Days' Fight off Portland,
England

OFF Portland on the south coast of England, as the sun rose on the morning of February the eighteenth, 1653, a fleet of seventy English men-of-war spread their snowy sails to the wind and dipped and tossed to the choppy Channel seas. This fleet, representing the entire naval force of England, was commanded by Admiral Robert Blake. As the darkness gave way to dawn, Blake paced slowly to and fro on the quarter-deck of his flagship, the *Triumph*. He was one of England's greatest admirals, a genius both at leading men and maneuvering ships in battle. He has been described as the man who "established England as the great naval power of the world."

"We should sight them soon, eh, Deane?" he asked of the man who paced beside him, Admiral Richard Deane.

"Yes, if the master of that hoy told the truth, they should be past the Channel Islands by now," Deane agreed. "We will catch them before the day is out; of that you may be certain."

"Aye, and pay them back for Dungeness," said Blake. "This time Tromp will not have two ships to our one."

"No, 'tis an even match today," Deane assented, "and, God willing, we will trounce them once and for all ere the day is done."

Word had been brought to Blake that the Dutch Admiral, Tromp, was beating up Channel with seventy-five men-of-war, escorting a convoy of two hundred richly laden Dutch merchantmen. Since the previous night the English fleet had been sailing back and forth across the entrance to the Channel in order to be sure of intercepting them. As usual, the English ships were divided into three squadrons, the Red, the White and the Blue. Blake, on this morning, was in command of the Red, while Admiral Sir William Penn commanded the Blue and Admiral George Monck the White.

A number of the English ships were first- and second-raters—full-rigged ships of a thousand tons or over and armed with from sixty to seventy guns. These were imposing in appearance, for their towering sterns, forecastles and sides were elaborately ornamented. Others of the English fleet were small craft—hoys, yachts, pinks and ketches. These were small sloop-rigged craft, lightly armed but fast terriers of the sea designed to dash in, deliver their attack and then swiftly slip away from beneath the big guns of the enemy—much like our gallant destroyers of today. As has always been the English custom, these vessels were sturdily built and partly for that reason were slower and drew more water than many of their Dutch adversaries. In the matter of speed, moreover, the Dutch frequently had the advantage, owing to the fact that they were more careful about keeping the underwater parts of their ship's hulls clean. In order to achieve this, they made a practice of coating them with tallow to permit them to move more easily through the water. Because of their heavier construction, how-

ever, the English ships could carry more and larger guns, which told heavily in their favor whenever they were not hopelessly out-numbered.

England and Holland had been waging bitter war for half a year. It was a war of ships being waged for the highest stakes—nothing less than to determine which nation should have supreme command of the seas. Rivalry between these two great seafaring nations had been in existence for many years and it had long been recognized by the leaders of both that, sooner or later, their commercial jealousy would flare out in open warfare. The Dutch had built so many ships and succeeded in securing so many cargoes for them that they had become known as the "waggoners of the sea." England, with her great victory over Spain still fresh in mind, and with a rapidly-growing merchant navy of her own, was not content to stand idly by while the Dutch attempted to usurp her place as mistress of the seas.

This was the underlying cause of the war, but actual hostilities had been provoked by an incident that occurred in May, 1652. For many years England had demanded that, as an acknowledgement of her sovereignty of the seas, the ships of other nations must dip their flags or lower their topsails whenever they passed an English man-of-war. On the twelfth of May, 1652, an English ship under the command of a Captain Young was sailing down channel and encountered a convoy of Dutch merchantmen beating up channel to their home ports. Captain Young watched with satisfaction as one Dutch vessel after the other dipped its flag. But—what was this? One of the Dutchmen sailed past without giving the customary salute. Captain Young immediately ordered a broadside to be fired at the offending foreigner. A short but indecisive engagement followed.

From this time on, each country knew that war was inevitable. The following week Admiral Blake, with fifteen ships, beat into Dover Roads where a fleet of fifty Dutch vessels was at anchor sheltering from a storm, and fired a cannon to remind the Dutch commander he had not saluted Dover Castle. The Dutchman, the redoubtable Admiral Tromp, replied with a broadside. Blake, resolute and convinced of the superiority of his men and their skill at the guns, ordered a general engagement. In an instant the roar of hundreds of cannon filled the air as the English attacked and the Dutch fought back. Fifteen ships against fifty! It was a typical piece of English audacity. The battle raged for five hours, every ship giving of its best, and when night fell Tromp was glad to escape into the darkness. Two of his ships had been sunk and the remainder had been so savagely handled that they were in no condition to continue the fight.

Other engagements followed—one off the Goodwin Sands in September in which several Dutch ships were sunk, but no English vessels were totally disabled; and one off Dungeness in November.

The *Triumph*

In this battle Blake had forty-two ships against Tromp's one hundred and one. The English, overwhelmed by vastly superior numbers, lost two ships and were forced to retreat to Dover. In this battle Blake had had the *Triumph* as his flagship, and she, with the *Vanguard* and *Victory,* had fought as gallant and courageous a battle as any in the long annals of the navy. These three ships, for a considerable time, were engaged against twenty of the enemy at once.

The winter passed and in February, as related above, Blake, with a completely reorganized fleet, was ready once more to meet the enemy. Shortly after sunrise on the morning of the eighteenth, as he and Deane were voicing their determination to give their enemy, Tromp, the worst drubbing he had ever received, there came the hail that all on board the *Triumph* had been impatiently awaiting.

"Sail ho!" cried the lookout from the *Triumph's* masthead. "The Dutch are in sight! A league and a half to windward!"

Blake ordered signals to be hoisted, directing the Blue and White squadrons to close up and join with him in launching the attack. A great and decisive battle was about to begin. Fought between equally matched fleets, the entire naval forces of the two leading naval powers of Europe, it was to last for three thunderous days, and result in as great a victory as British ships have ever won.

The wind, blowing from the west, favored the Dutch, and the English were put to a further disadvantage, for their three squadrons were quite widely separated when Tromp's fleet came in sight. Penn, with the Blue squadron, was a mile to leeward of the *Triumph*; Monck, with the White, was four miles to leeward.

Every effort was made to beat these vessels up to windward, so that the entire English force could join in battle at the same time. But it was to no avail. The westerly wind held them back, and Blake and the dozen or so large vessels of the Red squadron were forced to stand up alone against the full and flaming might of the entire Dutch fleet.

Blake, had he chosen to do so, could doubtless have fallen back and joined forces with the other English ships. A lesser commander, or one less fully imbued with that combination of cool calculation of all risks and a dash of recklessness that sometimes makes for genius, might well have chosen this safer course. But not Blake. Undaunted by the enormous odds against which his squadron would have to fight at the outset, he drove the *Triumph* to windward straight toward Tromp's flagship, the mighty *Brederode*.

The westerly wind, bearing the Dutch ships onward, soon brought the two forces together. Tromp held his fire until he was close to the English line—within musket range, according to some accounts. Then he poured a broadside into the *Triumph*. Doubling on himself, he turned his ship to present her other battery and discharged a second broadside at close range. Then, sailing down to leeward, he bore up sharply and loosed a third broadside into the *Triumph's* other side.

The other Dutch ships had closed in, surrounded the English squadron and were pouring in a murderous fire from all directions. Like lions at bay, the out-numbered English fought back, bursts of flame and smoke from their cannon following one another so rapidly that their ships appeared to be on fire.

As usual, the *Triumph* was the center round which the battle raged. As in her former battles, she continuously fought several enemy ships at once, the *Brederode* being her chief opponent. Blake, imperturbable and calm amidst the deafening roar of cannon and the indescribable confusion of battle, stood at his post on the quarter-deck, and issued his orders with a quiet resolution that inspired all who were near him with unbounded confidence.

The battle had started at eight o'clock in the morning and not until noon was Penn able to bring his Blue squadron into the line of battle, and so help relieve the terrible pressure to which his leader had been subjected. Monck soon joined in the fray with the vessels of the White squadron, and from that time on the tide of victory set in for the English. Ship for ship, the English were definitely superior. Now that they were nearly in equal force with the enemy, they made the most of it and blasted the Dutch with a fury unequalled in any previous engagement between the two fighting forces.

While the main body of the English fleet hammered at close quarters at Tromp's stubbornly resisting men-of-war, some of the smaller English vessels sped off to attack the merchant convoy. As darkness gathered, Tromp was glad to be able to escape from the general engagement and hurry after the convoy to protect it from further damage. Moreover, he was anxious to count his own losses and save his fighting ships from further battering.

The result of the first day's fighting was a decided victory for the English. They had had one ship sunk and four captured, but these were later recaptured and sent into port. The Dutch loss, on the other hand, amounted to five ships—three sunk, one captured and one blown up.

The *Triumph,* which throughout the day had led the fighting and had dealt and received an incredible number of blows, was badly shattered in both hull and rigging when the firing finally came to an end at nightfall. Her masts were either down or going over the side; her hull was holed in numerous places; a hundred of her men had fallen during the mad inferno of the day. In the heat of the battle Blake was wounded in the thigh by a jagged wooden splinter, and his flag-captain and secretary were killed by his side. Although both Blake and his flagship were crippled as a result of the first day's battle, the *Triumph* remained with the fleet, as it bore off to the eastward during the night in order to keep in touch with Tromp, hoping to renew the engagement on the following day.

The two fleets worked slowly along the Channel toward the Straits of Dover during the night, and as soon as the English could get near enough to engage the struggle began again, to be continued all day and the day after. Under cover of the darkness, Tromp had arranged his fighting ships in the form of a vast crescent which screened the merchant vessels of the convoy against the English attack. But the English now had the wind in their favor, were able to maneuver more freely, and used this circumstance to good advantage. Time and again, single vessels or groups of three or four pressed in toward the Dutch line, broke through it and harried the fleeing merchant ships—these "waggons of the sea" whose success in securing trade had had so much to do with bringing about the war. Innumerable actions were fought between the opposing men-of-war, and, as one contestant described it, there was "warm work" throughout the day until night again put an end to the fighting.

While Blake and the *Triumph* had been the mainstays of the

English fleet on the first day of the battle, the hero of the second day's fighting was Captain John Lawson, Vice-Admiral of the Red. Early in the afternoon, he drove his ship, the *Fairfax,* against the Dutch half-moon protective screen, and, with all guns blazing, beat into submission two of the largest enemy men-of-war. One of these was a vessel of more than 1,300 tons, which carried the flag of a Dutch rear-admiral. Then, surging forward into the convoy, Lawson lay about him to such good effect that a round dozen of the merchantmen surrendered and were taken captive.

But Lawson was well backed up by the other English ships, many of which carried out exploits no less daring and spectacular. Among the Dutch, Admiral De Ruyter, the second in command, fought like a lion, but toward evening his ship was so badly battered that she had to be taken in tow. As darkness came on, the English were still fighting as vigorously as when they began. So clearly was the battle going against the Dutch that the merchant vessels of the convoy threw cargo overboard to lighten themselves and so increase their speed. During this day the English lost one ship, the *Sampson,* but captured or destroyed six or seven of the enemy's men-of-war.

The pursuit recommenced on the third day, and the English attacks, aided by a strong west wind, became still more furious and more successful. The Dutch counter-attacks redoubled in energy, as the leaders strove to make up for the stinging humiliation of the previous defeats. And, as Admiral Penn remarked later on the great three-day long running battle, a Dutchman is never so dangerous as when he is desperate.

As the day started, the English saw that Tromp was shepherding his convoy toward the shallow waters of the French coast near Calais, evidently in the hope that the English ships, with their deeper draughts, would not be able to close in on him. As before, the Dutch fighting ships were spread out in a great half-moon formation.

Once again, the English pressed forward and laid their ships alongside the nearest Dutchmen. A dozen encounters went forward simultaneously, and the fighting, as described by those who took part in it, was of the most terrible description. Ships were taken and retaken; boarding parties were driven off or cut to ribbons; time and again there were fierce hand-to-hand encounters with guns, muskets and cutlasses on decks choked with desperate, wildly cheering, half-frenzied combatants.

Toward the middle of the afternoon, the greatest single exploit of that day of countless deeds of heroism occurred. Admiral Penn, with a squadron of his swiftest, heaviest-hitting ships, broke open a wide gap in the Dutch battle line, drove through it and captured some fifty merchant vessels. This was one-quarter of the entire convoy, and a heavy loss to the commerce-loving Dutch. In addition, four or five more Dutch men-of-war were captured or sunk during the course of the day's fighting. So sorely were the Dutch tried by the furious onslaught of the English that some of their captains are said to have given up the struggle as hopeless, and to have surrendered their ships freely.

At all events, when the third day's fighting came to an end at nightfall, Tromp realized that the only course open to him was to attempt to escape under cover of darkness. Accordingly, he led his flat-bottomed ships into the shallow waters of the French coast where the English could not follow, and then, hugging the shore and aided by favorable wind and tide, ordered his vessels to make all speed for home. By a rare combination of skill and good fortune, the Dutch were able to slip along the coast and keep out of reach of the English until they reached the Texel and safety.

Altogether the battle was a great victory for the English, and, although there were several further engagements between the two fleets, the battle of Portland is generally regarded as the decisive event of this war with the Dutch.

Even more, it is considered to have been one of the decisive battles of history, for it gave Britain supremacy on the seas, a position which, through thick and thin, she has retained to the present day.

10

The Royal George

Admiral Hawke's Flagship at the Battle of Quiberon Bay

THE Bay of Biscay is noted for its violent storms, but few of the gales that have swept across it from the howling North Atlantic have blown so furiously as the one that raged on the twentieth of November, 1759. It was a tremendous gale from the northwest, with howling blasts of wind, torrents of driving rain and ominous, dark weather, with the sea lashed to fury and cruel, gigantic waves running "so high that no boat could live for a moment amongst them," according to one who drove through the midst of the storm at its greatest height.

Through the murk and storm rack coming in from the open sea, a squadron of twenty-one English men-of-war struggled, led by the *Royal George* of a hundred guns, at whose masthead flew the flag of Edward Hawke, Admiral of the Blue. As the ships pressed on—and they seemed to be in tremendous haste—they now sank deep in the trough of the waves, now surged upward, rolling and staggering, and plunged forward on the crest of an enormous breaker. So violently were the waters moving that, even as the ships' bows rose and pointed toward the sky, swift-moving, heavy cross-seas beat on their sides and broke in deluges of seething foam across their laboring decks. At the wheel of each ship eight of the strongest seamen held the spokes, straining every muscle in the desperate effort to hold their wallowing monsters to the course.

Between the English vessels and the coast of France, a French squadron of twenty-three ships under Admiral de Conflans, with his flag in the *Soleil Royal,* was fighting the same storm. These ships had sailed from Brest a few days previously and were bound for the harbor of Vannes, in Brittany, on the shores of Quiberon Bay. Here an army of twenty thousand men, and ships for transporting them, had been gathered together and made ready for an invasion of England. De Conflans' warships were to rendezvous with the army at Vannes and, after the troops had boarded the waiting transports, were to sail with them to England, acting as a guard against any English men-of-war that might attempt to stop them. Other troops were to be ferried across the channel from Flanders once de Conflans had succeeded in carrying out the first part of the invasion plan.

On the same day that de Conflans sailed from Brest, Hawke had sallied forth from Torbay and, upon arriving off the French coast, had learned from an English merchant vessel, the *Love and Unity,* that the French fleet had but a short while before disappeared in the mists to the south. Divining the French plan, Hawke set after them with all possible speed.

On the morning of the twentieth of November, with the ships laboring and straining in the great gale from the west, the *Maidstone,* an English frigate sent out to scout ahead of Hawke's main body, signaled that the enemy was in sight. This was shortly afterwards confirmed by the *Magnanime,* which Hawke had sent ahead to discover how close the fleet was to the coast. Hawke at once ordered a signal hoisted on the *Royal George*—"Form line abreast"—in order to bring up all the rearward ships for the attack.

Toward ten o'clock in the morning, Hawke, peering through his telescope from the *Royal George's* heaving quarter-deck, could see that the French were making the fastest speed they could to port, intent upon escape rather than doing battle.

"Let them run," said Hawke to the officers near him. "We'll catch them before they reach the bay. They still have thirty miles to go."

But every minute counted and, to use his vessels to the best advantage, Hawke now signaled the seven ships nearest the French to draw into line-of-battle ahead of the *Royal George,* and endeavor to stop the French ships until the rest of the English squadron could overtake them. He signaled to the ships astern of the *Royal George* that they were to form into line-of-battle as they pitched and pounded on through the mountainous seas, "that no time might be lost in the pursuit."

As he made the signal, Hawke at the same time ordered that the *Royal George's* topgallant sails be set. In all probability, he took this action to show the other English captains that he was resolute upon their making all possible speed, despite the fury of the weather in which, ordinarily, the heavy-gunned men-of-war would have hove to under reefed topsails. Hawke was not disappointed by his captains. One and all, they shook out their topsail reefs and added what other sails they could.

And so, for the remainder of the morning and until half-past two in the afternoon the pursuit continued. The French, as Hawke put it in his report, "kept going off under such sail as all their squadron could carry and yet keep together, while we crowded after him with every sail our ships could bear."

At half-past two, the long-awaited moment, so valiantly striven for, arrived—the moment when the English ships could open fire. It was then that the leading English vessels—the *Dorsetshire, Defiance, Magnanime* and *Warspite*—came up with the rear of the French squadron and fell upon it like a pack of wolves. De Conflans, at this moment, was leading his fleet around the Cardinals, a dangerous chain of rocks to the north of Quiberon Bay, which, with the protection of its shore batteries, was still some eighteen to twenty miles distant.

The rearmost ship of the French squadron was the *Formidable*, under Rear Admiral de Verger. Ship after ship of the advancing English fleet attacked her as they drew abreast. The *Dorsetshire*, of seventy guns, first loosed a close-range broadside as she swept by, driving hard to overtake the French van. The *Defiance*, another seventy-gun ship, following hard on the *Dorsetshire's* heels, next roared thunder and spouted flame as she, too, sped by to try to overtake de Conflans.

Scarcely had the smoke from the *Defiance's* guns been whipped away by the gale than the *Magnanime*, under Lord Howe, came charging down from windward. Howe's intention was to press on past the *Formidable*, doing what damage he could in passing, but, as he came abreast of the Frenchman, a shot carried the *Magnanime's* foreyard away and checked her speed. "Black Dick"—as Howe was known in the navy—instantly changed his plans, turned to port and closed with the enemy. He "bore down upon the Rear Admiral," wrote an eye-witness, "and getting under his lee opened a most tremendous fire from his thirty-twos and twenty-fours." Hurled forward by the gale, the great bulk of the *Magnanime* was thrown against the Frenchman and tore away the port lids of the lower tier of guns.

As Howe freed his ship and drew away to continue the attack, the *Warspite* came up and joined in the fray. An inferno ensued as the three ships lay close together, rolling from side to side. The flashing and roaring of the guns and drifting clouds of yellowish smoke added to the already hellish fury of the elements. Under the blows of the English ships, the *Formidable* was soon dismasted and reduced almost to a wreck. "In half an hour," said an eye-witness, "they made a dreadful havoc in the *Formidable,* whose fire began to slack."

By now the *Royal George,* with Hawke's blue flag flying out at the main, was bearing down upon the scene of action. As she rounded the Cardinals just before four o'clock, Hawke was able to see the *Formidable* striking her colors to the *Resolution,* which had joined in the attack on the unfortunate vessel. Studying the situation from his closer vantage point, he saw that the rear of the French line was being fiercely engaged by the leading English ships, while the French van and center were crowded together in a confused mass inside the entrance of the bay.

In an effort to disentangle his ships and bring them into a defensive formation, Admiral de Conflans signaled for each ship to turn in succession. This seems only to have made matters worse. "The confusion was awful," wrote a French officer. "When the van, in which I was, tried to go about, part could not do it. We were in a funnel, as it were, all on the top of each other, with rocks on one side of us and ships on the other."

The *Royal George*

On came the *Royal George,* while the French ships struggled to get clear of one another and prepare as best they could to meet the attack. Hawke had but one goal in mind for his own big ship. It was to bring her alongside the *Soleil Royal,* the French flagship, and force her to surrender.

This was no easy task. The wind was now howling more fiercely than ever; the sea, even in the bay, was running high. But the gravest danger of all was that of the *Royal George* crashing on one of the sharp-fanged granite reefs or treacherous shoals of quicksand that fringed the entrance to the bay. "A network of shoals and sand-banks," is how one French writer describes Quiberon Bay, "with heavy surf breaking along the shore on the calmest days of summer, and ugly cross-currents swirling to and fro with the strength and rush of a mill race"; a haven "lined with reefs that the navigator never sees without alarm, and never passes without emotion."

It was into this devil's cauldron, with the unknown shore roaring under his lee, that Hawke proposed to drive the *Royal George.* The sailing-master of the flagship was charged with the duty of navigating her and keeping her clear of rocks and shoals, but he had scant knowledge of the waters leading to Quiberon Bay, for the French had done their utmost to keep such information from their enemies. Fearful of the tremendous risk involved in rushing through so dangerous a stretch of water, with visibility lessening each minute as the darkness gathered, the sailing-master advised Hawke that it would be suicide to attempt to reach the French. For Hawke, however, this was no matter of taking one or two ships. The battle was vital to England's existence as a nation. If he should fail, and the threatened invasion should be carried out, England might be subdued and reduced to a second or third-rate power. There was but one thing to do. Risk all to save all.

"You have done your duty in warning me," Hawke said to his sailing-master. "Now lay us alongside the *Soleil Royal!*"

Within a few minutes the *Royal George* was inside the bay and close to the concentrated power of the French fleet. Seeing that Hawke was making for the *Soleil Royal,* one after another of the French vessels beat up to try to intercept him. The first to draw alongside was the *Tonnant,* bearing the French Vice-Admiral. As the *Royal George* rolled heavily to starboard and then steadied for a moment, the orange-yellow flash of her port battery glowed bright; the thunder of her guns rose above the screaming of the gale, and the *Tonnant* shuddered from truck to keelson as the broadside found its mark.

Several other French ships did their utmost to head off the plunging *Royal George,* but she dealt with one and all, beating them aside as her great bow flung away the foaming seas. Hawke now was closing with the *Soleil Royal,* and directed his sailing-master to get across her stern so a raking broadside could be delivered. At this moment, the *Superbe,* a 70-gun ship, made a gallant effort to save the flagship. Surging ahead, she thrust herself between the *Royal George* and the *Soleil Royal.* Again the *Royal George* spoke and her broadside struck the *Superbe* like a blow from a giant's fist, just as the French ship was lifting on a breaking roller. Down she went like a stone, riddled by that one terrific hail of shot, her three topmasts disappearing under the waves "in a hideously sudden manner." The *Royal George's* people gave a cheer, according to an officer who was present, but it was a faint one, for the sailors were stunned by the suddenness of the disaster and the miserable fate of the hundreds on board the *Superbe.*

During this engagement the *Soleil Royal,* in endeavoring to avoid Hawke's bold attempt to rake, had fallen to leeward and, in trying to tack to recover her position, she collided with two other ships. Then, as she was drifting toward a shoal, she was forced to steer still further away from the fight and finally to anchor deep in the bay.

While the *Royal George* had been battling almost single-handed against the ships clustered around the *Soleil Royal,* the other English ships had been giving an equally good account of themselves. The *Torbay* had engaged the French *Thésée* so heavily that the latter had opened her lower gun-ports to bring more cannon into play. This was her undoing, for, as she rolled to the next wave, the water poured in and engulfed both ship and crew. The *Heros* was shattered by the *Magnanime,* and blown ashore by the gale in a helpless condition, while, as already related, the *Formidable* had struck to the *Resolution.*

Night now put an end to the battle, and the English ships anchored near the entrance to the bay to wait for daylight. In the morning, the French, fearful of another battle as relentless as the one they had just been through, sought to escape and, consequently, lost most of their remaining ships. The *Soleil Royal* cut her cables at daybreak, and was driven ashore, where the French burned her. Seven ships slipped along the coast to the north, but soon ran ashore. An eighth, the *Juste,* was wrecked on a shoal in the bay. Only eight ships succeeded in getting away by sailing to the south and seeking refuge in the harbor of Rochefort.

Considering the completeness of Hawke's victory, the magnificent courage and seamanship which carried it through and the tremendous difficulties overcome, the battle of Quiberon Bay is regarded as the most brilliant English victory between the Armada and Trafalgar. Hawke and the *Royal George* had saved England from untold horrors and further struggle, for the last possibility of a French invasion had been shattered and the finishing blow had been given to the naval power of France.

"The guns that should have conquered us they rusted on
the shore,
The men that would have mastered us they drummed and
marched no more,
For England was England, and a mighty brood she bore
When Hawke came swooping from the West."

11

The Endeavour

Captain James Cook's First Voyage of Discovery

On the afternoon of August the twenty-fifth, 1768, the bark *Endeavour* sailed from Plymouth, England, under the command of Lieutanant James Cook, R. N., having on board a number of scientists, bound for the Marquesas Islands to observe a transit of the planet Venus. The expedition and the reason for its being undertaken had caused a great deal of interest throughout the British Isles. It had first been proposed by the Royal Society, the most important scientific body in England. After royal assent had been obtained, the Admiralty had provided the vessel to carry the astronomers and other scientists to their destination in the Pacific Ocean.

Once the *Endeavour* was clear of the land and bowling along down channel, Cook left the officer of the watch in charge of the ship and went below to his cabin. He drew his keys from his pocket, unlocked one of the drawers of his desk, and drew out a large envelope, addressed to him from the Admiralty. It bore the words "Secret and Confidential." Here were the secret orders for the voyage.

Cook had already surmised that the Admiralty had other matters than the transit of Venus in mind when he was appointed to command the *Endeavour*. He was now about to discover what these were, and he read as follows:

"And whereas there is reason to imagine that a continent, or land of great extent, may be found to the southward of the tract lately made by Captain Wallis in His Majesty's ship the *Dolphin* (of which you will herewith receive a copy) or of the tract of any former navigators in pursuits of the like kind; you are therefore . . . required and directed to put to sea with the bark you command, so soon as the observation of the transit of the planet Venus shall be finished, and observe the following instructions."

His directions were to sail southward through the Pacific Ocean in order to discover the great "Southern Continent" that had long intrigued geographers and was believed to be in the neighborhood of Australia or New Zealand. These two bodies of land had already been seen by European navigators, such as the early Portuguese, the Dutch explorer Tasman and the Englishman Dampier. Some believed they might form part of the Southern Continent; others thought they were islands. No one really knew whether the continent existed, though many believed it did. Marco Polo's "Land of Beach," which abounded with elephants, spices and gold, was supposed to form part of it. Lieutenant Cook was now instructed to solve this riddle, to find the continent, report on its products and open up trade with the natives, if natives there were.

The lieutenant replaced his instructions in his drawer and turned the key. He was proud of the confidence the Admiralty had in him, and profoundly aware of the importance of his mission. There was

much to plan for in a voyage into the uncharted waters of the great South Sea. Cook sat quietly thinking of what might lie ahead. Then, smiling quietly to himself, he rose and went on deck.

For the rigors of a voyage such as this one, no better ship than the *Endeavour* could have been selected. In the introduction to the narrative of his second voyage, Cook described the kind of vessel required for such long distance seafaring:

"The success . . . will more chiefly depend on the kind, the size, and the properties of the ships chosen for the service, as the greatest danger to be apprehended and provided against on a voyage of discovery, especially to the most distant parts of the globe, is that of the ship's being liable to be run aground on an unknown desert, or perhaps savage coast. So no consideration should be set in competition with that of her being of a construction of the safest kind, in which the officers may, with the least hazard, venture upon a strange coast. A ship of this kind must not be of a great draught of water, yet of a sufficient burden and capacity to carry a proper quantity of provisions and necessaries for her complement of men, and for the term requisite to perform the voyage.

"She must also be of a construction that will bear to take the ground, and of a size which, in case of necessity, may be safely and conveniently laid on shore to repair any accidental damage or defect. These properties are not to be found in ships of war of forty guns, nor in frigates, nor in East India Company ships, nor in large three-decked West India ships, nor indeed in any but North-country-built ships, as such as are built for the coal trade, which are peculiarly adapted for this purpose."

The *Endeavour* was such a ship. She was a stout, strong vessel designed for safety in all weathers. Launched to be a humble coal-carrier, she was destined to become one of the world's most celebrated ships of discovery.

Her commander, Lieutenant James Cook, was an extraordinary man and as well fitted for the voyage as was the ship. He was the son of a farm laborer, whose highest ambition was that the boy become a haberdasher. To this end, Cook had been apprenticed but he soon escaped his master and ran away to sea. For some years he worked as a common sailor on sailing vessels in the Baltic and North Sea trades; then he entered the navy as a common seaman. In 1755, purely by chance, he was drafted to serve on a vessel making a survey of the Labrador coast. He showed such a marked aptitude for survey work, that his commanding officer commended him highly, and when a skilled hand was needed to pilot the fleet bearing General

Wolfe and his army to Quebec, in 1759, Cook was chosen. As a result of his work during this expedition, the ex-haberdasher's apprentice was given a commission—a rare happening in the navy of that day.

On the outward voyage to the Pacific, the *Endeavour* touched at Madeira and Rio de Janeiro, then rounded Cape Horn and steered to the northwest on a direct course for the island of Tahiti, finally chosen instead of the Marquesas as the best spot from which to·observe the transit of Venus. Tahiti was reached, after an uneventful passage, on the fourth of April, 1769, eight months after the expedition's departure from Plymouth.

The transit was successfully observed, and, in July, Cook sailed to investigate neighboring islands. He visited seventeen and, while at Raiatea, he took possession of them for England. He named them the Society Islands—the name they bear today—because they lay so close together.

In August, the *Endeavour* was pointed toward the southwest to carry out the secret orders given to her commander. Day after day, a tiny speck upon the illimitable blue reaches of the vast South Pacific Ocean, she surged onward, over seas no European ship had sailed before. When a month had passed, Cook looked daily for the coast of the Southern Continent, which, if it existed at all, should be in the region the *Endeavour* had now reached. But no land was to be seen. A long rolling swell, which could only have been formed by traversing hundreds of leagues of open water, swept up from the south.

Satisfied that no continent was near, and having gone as far to the south as his instructions commanded, Cook turned toward the west and early in October sighted the northern island of New Zealand. Since the visit paid by the Dutch navigator Tasman, well over a century before, no European vessel had called at New Zealand. Cook sailed the *Endeavour* around both the main islands and, despite the unfriendliness of the native Maoris, obtained valuable information. Six months were given to this work which proved, among other things, that New Zealand consisted of two islands and was not the northern extremity of the great Southern Continent.

Time after time, the Maoris attacked Cook and his sailors when they attempted to come ashore. In the end, their ferocity prevented any exploration of the interior of the islands. A typical entry in the narrative of the voyage states that at Queen Charlotte's Sound, where the *Endeavour* was careened to clean her hull, the natives greeted the explorers by "heaving a few stones against the ship." The children of these natives told later Englishmen that their fathers had believed the *Endeavour* to be a very large bird with beautiful white wings. The small boat that put off from her side they thought was a young bird carrying goblins armed with thunderbolts. The hostility of the natives did not prevent Cook from pursuing his favorite art, that of surveying coasts. He made a chart of the islands that, for its extraordinary accuracy, is one of the major achievements in the long history of exploration.

It was now the end of March, 1770. The *Endeavour's* work at New Zealand was completed, and Cook was to choose the route by which he should return to England. The Admiralty expected him to return either by way of the Cape of Good Hope or Cape Horn, taking the most direct route. There was another possibility, and this appealed the most to Cook. After holding a conference of his officers, who unanimously agreed to the course he proposed, it was decided to make for the east coast of Australia, then called New Holland, because of Tasman's voyages.

With the exception of Tasman, the earlier Portuguese, British and Dutch explorers had visited only the barren northern and western coasts of Australia. It remained for Cook to discover the rich and fertile southeastern part of the continent.

The *Endeavour* left New Zealand behind on the thirty-first of March and steered westward into a red and gold sunset that seemed a promise of good fortune. Land was sighted on the nineteenth day and, after coasting to the northward for several more days searching for a good harbor, Cook brought the *Endeavour* to anchor in a well-sheltered bay. Because of the numerous sting-rays in the water, the bay was first called Stingray Harbor. Later, after the scientists on board the *Endeavour* found countless new flowers and shrubs, the name was changed to Botany Bay. Here, a few years later, England established a convict settlement.

From Botany Bay, Cook sailed northward along the coast, accurately charting every bay and promontory and other features of the shore-line. These were of invaluable assistance to later navigators.

An exceptional navigator, Cook had so far sailed the *Endeavour* through calm and storm, and for many thousands of miles along uncharted coasts on which many another seaman might well have come to disaster. Now, owing to no fault of his own, the good ship came near to going to the bottom with all on board. On his progress up the Australian coast, Cook had kept close in to the shore and this course had taken the ship inside the Great Barrier Reef and its formidable hazards. Never charted, Cook had no means of knowing of its existence or of the suddenness with which its coral fangs rose from great depths to within a few feet of the surface.

At sunset, on the tenth of June, a coral shoal was seen from the masthead of the *Endeavour*. Cook prudently decided to veer away from the coast and cruise in deeper waters throughout the night, never suspecting that the Barrier Reef lay in his path. There was a fair steady-blowing wind and the ship sailed off before it. The depth of water began to vary with abnormal suddenness. The lead was kept going constantly, however, and soon the water deepened. Cook, believing that they were clear of reefs, turned in for the night.

Just before eleven o'clock, a sounding showed the water to be seventeen fathoms. In a few seconds, before the lead could be heaved again, the ship plunged headlong on the Barrier Reef. The waves lifted her and she crashed down with a terrific impact, violent enough, it seemed, to break her keel.

In an instant, Cook was on deck, cool and calm. He was not given to over-statement, but he was well aware of the crisis.

"It was," he wrote, "an alarming and terrible circumstance, and threatened immediate destruction."

He at once sent men to the pumps and ordered anchors carried out in small boats, so that an attempt could be made to haul the ship off the reef. It was high tide when the *Endeavour* struck. If she could not be freed at once, she would have to remain where she was, with the hole in her bottom becoming steadily larger, until the next high water. The ship's boats could not take all those on board; the pounding and grating on the reef meant certain destruction unless the ship were freed.

When the anchors had been carried out, all hands manned the capstan and the windlass and tried to heave in on the anchor cables, but their effort was of no avail. The *Endeavour* refused to move. There was but one thing to do, namely, to lighten the ship, and Cook gave orders for fifty tons of ballast, old stores and guns, to be thrown over the side. As this work was nearing completion, the tide approached the full; the time for another attempt to heave the ship off was at hand. It was high time, for the water lapping into the hold was gaining on the pumps.

Cook, with his customary foresight, made careful preparations to "fother" the ship, the moment she was refloated, that is, to lower over her bows a sail to which wool and oakum were sewn, and drag it along the bottom of the ship until it covered the leak. When all was ready, Cook sent every possible hand to the capstan and the windlass, warning them that their lives depended on their breaking the ship loose from the reef. It was a terrific struggle. But the lightening of the ship had eased her enough to allow her to be heaved free. Her keel grated slowly along the coral; she slipped off and floated in deep water. The fothering mat was then hauled into place over the leak and all hands were sent to the pumps. Within a quarter of an hour the ship was pumped dry.

The *Endeavour* was taken in to the shore and beached, so that the damage might be repaired. Cook then resumed his northward course along the coast, passed through Torres Strait, between Australia and

New Guinea, and brought the ship safely to Batavia, Java. This ended the exploring part of the voyage, for the route from Batavia to Europe was well known to navigators. The *Endeavour* sailed from Java on December the twenty-sixth, passed to the southward around the Cape of Good Hope, and on the thirteenth of July, 1771, anchored in the Downs, having returned at last to England.

The *Endeavour's* voyage was, without question, one of the most remarkable ever made. One historian has said that it was "the greatest which the history of discovery could record."

Cook made two more voyages of discovery. On the first, he sailed again to the South Pacific and struck far to the south, resolved to find out if the Southern Continent really existed. He was turned back by the great Antarctic ice barrier and was satisfied that if the Southern Continent did exist it was too cold and snow-covered to be of any practical value. On his last voyage, Cook sailed around Cape Horn to the coast of California and then northward, his aim being to find if there were a western outlet to the Northwest Passage. In this search he was not successful, but during the voyage he discovered the Sandwich or Hawaiian Islands, and took possession of Vancouver Island for the British Empire.

On his last voyage, Cook met an untimely death. While at the Sandwich Islands, on his voyage homeward from the northwest coast of America, he was killed by a band of natives, who had stolen some equipment from his ship, the *Resolution*.

Perhaps the best description of Cook is the one that calls him "the finisher of the main tract of oceanic discovery." His voyages opened up Australia, New Zealand and numerous islands of the Pacific to European colonization and development. The voyage of the *Endeavour,* in particular, had consequences of the greatest importance, for it resulted in the rich territories of Australia and New Zealand becoming members of the British Commonwealth of Nations.

12

The Bonhomme Richard

John Paul Jones' Flagship in the Battle with the Serapis

EARLY in the morning of August the fourteenth, 1779, an oddly-assorted squadron of American men-of-war sailed from the port of Lorient, France, and headed north toward the mists and grey-green racing seas of the English Channel. The squadron was commanded by Captain John Paul Jones in the flagship *Bonhomme Richard,* which was followed by four smaller vessels—the 32-gun frigate *Alliance;* the *Pallas,* a merchant vessel armed with thirty guns; another armed merchant ship, the brig *Vengeance;* and the 18-gun cutter *Cerf.* This small and weakly-armed force, of which only the *Alliance* and the *Cerf* had been built for war purposes, had as its purpose a commerce-destroying raid on the shipping surrounding the British Isles.

That swift and powerfully armed British frigates and ships-of-the-line were certain to be encountered did not apparently daunt Paul Jones. What he lacked in material equipment, he would make up for with sublime self-confidence, the ability to inspire his men to the greatest heights of courage and a resolution that refused to admit the possibility of defeat, no matter how great the odds might be.

The *Bonhomme Richard* was without question as sorry a parody of a fighting ship as ever carried stout hearts into the carnage of naval action. She was a reconditioned merchant vessel, originally named the *Duc de Duras;* an old, slow, leaky craft that had outlived her usefulness in the trade between France and India. Benjamin Franklin, at that time representing the American colonies at Paris, had obtained her from the French ministry of the Marine, and it was in gratitude to him that Paul Jones re-christened her the *Bonhomme Richard,* the French translation of Franklin's *nom de plume* as the author of "Poor Richard's Almanac."

Jones had a difficult time getting guns for his new flagship, but he finally obtained six old 18-pounders, which he mounted on the lower gun deck, and twenty-eight 12-pounders, which he ranged along each side of the main deck. In addition, eight 9-pounders were mounted on the forecastle and the quarter-deck. All the guns were old, and tragic consequences were to arise because of this.

Striking out from the French coast into the Atlantic, the squadron skirted along the west coast of Ireland, then around the northern tip of Scotland. Few days went by without the capturing or sinking of one or more British ships. Then, after sailing down the eastern coast of Scotland, the squadron arrived off the mouth of the Humber. Here, Paul Jones learned that, owing to news of his activities, the entire coast was in wild excitement and alarm. The size of the American force had been so exaggerated, and the terror inspired by the mere mention of the name Paul Jones was so great, that the people feared an invasion and were burying their plate and other valuables.

About noon of the following day, September the twenty-third, while the American squadron, in chase of a brigantine, was nearing Flamborough Head from the south, a large vessel, promptly followed by several others, suddenly rounded the promontory from the north. Other ships immediately appeared, coming into view one after the other in quick succession. The Americans counted the strangers with increasing amazement and consternation, and in twenty minutes they found themselves in the presence of a fleet of forty-two ships.

Paul Jones, after a long and careful search through his spy-glass, ascertained that the vessels were a convoy of forty merchantmen, guarded by two frigates. These proved to be the *Serapis* of fifty guns, commanded by Captain Richard Pearson, and the smaller *Countess of Scarborough.* Jones immediately gave the signal for a general chase. The *Serapis* soon hoisted three little black balls, which fluttered out into signal flags from the masthead. At the same time a gun was fired to windward. This was the signal of an enemy, and the merchantmen hastily put about and fled for their lives. But the frigates came on boldly, their drums beating loudly to quarters and the shrill piping of their boatswains' whistles sounding above the noise of wind and waves.

As the British frigates steadily drew nearer, the *Bonhomme Richard* was speedily cleared for action. The royal yards were sent down; the guns were cast loose and made ready; the powder-boys brought up cartridges of powder; the marines took up their stations fore and aft to resist boarders, or if luck served, to board the enemy themselves. Other marines, armed with muskets, clambered to the tops to fire on the decks of the enemy ship.

The breeze died down and darkness fell before the ships drew within range. The odds between the two forces were even, for, of the American ships, only the *Bonhomme Richard* and the *Pallas*

were close enough to engage. As the gloom of night deepened and the ships edged toward each other to grapple in a deadly struggle, a profound hush settled over the scene. The fresh splashing of the waves, as the great frigates tossed them aside, and the seething of the foaming waters alone served to break the eerie stillness.

The two larger ships drew close together at seven o'clock, and at the same time the *Pallas* ranged up alongside of the *Countess of Scarborough*.

"What ship is that?" hailed the *Serapis*.

"I can't hear what you say," replied Paul Jones, wishing to close the range before opening fire.

"What ship is that?" came the hail again. "Answer, or I shall fire."

The answer came in a blinding sheet of flame as the *Bonhomme Richard* let go her full broadside. Almost at the same instant, the *Serapis* replied. The great battle—"the most remarkable naval duel in history"—had begun.

For an instant all was quiet. Then began the heat of the action; the men on each ship hurried to reload the guns and fire. At the very first broadside, two of the six 18-pounders on the *Bonhomme Richard's* lower gun deck burst, killing most of the men that worked them and blowing up the deck above. The remaining 18-pounders were abandoned for fear that they also would burst. By this disaster the *Bonhomme Richard* not only lost her most powerful battery, but also sustained a serious loss in killed and wounded.

Paul Jones now drew ahead and crossed the *Serapis'* bow, raking her fore and aft with his port battery. The *Serapis* filled away, then took up a position on the *Bonhomme Richard's* port quarter. The men were by this time working their guns like demons and the cannonading had become furious, enveloping the two ships in dense clouds of smoke, illuminated by continuous lurid flashes. The roar of the guns was tremendous and echoed and re-echoed over the sea and the nearby headlands. Soon the musketry in the tops mingled its sharp rattling fire to the thunderous booming of the batteries; the frenzied bellowing of the sweating gunners and the shrieks of the wounded on both ships united in one tumultuous uproar.

Within thirty minutes of the opening of the battle, the *Bonhomme Richard* had received several shot below the water-line. The loss of the 18-pounder battery had compelled Captain Jones to rely entirely upon his fourteen 12-pounders on the main deck. These guns were worked with desperate energy, but in three-quarters of an hour the entire battery was disabled or silenced, while seven of the quarter-deck and forecastle guns had been dismounted. This left the *Bonhomme Richard* with only the 9-pounders on the quarter-deck to withstand the crashing broadsides of the far less seriously injured *Serapis*. Seldom had any ship been faced with such enormous odds.

Paul Jones cared nothing for the odds. His sole aim was to sink the enemy or force her to surrender. He ordered a 9-pounder shifted from the starboard side—which was away from the *Serapis*. This gave him three 9-pounders pointed toward the enemy. Under Jones' personal supervision, these guns were loaded and swept the enemy's deck with telling effect. Then they were double-shotted with round shot and directed against the *Serapis'* mainmast.

After the firing had lasted an hour the moon rose, and, with the greater visibility, Captain Pearson drove his ship ahead, aiming to cross the *Bonhomme Richard's* bow and rake her. He miscalculated his distance, however, and was forced to straighten out the *Serapis* directly ahead of the *Richard,* which, surging forward, plunged her bowsprit over the British frigate's stern. No gun on either vessel could be brought to bear on the other and there was a sudden lull in the uproar.

The silence was broken by a hail from the deck of the *Serapis*.

"Have you struck your colors?"

Paul Jones, standing defiantly on the quarter-deck of his ship, which was leaking and afire in a dozen places, and with only five of her smallest guns left in action, roared back in a dauntless voice:

"No! I have not yet begun to fight!"

As the two frigates drifted apart, the *Serapis* swung around, headed toward the *Bonhomme Richard,* and ran her jib-boom through the American ship's starboard mizzen shrouds. Knowing that his only chance lay in a fight at close quarters, Paul Jones lashed the spar to the rigging. The ships stayed in this position for a moment, but the wind then swung them around side by side, the *Serapis'* bowsprit breaking off as she turned. The Americans quickly secured the ships together by passing a hawser over the stump of the Britisher's bowsprit. The *Serapis'* spare anchor, at the same moment, hooked on the *Bonhomme Richard's* quarter, holding the two ships together aft. In this position, side by side and heading in opposite directions, the two frigates fought out the remainder of the action.

The battle now recommenced with terrific fury. The ships were so close that the British gunners had to jump into the shattered gun deck of the *Bonhomme Richard* to pass their ramrods into the muzzles of their guns. The *Serapis'* lower battery of 18-pounders, facing the *Bonhomme Richard's* guns, blown up at the first discharge, now sent broadside after broadside through the American ship's hull. The whole side was battered in and the waves washed in and out as the *Bonhomme Richard* rolled from one side to the other. Owing to the appalling condition of the gun deck, all the Americans had taken stations on the main deck or in the rigging.

The *Bonhomme Richard's* men now threw consternation into the hearts of their antagonists. So fierce was their musket fire from the tops that every officer and seaman was driven from the *Serapis'* deck, while the diminutive 9-pounders on the quarter-deck and one or two 12-pounders, which had been brought into action again, were worked so effectually that the cannon on the British frigate's main deck were disabled one after the other.

Between nine and ten the British attempted to board, but were driven back with pikes and pistols wielded by a desperate band of blood-stained, powder-grimed Americans. The roar of the British guns and the rattle of the American musketry rose to a new crescendo, suddenly climaxed by a terrific explosion aboard the *Serapis*. A seaman on the *Bonhomme Richard's* mainyard had flung a hand grenade into the Britisher's main hatchway. It struck a heap of powder cartridges which exploded, making a fiery inferno of the whole after-part of the ship. More than twenty of the *Serapis'* crew were killed and many others were critically wounded.

At this moment the *Alliance* appeared, bearing down from windward. Paul Jones turned to Richard Dale, his first lieutenant, and asked, "Do you see that, Dick? With her help, the battle is over."

The *Alliance* came swiftly on, but to the utter astonishment of everyone she fired, not at the *Serapis*, but full into the *Bonhomme Richard*. Her captain, Pierre Landais, a Frenchman, had long been suspected of disloyalty, even insanity. What caused him to attack the *Bonhomme Richard* has never been definitely determined; but it was probably crazy jealousy of Paul Jones.

"We called him for God's sake to forbear," Paul Jones reported after the battle. "Yet he passed along the off side of the ship—which was the port side, the enemy being on the starboard side—and continued firing. . . . Every tongue cried out that he was firing into the wrong ship, but nothing availed. He passed round firing into the *Bonhomme Richard*, head, stern and broadside, and by one of his volleys killed several of my best men and mortally wounded a good officer of the forecastle."

After this incredible outburst, the *Alliance* swung about and sailed away as suddenly as she had entered the action. Her vicious broadsides

had hulled the *Richard* and started new fires. The leaks gained on
the pumps and the freshening fires spread to within a few feet of
the magazine.

The *Bonhomme Richard's* surviving officers now advised their captain to surrender; but Jones would have none of it. He ordered his
men to their guns, threatening to kill the first one who hesitated to
obey, and the sight of his pistol and the expression on his face forced
them to prompt obedience. To the dismay of those on board the
Serapis, the American's fire grew steadily more devastating. One by
one, the remaining British guns were silenced. Paul Jones gave
the command to board. With wild shouts, the Yankee sailors leaped
over the bulwarks and down into the waist of the *Serapis,* driving the
Britishers before them. Captain Pearson, seeing the enemy in full
possession of the fore part of his ship and hacking their way relentlessly aft toward the quarter-deck, seized the ensign halyards and
with his own hands hauled down his flag. The next moment the
Serapis' mainmast tottered and crashed over the side, bringing down
the mizzenmast with it.

"He has struck! The ship is ours!" went up the cry.

In the sudden silence that followed, the voice of Paul Jones rang
out the order, "Cease firing!"

The battle was over—a battle "unsurpassed in naval history for the
endurance displayed by both sides." Both of the contending frigates
were in frightful condition. "A person must have been an eye-witness,"
Paul Jones reported, "to form a just idea of the tremendous scene of
carnage, wreck and ruin that everywhere appeared." Despite heroic
efforts made to save her, the *Bonhomme Richard* sank the following

morning. In his journal, Paul Jones described her end with moving eloquence:

"No one was now left aboard the *Richard* but our dead. To them I gave the good ship for their coffin, and in her they found a sublime sepulchre. She rolled heavily in the long swell, her gun-deck awash, and sank peacefully in about fifty fathoms.

"The ensign-gaff, shot away in the action, had been fished up, and put in place soon after firing ceased, and our torn and tattered flag was left flying when we abandoned her. As she plunged down by the head at the last, her taffrail momentarily rose in the air; so the very last vestige mortal eyes ever saw of the *Bonhomme Richard* was the defiant waving of her unconquered and unstricken flag as she went down. And, as I had given them the good old ship for their sepulchre, I now bequeathed to my immortal dead the flag they had so desperately defended for their winding sheet!"

13

The Formidable

Admiral Rodney's Flagship at the Battle of the Saints

SEATED at the great oaken table in his cabin on board the 100-gun ship-of-the-line *Formidable,* at anchor off the West Indian island of St. Lucia on a sunny morning early in April, 1782, Admiral Sir George Rodney was writing a despatch. Quite evidently, he was weighing every word with care, for from time to time he read over what he had written, and pondered on it. At last the despatch was completed and the Admiral gave it a final reading to make certain that it drove home the facts that bore so heavily on his mind. What he had read ran in part, as follows:

"The great event that must restore the empire of the sea to Great Britain is near at hand; let me but live to hail my most gracious monarch sovereign of the ocean, and then my happiness will be complete."

Things had been faring none too well for Britain in this year's first part. One difficulty had followed another in her current wars with America, France, Spain and Holland, and it was feared that, unless a decisive victory could be gained against her continental enemies, her long-maintained position as mistress of the seas would be taken from her by the fleets of France and Spain. Cornwallis's surrender at Yorktown the year before had been a bitter blow, and the success

of the American colonies had roused both France and Spain to increased efforts against her.

Both countries had despatched fleets to the West Indies, their plan
being to seize Jamaica, the center of British power and British trade
in the West Indies, and, this accomplished, to make "a formidable
descent upon Great Britain." The French had already captured the
islands of St. Eustatius, St. Kitts and Nevis. To counter these audacious
plans, which, because of the combined power of the navies arrayed
against England, appeared to have every chance of success, Admiral
Rodney with eighteen line-of-battle ships had been sent to Barbados
early in 1782, there to join forces with Admiral Sir Samuel Hood, under
whose command were eighteen of Britain's most powerfully-armed
ships of the line. Against these, the French Admiral De Grasse had
thirty-four ships at Martinique, and at San Domingo there was a
squadron of thirteen Spanish vessels.

Upon Rodney and Hood rested a responsibility of tremendous
proportions. If they should fail in their endeavor to engage and defeat
the enemy fleets, English power in the West Indies would be annihi-
lated; her hold upon Gibraltar, Malta and India might be destroyed;
England herself might be invaded. The danger was real, and there
were many who believed that England was doomed, that at long last
her mastery of the seas was to be brought to an end.

Rodney, in spite of the widespread feeling that his ships were to
go into battle with the odds of success strongly against them, felt
serenely confident of success. This is shown by the despatch already
quoted, and in a letter written to a brother officer: "Their fate is only
delayed a short time, for have it they must and shall."

His opportunity to let them have it came within a few days. The frigates stationed off Fort Royal, in Martinique, to watch the movements of De Grasse, brought word that the enemy's fleet, together with a convoy of merchantmen and supply ships, was putting to sea. That same morning Rodney signaled the English ships from the *Formidable*, ordering them to follow him to intercept the French. Their fleet was only forty miles away to the northward, and, even though the wind was light, Rodney anticipated little difficulty in overtaking them.

During the night of the eighth of April the English fleet passed Martinique. The next morning it was off the western coast of Dominica, and, away to the northward, near the blue horizon, the white sails of the French fleet and its convoy were in sight. Eager as they were to close with the enemy, the English were forced to curb their impatience, for, scarcely had the sun risen, than the wind died away, and the tall men-of-war, with loose-hanging sails, moved at only a snail's pace through the water.

Rodney's fleet was now formed in three divisions. Hood, in the *Barfleur,* commanded the van. Rodney, his flag flying in the great three-decker *Formidable,* led the center. The rear was commanded by Read-Admiral Samuel Drake, a descendant of that Drake who had terrorized the enemies of England in Elizabethan days.

A light breeze sprang up toward mid-morning, which, although not felt by most of the English ships, filled the sails of Hood's nine vessels in the van. Little by little, these drew away from the fleet. and soon were near enough to the French ships to open fire. If De Grasse had seized the opportunity of falling with all his ships upon

Hood's isolated squadron, there is little doubt that he might have done them serious harm. Luckily, however, he chose to send his second in command, Vaudreuil, to hold Hood off, and the latter contented himself with staying at a distance and firing, according to the French custom, at the masts and rigging of the English ships, hoping to disable them and force them to break off the pursuit. Rodney now put out boats ahead of the *Formidable*, and some of the other English ships followed his example. By towing and taking advantage of every breath of air, these vessels managed to come within range, and the French then hauled off to windward, the action coming to an end about two o'clock in the afternoon. Several of the English ships were damaged, but not seriously enough to force them to leave the fleet. The French ship *Caton* was so badly injured, however, that she was detached and sent in to Guadeloupe for repairs.

In the afternoon the wind fell again, and all that night and the following day the fleets lay in sight of each other, practically becalmed. It now became apparent that De Grasse, with the little wind available, was attempting to reach what is known as the Saints' Passage, a twenty-mile channel separating Dominica from Guadeloupe, along the northern side of which stretches a line of islets which Columbus discovered and named on All Saints' Day.

During the morning of the eleventh of April, De Grasse did his best to work his fleet through the Saints' Passage, tacking time and again, but baffled by the light airs and the periods of utter calm. By mid-afternoon most of the French ships had entered the passage, but others were still in the open sea to the westward. Rodney by this time had succeeded in closing up the gap between the two fleets to such an extent that he would soon be able to open fire on these rearmost ships. This De Grasse was determined to prevent. Turning about, he came back before the wind out of the strait. At sunset the two fleets were to the westward of the Saints' Passage, too far apart to engage, but certain that battle would be joined before another day had passed.

When day broke on the twelfth, Rodney had gained the weather gage, and the two fleets at last were within striking distance. Rodney's moment to let them have it had arrived.

Both fleets were now in line-ahead formation and converging; the English heading about northeast, and the French heading almost directly south, their ships scattered over an area of eight miles. The English battle line was in reverse order, being led by Drake and the rear division, with Rodney's *Formidable* in the center, and Hood following. Under billowing clouds of white canvas, the seventy great ships drew slowly closer together, as the first bright rays of the sun flashed across the deep blue of the Caribbean and warmed the green slopes of Guadeloupe and Dominica, rising heavenward beyond the long French line.

Shortly before eight o'clock the first shots were fired, the ninth ship of the French line, the *Brave,* commencing to blaze away at the *Marlborough,* the leading English ship. Scarcely had the *Marlborough* replied with a thundering broadside, than the ship next astern of her came within range and roared into action. Then one ship after the other entered the fray, until, as the two lines slowly passed each other heading in opposite directions, every vessel was ablaze with the fire-flashes of her guns, and an unceasing thunder filled the air. Each line was now about six miles in length, and over that great distance there rose the clouds of yellowish smoke, the crashing impact of cannon balls against wooden sides and bulwarks, the falling of masts and spars, and the excited cheering and shouting of the gunners and their mates.

All morning long the firing continued, with each side giving as good as it received. Then, a little before noon, the wind freshened and blew steadily from the southeast. It was the merest whisper of a breeze, that one could scarcely feel against one's cheek, but almost without exaggeration, it may be said that it, coupled with Rodney's genius, saved England and changed the course of history.

Just as this breeze sprang up, Rodney and Sir Charles Douglas, the Captain of the *Formidable,* were looking intently at the French battle-line, observing the effects of the English firing. Suddenly they saw the sails of the French ships flatten back against the masts. Then, as the breeze continued, the speed of the Frenchmen was checked and their bows were forced partly round toward the English line.

The slow onward progress of the stately French line was stopped. Then Rodney saw a wide gap opening up between the *Glorieux* and *Diademe,* the two enemy vessels opposite the *Formidable.*

"Do you see that opening, Sir?" said Douglas, pointing.

"Yes, yes," replied Rodney. "If we are quick about it, we can cut their line."

For a moment or two he hesitated. He would assume grave responsibility if he should leave his own battle-line at that juncture, for the ironclad "Fighting Instructions" of the British navy expressly forbade breaking the line or changing the order of battle during an action. Should he obey the "Instructions" and possibly fight an inconclusive battle, or should he disregard the regulations, and risk his reputation, laboriously built up throughout a lifetime of devoted service, in an attempt to shatter French sea-power once and for all?

Rodney's innate courage prevailed, backed by the conviction that his proposed action was tactically sound. It is not difficult to imagine him saying to himself, with the same spirit as that shown by the American admiral, Farragut, "Damn the regulations. Go ahead."

Turning to Sir Charles Douglas, he told him to swing the *Formidable* to starboard and to steer for the gap in the enemy line. At the same moment, the five ships next astern were signaled to follow the flagship.

Then, as the great three-decker thrust her high bows between the *Gloreiux* and *Diademe,* her hundred great guns flamed and thundered in a mighty crescendo of destruction, pouring broadside after broadside into the enemy ships. After her came the five other ships of Rodney's division, firing furiously from both sides as they passed through the gap. Once through, and to windward of the French, the *Formidable* directed her fire anew on the *Glorieux* and *Diademe,* which were soon reduced to wrecks.

All of the *Glorieux's* masts were sent crashing over the side by English cannon balls, and her captain was killed outright. One of the seamen rescued the ship's ensign—a broad white field covered with the golden lilies of France—and held it aloft on a pike. One of the *Formidable's* musketeers pierced his arm with a bullet, but he quietly shifted the flag to his other hand. A lieutenant then nailed the flag to the stump of a shattered mast. The *Formidable* now poured a murderous fire into the unfortunate ship, and other English vessels descended upon her. Her bulwarks were splintered in a hundred places; her decks were ploughed and ripped by scores of shot, her guns were blasted from their mountings and thrown backward into the midst of the troops and men-of-war's men crowded upon her deck. Finally, a wounded officer staggered to the broken mast, tore away the streaming ribbons which once had been the flag of France, and the ship surrendered.

Meanwhile, Hood in the *Barfleur* had battered his way through the French line, cutting off the twelve leading ships from those in the center. Thus, the French line was separated into three isolated fragments. Due to the falling away of the wind, the twelve ships of the French van drifted helplessly away from the scene of the battle, leaving Hood free to join with Rodney in hammering the six French vessels of the center. Drake, meanwhile, was actively engaged in punishing the ships of the French rear under Vaudreuil.

Three of the French ships were now so relentlessly cannonaded that they were forced to strike. The *César,* falling off to windward, was surrounded and overpowered by sheer weight of metal. After her flag was lowered, she was set on fire by accident, and went flaming to her end. The *Hector* was the next to strike. After fighting a magnificent battle all afternoon, "with her sides like a blazing furnace vomiting fire and iron," she was forced at the last to give in and lowered her flag as the sun was nearing the horizon. When she surrendered, her captain was dead, and there were six feet of water in her hold. The next ship to surrender was the *Ardent,* which fell to the guns of Hood's division.

But a still greater prize was to be taken before the battle ended. This was the great *Ville de Paris,* a three-decker of one hundred and ten guns, considered the finest and most powerful ship of war afloat. She was the flagship of Admiral De Grasse, and had been in the thick of the fighting all day. Now, as evening drew on, her masts and spars were down, her rudder was shattered, and her crew were serving their guns with powder ladled out of powder barrels that had been brought up from the holds after the last of the cartridges had been rammed into the guns.

Just as the sun was touching the horizon, Admiral Hood in the *Barfleur* ranged alongside the sorely-wounded ship. In Hood's own words, "As soon as I got within random shot he began to fire upon me, which I totally disregarded till I was satisfied by firing a single gun from the quarter-deck that I was fairly within point-blank, when I opened such a tremendous fire as he could not stand for more than ten minutes, when he struck. This was at sunset, and my boat had scarcely got aboard, when Sir George made the signal and brought-to, and continued to lay-to the whole night."

And so, as the swift tropic darkness settled down over the stilled waters, the epoch-making battle came to an end, epoch-making not only because it saved the West Indies, saved England herself from quickly-gathering disaster, and restored her position as the first nation in the world, but also because of Rodney's genius and daring in handling the *Formidable* so as to break the enemy's line-of-battle. Regarding this action, it should be pointed out that Rodney is recognized as the greatest of all tacticians between the times of Blake and Nelson, although Hawke was very nearly his equal. Moreover, he had long pondered the advisability of abandoning the old practice of keeping the fleet in line-of-battle during action, and instead, breaking up the enemy line as he did at the battle of the Saints.

Through his handling of the *Formidable* at the critical moment of this battle, in accordance with plans that he had many times considered, but had never before felt free to execute, Rodney set a precedent which inspired the British commanders who followed after him to a fiercer, more flexible, and more headlong style of sea-fighting.

It was the success of the *Formidable* at the battle of the Saints which made it possible for Nelson to apply the famous "Nelson Touch" at Trafalgar, break French and Spanish sea-power utterly, and make England once again the undisputed mistress of the seas.

14

The Grand Turk and other Famous Ships of Salem

WHILE all the seaport towns of New England and, to a lesser extent, those of the more southerly colonies were active in shipbuilding from the earliest colonial days, Salem was without question the most illustrious of all the early American maritime cities. The ships and sailors of old Salem symbolize the early, struggling days of American oversea voyaging; the years during which the Stars and Stripes were first carried to the farthest corners of the globe.

These men were "the incomparable seamen who . . . first carried the American flag to Hindustan, Java, Sumatra and Japan, who were first to trade with the Fiji Islands and with Madagascar, who had led the way to the west coast of Africa and to St. Petersburg, who had been pioneers in opening the commerce of South America and China to Yankee ships."

Salem ships were active in the rum and molasses trade with the West Indies from 1650 onward, but the period of real expansion did not come until after the Revolutionary War. During the war, Salem merchants and ship owners had fitted out a number of splendidly built privateers to prey on British shipping. These ships were available for overseas trading when the war came to an end, and the Salem merchants lost no time in sending them on distant voyages. In the following forty years, or from about 1780 to 1820, Salem ships by the hundreds ventured to far distant harbors, furrowing uncharted and almost unknown waters, in an outburst of pioneering activity equaled only by the merchants and adventurers of Elizabethan England.

The greatest merchant in Salem during this period of the old port's most spectacular achievement, and the man chiefly responsible for initiating the world-wide enterprise of the Salem merchant fleet, was Elias Hasket Derby. He was often called "King Derby."

Elias Derby's father was Richard Derby, whose career as a captain and merchant embraced the greater part of the maritime history of America during the 1700's. His brother, John, also a great and venturesome seafarer, had several famous exploits to his credit. When war was declared against Great Britain in 1775, it was John Derby who carried the first reports of the battles of Lexington and Concord to England. The official British despatches were sent by the "Royal Express Packet" *Sukey*. Though John Derby sailed four days later, he drove his little 62-ton schooner *Quero* so hard across the Atlantic that he beat the *Sukey* by several days. Eight years later, in his full-rigged ship *Astrea,* he was the first to arrive in America with the news that a treaty had been signed with Great Britain. John Derby was also one of the owners of the ship *Columbia* which, in 1792, was the first vessel to explore the Columbia River in Oregon and thus, by right of discovery, gave this region to the United States.

Elias Derby was active during the Revolution in equipping privateers and, with the object of achieving greater speed, he materially improved the design of Salem-built ships. At the close of the Revolution, he owned four ships, all large vessels, for they ranged from three hundred to three hundred and fifty tons' burden.

Derby inaugurated his far-flung trading activities the moment the seas were cleared of hostile armed vessels. He sent his bark, the *Light Horse,* to little-known St. Petersburg in 1784 to bring home a cargo of hemp and iron. Next, he despatched his best ship, the *Grand Turk,* to the Cape of Good Hope—the first American vessel to make a trading voyage to this part of the world. The *Grand Turk* was the pride of Salem. Though less than one hundred feet long, and of only about three hundred tons' burden, she was, at the time of her launching in 1781, the largest vessel yet built in a Salem shipyard. She was known everywhere as "the great ship."

Largely "by guess and by God," for the charts aboard her were inaccurate and the navigating tables totally inadequate, the *Grand Turk* made a safe voyage to Table Bay, the site of the present Cape Town. While there, she was visited by a Major Samuel Shaw who has left us the best account available of the commercial aims and eventual success of the voyage.

"The object," he wrote, "was to sell rum, cheese, salt, provisions and chocolate, loaf sugar, butter, etc., the proceeds of which in money with a quantity of ginseng and some cash brought with him, Captain Ingersoll intended to invest in Bohea tea; but as the ships bound to Europe are not allowed to break bulk on the way, he was disappointed in his expectations of procuring that article, and sold his ginseng for two-thirds of a Spanish dollar a pound, which is twenty per cent better than the silver money of the Cape. He intended remaining a short time to purchase fine teas in the private trade allowed the officers on

board the India ships, and then to sail to the coast of Guinea to dispose
of his rum, etc., for ivory and gold dust; thence without taking a
single slave to proceed to the West Indies and purchase sugar and
cotton, with which he would return to Salem. Notwithstanding the
disappointment in the principal object of the voyage and the conse-
quent determination to go to the coast of Guinea, his resolution not
to endeavor to retrieve it by purchasing slaves did the captain great
honor, and reflected equal credit upon his employer, who, he assured
me, would rather sink the whole capital employed than directly or
indirectly be concerned in so infamous a trade."

After completing his trading in Africa, Captain Ingersoll made
for the West Indies. At the Island of Grenada, he sold his cargo
to such advantage that he was able to purchase cargoes, and load both
the *Grand Turk* and the *Atlantic*.

In November, 1785, the *Grand Turk* cleared for the Isle of France,
or Mauritius, as it is known today, a small group of islands in the Indian
Ocean. Elias Derby gave secret orders to his captain, however, to

continue to Java and China. After an absence of nearly two years, the "great ship" returned in June, 1787, with a rich cargo of silks, nankeens and tea.

The *Grand Turk* was not, however, the first American vessel to make the long voyage to the coast of China and the great port of Canton. This honor belongs to the ship, *Empress of China,* which sailed from New York for Canton in February, 1784, and returned in May of the following year, after a voyage of fourteen months and twenty-seven days.

Convinced by the success of the *Grand Turk's* first voyage to the Far East that great profits were to be made in the trade, Mr. Derby sent his eldest son, Elias Hasket, Junior, to India to establish a base there for gathering cargoes for shipment to Salem and for the disposal of goods brought to the East in vessels of the Derby fleet. A partial record of some of his activities reveals how truly enormous were the profits of the pioneers in the Eastern trade. In 1788, for example, he sold a single cargo for a sum so large that with it he purchased two vessels, a ship and a brigantine, in the Isle of France. These two vessels were despatched to Bombay to load cotton. Two other Derby owned ships, the *Astrea* and the *Light Horse,* arrived shortly afterwards and were loaded for Salem at Rangoon and Calcutta. This done, young Derby secured a cargo for the brig *Henry* and in her set sail for home. After disposal of the different cargoes, the profits from these transactions proved to be well over a hundred thousand dollars.

In 1788, Mr. Derby sent the *Astrea* to Batavia, a port at which only a handful of American vessels had called up to that time. Other owners were also becoming aware of the wealth to be drawn from the Far Eastern trade and a number of Salem vessels were engaged in it. Canton and Batavia were the great meccas of the East; but little by little other ports were being opened up and new trades developed.

Thus, in 1793, a Salem captain by the name of Jonathan Carnes was skirting the coast of Sumatra, entering whatever strange harbors offered an opportunity for trade. While in the port of Bencoolen, he heard that wild pepper—then in great demand in the United States and Europe—was obtainable. Returning to Salem, he told a merchant friend, Jonathan Peele, of his discovery and induced him to equip a fast schooner, the *Rajah,* for a secret expedition.

In November, 1795, he cleared for Sumatra. A year and a half passed by and then, one day, the *Rajah* was sighted off the harbor of Salem. Her entire cargo was bulk pepper. People could hardly believe it. Pepper! One of the rarest and richest of cargoes, usually brought from the East in a package or two at a time. There was as much excitement as if the *Rajah* had come home, her holds filled with gold and silver, emeralds, diamonds and rubies. This cargo brought a sum equal to seven times the cost of the ship—and all the expenses of the voyage besides.

Salem merchants and captains almost groveled before Captain Carnes to get him to reveal the secret port at which he had loaded his fabulous cargo. But it was no use. He maintained absolute silence and the *Rajah* was able to make two more enormously profitable voyages before the other Salem captains, by dogging the mysterious ship, discovered the source of all this wealth. When this happened, a number of vessels at once engaged in the Sumatran pepper trade and

149

for half a century Salem was the center of this exceptionally profitable business.

Within three or four years after the close of the Revolutionary War, China, India, Africa and the East Indies were thus being visited with a certain degree of regularity by Salem ships. In 1796, Elias Derby, always a pioneer, again went beyond the accustomed trade routes by despatching the *Astrea* to Manila in the Philippine Islands. She was the first American ship to enter this port, and repaid her owners by obtaining a homeward bound cargo of sugar, pepper and indigo, upon which the customs duties alone amounted to twenty-four thousand dollars.

In the conduct of his fleet's operations, Elias Derby was dealing with virtually all of the then known world. While his larger ships were making their distant voyages, his brigs and schooners were gathering future cargoes for the Orient; voyaging to Gothenburg and St. Petersburg for iron, duck and hemp; to France, Spain and Madeira for wine and lead; to the West Indies for rum; to New York, Philadelphia and Richmond for flour, provisions, iron and tobacco. These shipments were assembled in the warehouses of Derby wharf and paid for in the teas, coffee, pepper, muslin, silks and ivory which the ships from the Far East were bringing home. In fourteen years Elias Derby's ships trading to the Far Eastern ports and Europe made one hundred and twenty-five voyages; of the thirty-five vessels engaged in this traffic only one was lost at sea.

Mr. Derby owned a fleet of forty vessels and when he died in 1799, he left an estate valued at more than a million dollars, then the largest fortune in America.

Vessels belonging to other merchants were also visiting distant and little-known harbors at this time. The ship *Franklin,* owned in Boston but commanded by Captain James Devereux of Salem, beat up through the China Sea and was the first American vessel to visit Japan. The following year the Boston ship *Massachusetts* touched at Nagasaki, and in 1801 the *Margaret* of Salem, after loading at Batavia, also sailed to the northward and entered the harbor of Nagasaki. Both these vessels were despatched to Japan by the Dutch East India Company which had held a monopoly of the island's commerce for two centuries.

The Salem bark *Lydia,* in 1801, made her way to Guam in the Ladrone Islands, then under Spanish rule. She had not sailed there in the hope of finding a cargo but, while lying in Manila, had been chartered by the Spanish Government to take the new Governor of the islands to his post. For this service she received the round sum of eight thousand dollars.

Second only to Elias Derby in Salem of the late eighteenth and early nineteenth centuries, Joseph Peabody made an important contribution to the upbuilding of America's commerce and prestige. His fleet was built up in the years immediately following Derby's death. He acquired the ownership of eighty-three ships, a fleet twice the size of that sailing under the Derby house flag.

The vessels of the Peabody fleet ranged as far over the high seas as those of Elias Derby. All told, they made thirty-eight voyages to Calcutta, seventeen to Canton, thirty-two to Sumatra, forty-seven to St. Petersburg and thirty to other European ports. Over seven thousand seamen were employed by the Peabody fleet during the life of its owner and the cargoes they brought back contributed mightily in customs duties to the struggling United States Treasury.

One of the best known of the Peabody ships was the *George,* built in 1814. Measuring only one hundred and ten feet in length, with a beam of twenty-seven feet, she was a notable commercial vessel of the day and, because of her trim appearance, she was universally known as the "Salem frigate." She was employed regularly in the East India trade and in twenty-two years made twenty-one voyages, the duties on these cargoes amounting to more than six hundred thousand dollars.

William Grey, the third great Salem merchant, lived at the same time as Joseph Peabody. He learned the complicated business of world trading under the watchful eye of old Richard Derby. He applied the knowledge gained in the Derby counting house so well that by 1807 he owned a fleet of thirty-six vessels—fifteen full-rigged ships, seven barks, thirteen brigs and one schooner. These ships represented a quarter of the total tonnage of Salem afloat at that time.

As the trade routes to India and the East Indies became better known and frequented by more and more ships, the Salem vessels pressed on beyond the usual trading centers and entered the little-known waters of the South Pacific in search of new and richer cargoes. No corner of the Seven Seas seems to have been too hostile or remote to be overlooked by the ship owners of old Salem. When Captain William Richardson in the Salem bark, *Active,* heard, in 1811, that the British East India Company was trading profitably with the Fiji Islands, he set his course for the islands and bartered his Yankee goods for native produce. "During the next half century the untutored people of the Fijis pictured the map of America as consisting mostly of a place called Salem whose ships and sailors were seldom absent from their palm-fringed beaches."

The Salem trade was at its height from 1800 until about 1820. Vessels from Boston, New York and Philadelphia were then launched in great numbers to compete with the Salem ships.

From 1820 to 1840, Salem ships were still active and making many voyages, but Boston had commenced to draw trade away. However, the glamor of the Eastern trade continued to pervade old Salem. Its waterside warehouses were filled with "hemp from Luzon; pepper from Sumatra; coffee from Arabia; palm oil from the west coast of Africa; cotton from Bombay; duck and iron from the Baltic; tallow from Madagascar; salt from Cadiz; wine from Portugal and the Madeiras; figs, raisins and almonds from the Mediterranean; teas and silks from China; sugar, rum and molasses from the West Indies; ivory and gum-copal from Zanzibar; rubber, hides and wool from South America; whale oil from the Arctic and Antarctic, and sperm from the South Seas."

It became evident about 1850, that the vast foreign commerce of Salem was coming to a close. The ships from Nova Scotia, engaged in coastwise trade chiefly, greatly outnumbered those signaling their arrival from the golden ports of the Orient and the islands of the blue Pacific.

How rapidly the foreign trade declined is shown by the successive entries in the records of the Salem Customs House: In 1860 the foreign entries were: from Nova Scotia 215, Java 7, Africa 25, Cayenne 10,

Montevideo 2, Zanzibar 4, Surinam 2, Rio Grande 2, Buenos Aires 2, and one each from Mozambique, Shields, Sunderland, Port Praya, Newcastle and Trapani.

In 1870 the foreign entries were: from the British provinces 117, Cayenne 3, Newcastle 2, and one each from Zanzibar, Rio Grande, Cape Verde Islands and Sunderland.

In 1878 the foreign entries were: from the British provinces 53, and none from any other ports.

So ended the era of Salem's glory. The other coastal cities—New York and Baltimore, Boston, Portsmouth, New London and New Bedford had, of course, all taken their part in the great adventure; but to Salem belongs much, if not most of the credit for leading the way. During the years of Salem's leadership, shipping was the great interest of the United States; it influenced our legislation and our literature, and the sea was a favorite career, not only for boys with their way to make in the world, but for the sons of wealthy men as well. Times have changed, but the memory of the Salem ships will never fade.

15

The Columbia

The First American Ship to Sail Around the Globe

WHEN the first American ships went out to China, one of the principal cargoes they carried was ginseng, a root growing wild in many parts of North America and prized by the Chinese for its supposedly wonderful medicinal properties. The Americans had learned about the Chinese fondness for ginseng from the English who bought it in America, carried it to London and re-shipped it to the Orient.

Other American products—tobacco, turpentine, tar and bearskins—were also taken out to China. As more and more vessels entered the China trade, it became apparent that a greater quantity of these goods, and of ginseng as well, was being carried to Canton than the market could absorb. Something else had to be found for the American captains to sell to the Chinese merchants in sufficient quantity to allow them to reload their ships with the fragrant teas and shimmering silks that were wanted so urgently at home.

This problem was largely solved toward the close of the eighteenth century by the owners and master of the Boston ship, *Columbia,* which opened up the fur trade between the Pacific Northwest and China. The furs carried by the *Columbia* and the many vessels that followed in her wake were the glossy black skins of the sea otter. These were eagerly purchased at high prices in Canton, and the profits were enormous. A single skin, purchased from the Indians for sixpence or a few trinkets, could be sold at Canton for as much as one hundred dollars. This was the golden lure that led to the first voyage of the *Columbia.*

For what proved to be the Americans' great good fortune, the Yankee ship owners and merchants were indebted to the English explorer, Captain James Cook, for the discovery that the fur of the sea otter was highly prized by the Chinese. Some of Cook's seamen noticed Indians wearing the furs, and, impressed by their unusually rich appearance, bartered knives and knickknacks to obtain some for their own use. During the passage across the Pacific, many of the skins were mislaid or spoiled by water, but when the ships arrived at Canton, the sailors were offered fabulous prices for the furs they had left. The Chinese buyers paid them ten thousand dollars for skins which had cost but a few cents. This unexpected wealth quickly went to the sailors' heads, and they nearly mutinied in an attempt to force their officers to re-cross the Pacific and load a full cargo.

When the journals describing Cook's last expedition were published in America, there were many who scoffed at the story about the sailors and their furs. Others, however, thought there was some truth in it. Among these, were six Boston merchants—Joseph Barrell, Charles Bulfinch, Samuel Brown, John Derby, Crowell Hatch and John Pintard—who decided to risk the venture of sending a ship to the northwest coast to load sea otter furs for China.

Two vessels were fitted out for the expedition, the *Columbia,* two hundred and twelve tons, Captain John Kendrick, and the

Lady Washington, ninety tons, Captain Robert Gray. Both ships were heavily armed, and both captains were ex-privateersmen, well versed in the handling of arms. The ships were loaded with an amazing assortment of gewgaws—snuff boxes, jews-harps, buttons, earrings. They carried, as well, scrap iron to be fashioned into simple tools.

There was great excitement in Boston while the ships were making their final preparations for departure. A new trade was to be opened up by Yankee vessels; a new source of wealth was to be tapped. Stories of the fabulous profits to be made were heard on every side, and many a school boy wished he could leave his books and be one of the company bound for the northwest coast. Special sea letters were obtained from Congress, requesting that civil treatment and fair trading privileges be accorded to the two ships, and a handsome medal was struck to commemorate the venture.

On September the thirtieth, 1787, the vessels were ready. They sailed from Boston harbor to the cheers of a crowd of enthusiastic well wishers. Their voyage was to have far more important results than those anticipated at the time, for the trade greatly strengthened American claims to the territory now constituting the northwestern States, and led to their becoming part of the United States instead of going to Great Britain. The voyage was of interest in another way, too, for the *Columbia* and *Lady Washington* made the voyage to the west coast by way of Cape Horn, the first American ships to attempt this hazardous passage. The earlier ships trading with China had gone by way of the less stormy Cape of Good Hope.

The first leg of the voyage, south to the tip of South America, was uneventful. Off Cape Horn, however, the two ships ran into a furious gale. Driving down from the west, the mountainous waves of the Horn, known and dreaded by all old-time sailing-ship men, swept over the little vessels, and forced them far to the east and south. Blinding snow storms blotted out the pale sun and hid the ships from each other. At the mercy of the screaming wind and the tremendous seas, the ships were driven apart.

Thereafter, each pressed on toward the northwest coast by itself, and, eleven months after leaving Boston, both ships arrived at Nootka Sound on Vancouver Island within a few days of each other. Each had had a desperate time. The *Lady Washington* had lost a man through Indian treachery. The *Columbia's* men had not been attacked by Indians, but were so seriously weakened by scurvy that the *Lady Washington's* crew had to help them furl their sails and anchor the ship.

Winter was setting in by the time the voyagers reached Nootka Sound, and it was too late in the season to commence trading with the

Indians. The ships were moored in a sheltered cove, and the crews set up a camp on shore. Here they dwelt throughout the winter, their principal occupation being to make the scrap iron of their cargo into what were then known as "chisels." These were rough tools about eight inches in length, which the Indians used amongst themselves as currency.

In the spring they bartered the "chisels" and other goods for furs. For six or eight "chisels" and a blanket or small mirror, the Indians usually would part with the very finest sea-otter skin. Sometimes, however, the Yankees made a lucky strike, as was the case at one Indian settlement where they obtained two hundred skins at a cost of one "chisel" apiece. Later on, at Canton, these skins were sold for more than six thousand dollars.

When all the available furs had been obtained, the *Columbia* set sail for China, in July, 1789, leaving the little *Lady Washington* behind on the coast. A stop was made at Hawaii, or "Owhyee," recently discovered by Captain James Cook, and the officers and men were delighted by the beauty of the white beaches, the majestic green-clad mountains, the languorous climate and the friendliness of the natives. Impressed by the enthusiastic descriptions of the islands given by the *Columbia's* men on their return, the masters of other American ships made it a practice to break their voyages at Hawaii to obtain fresh food and rest their men.

Upon the *Columbia's* arrival at Canton, her furs were readily disposed of. The story contained in the journals of Captain Cook's last voyage was proven to be true. With the money obtained from the sale of the furs, the agents of the *Columbia* purchased three hundred and fifty chests of Bohea tea for her homeward cargo. Sailing in February, 1790, the good ship stood to the southward, passed through Sunda Strait between Java and Sumatra, and then struck down through the Indian Ocean for the Cape of Good Hope. On August tenth, she arrived safely at Boston where she was hailed, not only for being the first vessel to engage in the fur trade, but also for being the first American craft to circumnavigate the globe.

The *Columbia's* owners were so enthusiastic over the tremendous possibilities of the fur trade that they immediately prepared the ship for a second voyage, and before the year was out she set out again for the northwest coast. While on this voyage, her captain discovered the great river of the northwest and, in honor of his ship, named it the Columbia River, thus adding a third distinction to the two which the *Columbia* had previously earned.

Other ships were, of course, put into the fur trade following the successful conclusion of the *Columbia's* voyage, and the Indians of the northwest soon became familiar with the white men from the east, all of whom they called "Boston men." The English they called "King George men." By 1801, the fur trade was employing fifteen American ships, most of them from Boston, which in that year gathered eighteen thousand skins on the northwest coast and sold them in Canton for more than half a million dollars.

While the trade was profitable, it was also one that required superb seamanship. The ships were very small, ranging from one hundred to two hundred and fifty tons, and it was no easy task to bring one of them safe and sound around Cape Horn where mountains of water sweep unendingly in from the South Pacific. Even greater dangers had to be contended with on the rugged and uncharted coast of north-west America.

The hostility of some of the Indians added another danger. The *Lady Washington* lost one man at Murderer's Harbor on her first voyage, as has already been related, and on her second voyage three of the crew were killed by Indians at Massacre Cove. Many other ships were attacked and, as a consequence, every vessel in the trade was heavily armed, not only with cannon, but also with muskets, pistols, cutlasses and pikes to be used in hand-to-hand encounters. As a further precaution, boarding-nets were tied up when Indians came alongside in their canoes to trade, and only a few were allowed to come aboard at any one time. All these precautions, however, could not do away entirely with the danger of attack. If a ship were becalmed or ran on one of the sunken rocks which abounded near the coast, it was likely to be attacked by Indians in big war canoes closing in on all sides.

Many of the ships that followed the *Columbia* made fortunes for their owners, but others were not so lucky. As more vessels visited the coast, furs became scarcer and the Indians asked for greater numbers of "chisels," blankets, muskets and other goods in exchange.

Then, too, the Indians came to want special articles; they would refuse to trade unless these were produced. One year, for example, a ship that had green glass beads got all the furs it could carry, paying only two beads for each skin. On another occasion, a captain could not persuade the Indians to take any cloth, usually a staple article of trade. Faced with the prospect of a profitless voyage, he put his wits to work and finally created a tremendous demand for his cloth by decorating it with cheap brass buttons. The same captain, Joseph Ingraham, of the

Hope, also conceived the idea of beating his scrap iron into iron collars instead of chisels, and these novelties brought him many hundreds of skins. Each iron collar was exchanged for three skins, each skin worth forty dollars at Canton.

No captain could foretell whether his voyage would end in a profit or loss. Doubtless a number of voyages were unsuccessful, but they were counterbalanced by those that brought exceptionally large rewards. The *Columbia* on her second voyage made a net profit of ninety thousand dollars from its cargo of furs. Captain William Sturgis, one of the principal figures in the northwest fur trade, on one occasion made nearly a quarter million dollars from an original investment of fifty thousand dollars in trade goods. Many others were just as fortunate.

This trade, opened up by the *Columbia,* continued for about twenty years, or until the war of 1812. Then as now, the British knew the value of sea-power and had ships stationed in every strategic port of the world. On the far-distant northwest coast their sloops-of-war were very active, and succeeded in driving off all the American vessels that came to trade for furs. When the war came to an end, a few ships re-entered the trade, but met with little success, for furs had become scarce. Moreover, the Indians put so high a price on those they offered that the trade was no longer profitable.

Though the fur trade is now but a memory, the ship that led the way to the northwest coast can never be forgotten. A great river rolling to the sea bears her name!

16

The Victory

Admiral Nelson's Flagship at the Battle of Trafalgar

CHEER after cheer rose from the decks of the English warships on station off Cadiz, Spain, on a September morning in 1805. It was a joyous, noisy, exuberant shouting and huzzaing that came roaring from the throats of these thousands of English sailors.

"Admiral Nelson!" they shouted, and again, "Admiral Nelson! Hurrah! The Admiral's here! Three more cheers, lads! The Admiral has rejoined the fleet! Hurrah! Hurrah! Hurrah!"

As the cheers echoed and re-echoed across the sunlit water, the stately *Victory*, which had brought Nelson from England, joined the slowly cruising English squadron. Her consorts, the graceful frigate *Euryalus* and the towering ships of the line, *Ajax* and *Thunderer*, took up positions on the flanks of the twenty-odd other English men-of-war present.

The presence of Nelson spread a feeling of confidence through the fleet. Elation and anticipation set the men's blood to tingling. His victories at Saint Vincent, Aboukir Bay and Copenhagen had given him a reputation such as no other English admiral had ever known. What was worth more, it had given his fleet captains and the seamen the utmost confidence in his ability to achieve success, no matter what might be arrayed against him.

163

For more than two years the English navy had been blockading France and keeping a watchful eye on all French warships and their allies, the men-of-war of Spain. Vigilant, alert, unceasing, through long months of monotony and through scores of tempests, the blockading vessels had kept the sea. In over two years Nelson had left his ship only three times, and then for less than an hour each time. For twenty-two months his Vice-Admiral, Collingwood, did not anchor.

Through all these wearisome months, the magic presence of Nelson had been an inspiration to the men and officers of the blockading fleet. His greatness of spirit, that selfless nobility which led him to place duty far above his personal interests, was felt by every man. It was no wonder that the storm-tossed veterans of the blockading squadron roared themselves hoarse when, after a short absence in England, their beloved Nelson returned, this time to lead them into battle.

Napoleon had been doing his utmost to get the English vessels out of the way or to destroy them. All his preparations for invading England had been completed. An army of one hundred and fifty thousand veterans had been gathered at Boulogne, and more than a thousand vessels had been prepared to transport it across the English Channel. But the French and Spanish warships that were to protect the army while making the crossing were widely separated, some at Brest, some in Spanish ports and others in the Mediteranean. To unite them at Boulogne to protect the crossing of the Channel was Napoleon's plan. To prevent this and to destroy the French fleet was Nelson's determination.

Napoleon, in August, had ordered Admiral Villeneuve, in command of twenty-nine French men-of-war at Ferrol, Spain, to make

post-haste for Brest. Everything was ready to invade England the moment escorting warships were at hand. Villeneuve was afraid of meeting a superior English force in the Bay of Biscay, however, and, instead of proceeding to Brest, set a southerly course and took his ships into Cadiz where the Spanish fleet lay at anchor. On the very day that he reached this harbor, Napoleon sent off from Boulogne an urgent dispatch directed to Brest, where Villeneuve should have been.

"Admiral, I trust you have arrived at Brest. Start at once. Do not lose a moment. Come into the Channel with our united squadrons, and England is ours. We are all ready. Everything is embarked. Come here for twenty-four hours and all is ended, and six centuries of shame and insult will be avenged."

Far from being at Brest, Villeneuve was at Cadiz. And now, a month later, Nelson was also at Cadiz and making his plans for battle. A few days after his arrival he wrote to Lady Hamilton:

"I believe my arrival was most welcome, not only to the commanders of the fleet, but also to every individual in it; and, when I

165

came to explain to them the 'Nelson touch,' it was like an electric shock. Some shed tears, all approved—'It was new—it was singular— it was simple!' and, from Admirals downwards, it was repeated—'It must succeed, if ever they will allow us to get at them! You are, my Lord, surrounded by friends whom you inspire with confidence.' "

The "Nelson touch" refers to the plan of attack Nelson had formulated for crushing the allied fleet. It was a radical departure from the customary method of fighting-fleet action, which ordinarily called for each fleet to form in line-of-battle and sail on parallel courses. The "Nelson touch," instead, stipulated that the British fleet should be formed in two columns, one led by Nelson in the *Victory,* the other by Collingwood in the *Royal Sovereign.* Both columns were to sail directly toward the enemy's battle line. One would break through the line and cut off about a third of the leading ships, while the others would break through at a point further down the line and separate the rearmost ships from the rest of the fleet. By this method of attack, the enemy fleet (which had thirty-three ships, against the British twenty-seven) would be divided into three groups, each smaller than one of the British columns. Every effort was to be made to overwhelm the ships cut off at the head and rear of the enemy battle line, before the center could come to the rescue. Nelson also believed that the novelty of the attack would puzzle the enemy and delay him in preparing an adequate method of defense or counter-attack. In this, events proved him correct.

On the morning of the nineteenth of October, while Nelson was cruising off Cape Trafalgar, the frigate *Euryalus,* which had been sent close in shore to watch the movements of the enemy in Cadiz harbor, signaled to the *Victory*: "The enemy's ships are coming out." Nelson ordered the fleet to prepare for a "General chase southeast," toward the Straits of Gibraltar, to prevent the allied fleet from entering the Mediterranean. Owing to lack of wind, all the French and Spanish ships were not clear of the harbor until the morning of the twentieth. Villeneuve set a course for Gibraltar, but changed his mind during the night, as his outlying frigates sighted some of the British fleet and signaled that they were closing in in great numbers. Despairing of reaching Gibraltar without a battle, and wishing to have Cadiz under his lee should the British attack, Villeneuve reversed his course and led his ships to the northward, planning to cruise off Cadiz and await events. When the turnabout was made, the *Euryalus* was close by, keeping watch. Her commander reported that the great allied fleet looked like "a lighted street some six miles long."

At dawn next morning, the twenty-first of October, the two fleets came in sight of each other. The French were now sailing to the southward, while the British, about nine miles to the westward, and to windward, were heading northward. On one side lay Cadiz, on the other Cape Trafalgar, and in the far distance the Straits of Gibraltar. The allied French and Spanish fleet was in a long column, except for twelve vessels under the Spanish Admiral, Gravina, stationed to leeward ready to beat up to any part of the allied line against which the British might concentrate their attack. The British fleet was sailing in two columns, ready to apply the "Nelson touch," with Nelson in command of the windward division of twelve ships, and Collingwood in command of the fifteen sail to leeward.

Nelson, sizing up the situation from the quarter-deck of the *Victory,* made the signals in quick succession: "Form the order for sailing"; "Prepare for battle;" "Bear up." With all sail set, the British columns forged ahead; but, because of the lightness of the wind, their progress was slow, and the entire morning was to pass before they could get to grips with the enemy.

Looking ahead, the British seamen could see the long line of great, heavy-gunned ships which they had sought for so long to bring to battle. Towering high above the others, was the enormous *Santissima Trinidad,* of a hundred and thirty guns, the largest ship afloat. Directly astern of her, and the eighth ship from the head of the line, was the *Bucentaure,* the famous flagship of Admiral Villeneuve. To left and right of these formidable antagonists floated the other men-of-war that for so long had contested Britain's mastery of the seas— *Formidable, Heros, Redoutable, Duguay Trovin, Intrepide, San Juan Nepomuceno, Principe de Asturias,* and a host of others. To an officer on one of Nelson's ships, "the horizon appeared covered with ships."

About nine o'clock the French-Spanish fleet wore together and reversed the order of its sailing, Villeneuve having decided to make for Cadiz as a port of refuge. But the British continued to draw nearer, Nelson's column, led by the *Victory,* being directed at Villeneuve's flagship, the *Bucentaure,* and Collingwood's division bearing down so as to break through the enemy line and cut off the twelve ships of the allied rear.

Toward eleven o'clock, as the engagement became more imminent, Nelson went below to write his last messages to his loved ones and enter in his diary the words of his immortal "Prayer before Trafalgar":

The *Victory*

"*May the Great God whom I worship grant to my Country, and for the benefit of Europe in general, a great and glorious victory; and may no misconduct in any one tarnish it; and may humanity after victory be the predominant feature in the British fleet. For myself, individually, I commit my life to Him who made me, and may His blessing light upon my endeavours for serving my country faithfully. To Him I resign myself and the first cause which is entrusted to me to defend.*"

Nelson then made the famous signal to his fleet: "England expects that every man will do his duty." Shouts and cheers rose as the signal was interpreted. The inspiration of the immortal words led each man to vow to do his best. Then was hoisted the signal for "Close action." The hour of battle had come.

At this moment, according to a midshipman on board the *Neptune,* "It was a beautiful sight when their (the enemy) line was completed, their broadsides turned towards us, showing their iron teeth, and now and then trying the range of a shot to ascertain the distance, that they might, the moment we came within point-blank (about 600 yards) open their fire upon our van ships—no doubt with the hope of dismasting some of our leading vessels before they could close and break their line. Some of the enemy's ships were painted like ourselves with double yellow streaks, some with a broad single red or yellow streak, others all black, and the noble *Santissima Trinidad* with four distinct lines of red, with a white ribbon between them, made her seem to be a superb man-of-war, which, indeed, she was."

The *Royal Sovereign* was the first of the British ships to reach and break the enemy's line. At a few minutes past noon, with guns blazing to both port and starboard, her great hulk moved between the Spanish *Santa Ana* and the French *Fougeux.* Nelson, watching from the *Victory,* turned to Captain Hardy, and said enthusiastically, "See how that noble fellow Collingwood carries his ship into action!" At the same time Collingwood was saying to Captain Rotherham, "What would Nelson give to be here?"

Followed by the *Mars, Belleisle, Tonnant, Bellerophon* and the other ships of his division, Collingwood strove to drive the rearmost ships of the enemy away from the rest of the fleet. Swinging the *Royal Sovereign* round alongside the *Santa Ana,* he engaged her fiercely muzzle to muzzle. The *Fougeux* poured in a galling fire from astern, while one French and two Spanish ships attacked the starboard side of the *Royal Sovereign,* which lay away from the *Santa Ana.* As the other British ships drove into the mélée and commenced their thunderous chorus, the pressure on the *Royal Sovereign* was lessened. Further relief was afforded by Nelson's onslaught against the enemy's center.

At half-past twelve the *Victory* bore down upon the *Bucentaure,* and as she swept majestically toward the thickest part of the enemy line, the broadsides of eight of their most powerful vessels opened fire upon her. Ear-splitting crashes resounded as the enemy strove to annihilate the British flagship; sheets of orange-yellow flame illuminated their colossal sides, and clouds of sulphurous smoke enshrouded their towering masts and spars. The *Victory* was silent for a moment. Then, as she rounded under the stern of the *Bucentaure,* she poured in a broadside that dismounted twenty of the Frenchman's guns and killed four hundred men. Every one of the *Victory's* guns was treble-shotted, and few single broadsides in the history of naval warfare have equaled this opening blast of the *Victory* in destructiveness and force.

Leaving the *Bucentaure,* the *Victory* ranged up alongside the *Re-*

doutable, the next ship in line, so close that the muzzles of the *Victory's* guns scraped the side of her opponent. While the great guns were blazing below, the soldiers stationed in the French tops kept up a furious fire upon the upper decks, and struggling masses of boarders strove to cross the *Victory's* bulwarks, only to be beaten back with terrible losses. The *Temeraire* now closed in on the opposite side of the *Redoutable* and, with her fire added to that of the flagship, the Frenchman was soon so battered as to be little better than a sinking wreck.

Two other enemy ships had loomed up through the smoke of battle, one of them the giant *Santissima Trinidad,* and had commenced to blaze away at the *Victory.* Three ships against one—it meant hot work for the *Victory's* gunners. Firing rapidly, they inflicted damage that helped to weaken the *Santissima Trinidad* so that she later surrendered. But the *Victory* was receiving, as well as giving, terrific punishment. One of her masts had crashed over the side; her wheel was shot away; there had been heavy loss on the gun-decks as well as the open upper deck. On the quarter-deck where Nelson was walking up and down talking to Captain Hardy, several men had been killed and wounded. One shot passed between Nelson and Hardy, burning the latter's foot and carrying away a shoe-buckle. The continuous rattle and clatter of musketry sounded from a party of sharpshooters in the mizzen-top of the *Redoutable,* who were striving to clear the *Victory's* decks.

Shortly before half-past one Nelson, who had steadfastly refused to cover up the brilliant stars on his coat, was hit by a bullet fired by one of the *Redoutable's* mizzentop men. Hardy was beside him when he fell, but was not in time to catch him. "They've done for me at last, Hardy," gasped Nelson. "I hope not," said the captain. And Nelson replied, "Yes, my backbone is shot through."

As he was carried below, Nelson covered his decorations with a handkerchief so that none of the crew would see them and realize that their leader had been struck down. His flag was kept flying and, to the very end of the battle, the fleet was not aware of its irremediable loss. He had not been ten minutes among the wounded in the cockpit when loud cheers from the *Victory's* crew, following on a sudden lull in the cannonading, told him that the *Redoutable* had surrendered. The firing rose again to a crescendo, as several fresh French ships bore down on the *Victory*. Hardy hurried on deck but, when the attack had been repulsed, came down with the news that fourteen or fifteen of the enemy ships had struck.

"That is well," Nelson managed to say, "but I bargained for twenty. Anchor, Hardy, anchor." And then, shortly afterward, as he felt his life slipping away, "Kiss me, Hardy. Thank God, I have done my duty!"

Before Nelson closed his eyes for the last time, and while his flag was still flying, seventeen enemy ships had been captured. In a series of fiercely-contested yard-arm to yard-arm actions between single ships and groups, the battle had become the "great and glorious victory" that Nelson had prayed for. In addition to the seventeen prizes, one enemy vessel, the *Achille,* was on fire and soon blew up; four were in flight far to the northwest and were subsequently captured; and the remainder were escaping with their wounded to Cadiz.

Although the victory of Trafalgar did not bring the long struggle with Napoleon to an end, it severely limited his powers of action. With French naval power broken, the danger of invasion, for long a menace overshadowing everything else in England, was completely done away with. Moreover, the battle re-confirmed Britain's position as the mistress of the seas.

Despite the magnitude of the victory and its results, the rejoicing in England was quiet and even half-hearted. The loss of Nelson seemed a terrible price to pay, even for such a sweeping victory.

17

The Constitution

WHAT the *Victory* is to England, the *Constitution* is to the United States. Each ship is a symbol of its nation's most cherished ideals and principles—freedom from oppression, justice and a democratic form of government. Each ship and its company fought for these ideals and helped its country to achieve the way of life for which its officers and men were ready and willing to sacrifice their lives.

The *Constitution* was one of six frigates authorized by the United States Congress in 1793 to provide a naval force to protect American commerce against the attacks of the Barbary Coast pirates. She was launched at Boston on the twentieth of September, 1797.

The plans of the *Constitution* and her sister frigates were drawn by Joshua Humphreys of Philadelphia, but many valuable suggestions for their construction were made by the commanders who had served in the American navy during the Revolutionary War. Humphreys' chief objective was to create a type of ship that could out-sail and out-fight any foreign-owned frigates then afloat.

His plans called for ships that would be about fifteen feet longer than the average 38-gun British frigate, but of the same or even narrower beam. The added length was designed to give them faster sailing qualities, since speed in sailing ships depends to a large extent on the ratio of beam to length.*

In addition to their greater speed, the new frigates carried heavier guns than any of the British frigates. These were 24-pounders, previously considered as too large for any craft other than a massive battleship of the line.

The *Constitution* first saw active service in the war against the Barbary pirates. She joined the American Mediterranean squadron as flagship in the summer of the year 1803, under the command of Captain Edward Preble, and in the following year led the fleet in numerous bombardments of the city of Tripoli. Time and again the great frigate ran close in shore and, in defiance of the powerful shore batteries, poured one roaring broadside after another into the forts and war-galleys of the Tripolitans. Finally, under the persuasion of these repeated bombardments, the ruler of Tripoli, who for years had exacted tribute from all the great maritime powers, realized that the United States was determined to fight him forever, if need be, in order to stop his preying on its merchant ships. In June, 1805, he begged for an end of the bombardments, freed the American captives he had taken from war and merchant vessels and signed a treaty in which he promised never again to levy tribute on American ships passing through the Mediterranean.

When war broke out between Great Britain and the United States in the year 1812, the *Constitution,* now under the command of Captain

* *The length of the frigates was 175 feet and their beam 43½ feet. The height of their mainmasts was 180 feet and their sail area was considerably greater than that of the British frigates of the period. This added still further to their speed which, in a strong wind and with all sails set and drawing, was frequently as great as 13½ knots.*

Isaac Hull, put to sea immediately to search for British frigates which might be brought to action. On the twelfth of July she left Chesapeake Bay, spread her full canvas to the wind and headed north along the coast, keeping a sharp lookout for enemy craft.

Her cruise was uneventful until the seventeenth of July, when, early in the afternoon, her lookout sighted a squadron of five large British frigates. This was more than Captain Hull had bargained for. He realized that it would be suicidal to engage so strong a force and consequently put about and set a southerly course to escape. A pursuit that is one of the most famous in all naval history followed.

There was little or no wind, and the *Constitution* and her pursuers at first moved silently forward over the glassy water at a snail's pace. On the morning of the eighteenth, it seemed to Captain Hull that the British frigates were drawing nearer. Determined not to be overtaken, he ordered the ship's small boats to be lowered and to take the frigate in tow. At the same time, streams of water were played on the sails to make them hold the wind better. The *Constitution* forged ahead a little more swiftly, gaining perceptibly on her pursuers.

The British soon detected what was happening and put out their own boats to tow. This brought them closer, and the leading frigate, the *Belvidera,* soon opened fire, some of her shot passing over the *Constitution.* Captain Hull thereupon resorted to another device—that of putting out kedge anchors in front of his ship and then pulling her through the water by pulling in the anchor cables. The *Constitution* forged ahead once more. But the British saw what was afoot and followed the American ships' example.

The chase continued for two days and two nights, towing and

kedging being employed continually, and the *Constitution* keeping her lead by only the slightest margin. The exhausted crews caught snatches of sleep whenever it was possible, but the officers remained continually on deck; when not on duty, they slept on ropes or sails, ready to be wakened at the slightest alarm.

On the evening of the second day, the *Constitution* finally managed to make good her escape. At about half-past six, a heavy squall of wind and rain was seen approaching. Captain Hull ordered all the sails to be kept fully spread until the squall was almost upon the ship. Then, at a sharp command, the Yankee crew swarmed into the rigging and, almost in less time than it takes to tell, furled all the light sails and snugged the frigate down for a gale. When the English commanders observed these seemingly frantic measures being taken, they thought that a squall of unusual violence must be sweeping toward them. They ordered sail to be shortened and bore up into the wind, thus heading their ships on a course opposite that of the *Constitution*.

This was just what Captain Hull had hoped for. As soon as the rain came down and hid his ship from the enemy, he ordered all sail to be set and the *Constitution* plunged through the water at a good eleven-knot speed. She was hidden from the British by the rain for nearly an hour, and, when the squall finally blew over, the enemy was many miles astern. Roaring on before a strong breeze throughout the night, the *Constitution* made good her escape.

After running the British squadron out of sight, the *Constitution* headed northward and put into Boston for a fresh supply of water. Sailing again on August the second, she cruised off Nova Scotia, taking a few prizes. She then set a southerly course, in the hope of finding more British shipping near Bermuda. A little after noon on August the nineteenth, when she was about seven hundred miles east of Cape Cod, a sail was reported from the masthead and, after an hour's scrutinizing through his telescope, Captain Hull was certain she was a British frigate.

The Britisher, which later proved to be the frigate *Guerriere,* was apparently anxious to engage, for she shortened her sails and braced her main topsail to the mast, waiting for the American to come down to her. Captain Hull drove his good ship onward at her best speed, and just as darkness was closing in, he came within range. As she drew close in to the *Guerriere* and ran alongside of her at about two hundred yards distance, the British ship opened fire; but Hull did not reply. He ordered the guns to be double-shotted—two round shot being loaded instead of the customary single shot—and trained on the enemy; but no gun was to be fired until he gave the word.

The *Guerriere* maintained her fire and many of her shots were coming uncomfortably close, while frequent exultant cheers were wafted across the water to the ears of the Americans. From time to time, the gun crews, crouching tensely beside their cannon, looked questioningly toward the quarter-deck; but Captain Hull gave no sign that he was ready to open fire.

Within a minute or two a shot from the *Guerriere* struck the *Constitution's* bulwarks and sent a shower of jagged splinters flying across the gun-deck, killing and wounding several men. As they were being carried below to the cockpit, First-Lieutenant Morris strode aft to the quarter-deck, where Captain Hull was calmly pacing back and forth.

"The enemy has opened fire and killed two of our men, sir," he reported. "Shall we return it?"

"Not yet, sir," was the response, and Morris, returning to his station, bade his men to wait.

Three times Lieutenant Morris asked if he could open fire, and three times he was answered with a calm, "Not yet, sir." But at last, having gained the position he wanted, about forty yards off the *Guerriere's* port quarter, Captain Hull gave the long-awaited signal. Instantly the frigate belched forth a storm of iron hail that carried death and destruction into her opponent.

The effect of this carefully aimed broadside delivered at short range was overwhelming. Splinters flew over the British frigate like a cloud, some of them reaching as high as the mizzentop. Her hull and bulwarks were ripped open in a dozen places. Captain Hull now gave the order for rapid and continuous fire and the American gunners bent to their work in grim earnest. The *Constitution's* side seemed to be a continuous sheet of orange-red flame, and clouds of sulphurous smoke poured from the muzzles of her guns. When Hull saw the destruction his broadsides were causing, he exclaimed with conviction, "By God, that ship is ours!"

Within ten minutes the *Guerriere's* mainyard was shot away and her hull, rigging and sails were badly cut up, while the *Constitution* had sustained no serious damage. In another few minutes a shot from the *Constitution* brought down the British ship's mizzenmast, and soon after, with a tremendous rending of timbers that drowned out even the roaring of the cannon, the *Guerriere's* foremast and mainmast crashed in an uproar to the deck and over the side. The British ship was now totally dismasted, her decks filled with wreckage, and her hull taking water in torrents. She drifted slowly away from the *Constitution* and, falling into the trough of the sea, rolled heavily from side to side, burying the muzzles of her main-deck guns in the water. Beaten and helpless, the great ship, which but a few minutes before had been as splendid a frigate as any afloat, struck her colors.

Her commander, Captain James Dacres, had been a friend of Captain Hull's prior to the war, and on one occasion had wagered that he would defeat the *Constitution,* if his ship ever had the opportunity to engage her. The loser of the wager was to give the other a good hat. Dacres had been wounded during the battle and, as he came up the side of the *Constitution* to surrender his sword, Captain Hull held out his hands and said, "Let me help you, Dacres, I know you are hurt."

"Thank you," said Dacres bravely. "I have brought you my sword."

"No, no, I will not take a sword from one who knows so well how to use it," was Hull's reply, "but I *will* trouble you for that hat."

The *Constitution's* victory was hailed with joy throughout the United States, for it was the first occasion on which an American frigate had defeated a British antagonist of equal strength and merit. "It took but half an hour," wrote Henry Adams, "but in that one-half hour the United States of America rose to the rank of a first-class power."

Captain Hull left the *Constitution* after her battle with the *Guerriere* and Captain William Bainbridge, a veteran of the war with Tripoli, took command. Under her new commander, the good ship sailed from Boston late in October, 1812, in company with the ship-sloop *Hornet,* their orders being to proceed to the Indian Ocean to prey on British shipping there. However, an action with the British frigate *Java,* off the Brazilian port of Bahia, prevented this design from being carried out.

The *Java* had left England in November, bound for India, and having under her protection two richly-laden merchant ships. On the twenty-fourth of December, being short of water, her commander, Captain Lambert, decided to put into Bahia, while the two Indiamen continued on toward the Cape of Good Hope.

Four days after Christmas the *Java* approached the Brazilian coast and, to the great surprise of everyone on board, sighted the *Constitution* cruising back and forth some thirty miles off the port of Bahia. Captain Lambert gave the order to clear for action. Captain Bainbridge, seeing the enemy run out his guns, maneuvered the *Constitution* so as to get to windward, bore down under full sail upon the *Java* and, when the ships were about half a mile apart, opened fire with his port battery. The *Java* did not immediately reply, but when the American frigate had closed in to within pistol shot, delivered her starboard broadside. The two frigates then ran along side by side, delivering and receiving a tremendous fire.

Captain Bainbridge was anxious to come to close quarters, but the *Java* now had the weather gage and kept at a distance. For half an hour she did no serious damage to the *Constitution,* but then a lucky shot crashed into the American ship's wheel and smashed it into splinters, at the same time wounding Captain Bainbridge in the thigh. He had already been injured by a musket ball, but had refused to go below for fear of the effect this might have on the crew.

The loss of the wheel was a serious mishap, for the *Constitution* now had to be steered by means of relieving tackles fastened to a tiller two decks below the quarter-deck. The men at the tiller could not see the sails and orders had to be transmitted by a chain of midshipmen. The *Java* now tried to rake her opponent fore and aft. Though disabled, the *Constitution* prevented this from happening and continued to blaze away with her broadside guns.

Bainbridge knew, however, that the *Constitution* in her crippled condition could achieve a victory only by pouring in a deadly fire at close quarters, and he soon decided that, regardless of the risk, he would close with the enemy. Setting his fore and main sails, he boldly headed his frigate for the *Java,* exposing her to a fore-and-aft raking fire. For some unexplained reason the British ship did not use this opportunity and, when her broadsides could have raked the *Constitution* from stem to stern, she discharged only one 9-pounder.

The *Java's* hesitation during this interval proved her undoing. On came the *Constitution,* nearer and nearer, and at close quarters she opened an unbelievable fire. It was the same inconceivably heavy and rapid flaming crescendo of destruction that had done for the *Guerriere.* The *Java's* jib boom and bowsprit were shot away and her running rigging was so badly cut to pieces that she could scarcely maneuver. A few minutes later, at a distance of two cables, the *Constitution* delivered a hail of shot that swept the Britisher's decks fore and aft. Her foremast crashed down and the main topmast followed. Then, as one of the *Java's* officers wrote, the *Constitution* "lay on our starboard quarter, pouring in a tremendous galling fire, while on our side we could never get more than two or three guns to bear, and frequently none at all." In a short while, the *Java's* mizzenmast was shot away and, according to the report of her commander, she was "an unmanageable wreck." Surrender was inevitable.

Following her victory over the *Java,* the *Constitution* returned to Boston to repair the damage sustained in the battle. This was so considerable that it was January, 1814, before she once more put to sea. Under the command of Captain Charles Stewart, she made a cruise through the West Indies during which she met but slight success, capturing only four prizes. Upon her return to Boston, she was blockaded in that port by a powerful British squadron and not until the seventeenth of December, 1814, was she able to give the enemy the slip and gain the open sea. This was to be her last cruise in the War of 1812 and she achieved her greatest triumph—the simultaneous defeat of a British frigate and a sloop-of-war.

Captain Stewart first ran down to Bermuda, where he captured a large merchant ship. He then set a course eastward across the Atlantic. Early in February he reached the coast of Portugal and thenceforward patroled between Portugal and the Madeiras, keeping a constant lookout for British ships. On the twentieth of February, while bowling along before a stiff breeze under short canvas, two vessels were sighted off the port bow, and on the same course as the *Constitution*. These proved to be the British 32-gun frigate *Cyane* and the 21-gun sloop-of-war *Levant*.

The *Cyane* was the nearest vessel and, as the officers of the *Constitution* studied her through their spy-glasses, they saw that she had two rows of gun ports, although one row appeared to be false ports painted on her sides. Some of the officers thought she might be a double-decked ship. One said to Captain Stewart, "If she really has two decks, she is at least a 50-gun ship."

"Well," Captain Stewart replied drily, "at least she is an English man-of-war; and we must flog them when we can catch them, whether they have one deck or two."

The *Constitution* was soon almost within range of the *Cyane,* was overhauling her rapidly and was ready to open fire at any moment, when there was a loud crash overhead and her men, looking aloft, saw that the main royal mast had snapped in two. This mishap forced Captain Stewart to give up the chase for half an hour, and it gave the two British ships time to draw close together. They could not now be attacked separately.

It was five o'clock when the *Constitution* once again got underway, gathered speed and drove forward in full chase. The two enemy ships were now about four miles ahead and formed in a line of battle, east and west, ready and waiting to rake the American frigate as she bore down from the north. Captain Stewart cleared for action and beat to quarters, the growling rumble of the drums carrying menacingly across the water to the ears of the Britishers.

At six o'clock the *Constitution* hauled up her courses and turned

184

to the west. Five minutes later she was three hundred yards abeam of the sternmost vessel, the *Cyane,* and opened fire from the long guns of her port battery. Both British ships promptly responded with their starboard guns, and for fifteen minutes there was the deafening roar of tremendous firing. By 6.20 P.M. such thick clouds of smoke had risen from the guns that accurate aim was impossible, and Captain Stewart gave the order to "Cease firing." He drove the big frigate ahead, through the darkness and smoke, to a position abeam of the *Levant.* Then, the guns having been reloaded with a double-shotted broadside, the *Constitution* poured it at close range into the enemy. It was a terrific blow which shook the *Levant* from truck to keelson, smashed through her bulwarks and dismounted several of her guns.

One of the most brilliant maneuvers ever executed by any ship in any naval engagement now followed. Captain Stewart, well aware of the danger of being raked by the *Cyane,* suddenly braced his main and mizzen topsails flat to the mast, shook all forward, let go his jib sheet, and, as though propelled by engines, quietly but swiftly backed the *Constitution* to a position abreast the *Cyane.* So rapidly was the maneuver executed that, almost before the enemy was aware of it, the American frigate was close alongside her new antagonist, with every gun of her formidable battery reloaded and double-shotted. A quiet order passed along her decks; the next instant the red flames of her broadside stabbed the darkness and one of her terrible broadsides tore its way into the British frigate.

Captain Stewart now maintained a heavy and rapid fire against the *Cyane* until he saw that the *Levant* was luffing across his course to rake. He would have to put a stop to this. Filling away under her topsails, the *Constitution* bounded forward and crossed the *Levant's* wake before the smoke from her last broadside had sufficiently cleared away to enable the English to discover her exact position. The Americans then poured in a tremendous broadside, raking the *Levant* fore and aft, and before she could recover from the dreadful hammering of this blow, the Americans raked her again with terrific effect.

Now it was time to turn again to the *Cyane,* which was once more trying to cross the *Constitution's* stern to rake. Captain Stewart wore his ship around and turned the tables on his opponent by scudding under her stern and letting loose another of his terrible double-shotted broadsides. The *Constitution's* guns flamed and thundered destruction, relentlessly hammering to pieces the bravely resisting Englishman. There seemed to be something superhuman about the *Constitution's* fire—no ship could long survive the awful blows of her furiously served guns. The *Cyane* was no exception. After ten minutes of gallant effort, she hoisted a light and fired a single gun as a signal of surrender.

For an hour the American and English ships lay close together, while prisoners were being transferred. Then, at 8 P.M., Captain Stewart started in pursuit of the *Levant,* which had made off to leeward. Seeing the *Constitution* approaching, the *Levant* close hauled her sails and, with topgallant sails and colors set, bore up toward her powerful antagonist. At 9.05 P.M. the ships passed each other and exchanged broadsides. Before the smoke had cleared away, Captain Stewart wore rapidly round, crossed the *Levant's* stern and raked. Shaken by this blow, the smaller English ship crowded on all sail and sought to increase the range. She was not to escape, however, for the *Constitution*

186

started in pursuit and at 9.30 P.M. opened fire with one of her chase guns. Soon she was nearly abreast of the *Levant* and was ready to deliver one of her full broadsides, but before the order was given, the commander of the *Levant* surrendered. It was the wisest course to pursue, since the English sloop was no match for the American frigate, and a further engagement would only have meant needless bloodshed and suffering.

This was the last important action in which the *Constitution* took part, and it marked a brilliant climax to her career. Under her three commanders, she had fought three of the greatest single-ship actions in the history of naval warfare. She had been one of the most important single factors in bringing the British and Americans together to negotiate a treaty of peace toward the close of the year 1814. Like the *Victory,* the *Constitution* is preserved as a glorious reminder of the days of wooden ships and iron men, and of the ideals for which her officers and sailors fought.

18

The Niagara

Oliver Hazard Perry's Flagship at the Battle of Lake Erie

TOWARD the end of March, 1813, a twenty-six-year-old Master-Commandant of the United States navy, Oliver Hazard Perry, left the village of Buffalo, at the eastern end of Lake Erie, and made his way in a sleigh over the ice to the hamlet of Presque Isle, on the southern shore of the lake. A forlorn sight met him when he reached his destination. There were a few dozen log houses and a tavern, all surrounded by deep snow. The dull, leaden sky of a wintry day hung over the scene like a pall.

Perry, who had asked the navy department to send him where he "could meet the enemies of his country," had been despatched to this desolate hamlet to undertake a task of almost unbelievable difficulty. This was nothing less than to build from the keel up a fleet of warships with which to attack and, if possible, defeat the British squadron, then in undisputed command of Lake Erie.

Through their possession of the vast tract of land then known as the Territory of Michigan, and now comprising a number of states, the English controlled the upper lakes, and were in a position to carry out their plans of extending the borders of Canada to the Gulf of Mexico, thus cutting the United States off from the West. Young

Perry's herculean task was to regain control of Lake Erie, the first step necessary to the recovery of the endangered territory.

With only too keen a realization of the enormous task that lay ahead of him, Perry began to build his fleet. There were to be two brigs, the *Niagara* and the *Lawrence,* a gunboat, the *Ariel,* and a schooner, the *Scorpion.* The *Lawrence* was named, by order of the secretary of the navy, after Captain James Lawrence of the frigate *Chesapeake,* who had lost his life in an engagement with the British frigate *Shannon.* The largest vessels, the two brigs, were each one hundred and ten feet over all, and had twenty-nine feet beam.

Perry worked under tremendous difficulties, for he had no rigging, sails, cannon, powder or shot. He was obliged to go to Pittsburgh in the dead of winter for equipment and to bring it to Erie on ox-drawn sledges over the almost impassable forest trails. When he returned from this tedious journey, he found that the British had abandoned Fort Erie, on the Niagara River opposite Buffalo. This made it possible to bring five vessels, the brig *Caledonia,* the schooners *Porcupine, Somers* and *Tigress* and the sloop *Trippe* up the river and add them to his squadron. By the united efforts of two hundred soldiers and many yoke of oxen, these vessels were warped up the swift current, six days being required for the task. When they floated on Lake Erie, Perry's force was immeasurably strengthened.

Perry now had nine ships, mounting fifty-four guns, while the English squadron against him consisted of six ships that mounted sixty-three guns. The English vessels, all somewhat larger, were the flagship *Detroit,* the ship *Queen Charlotte,* the brigs, *Hunter* and *Lady Prevost,* and the schooners, *Chippewa* and *Little Belt.* They were manned by a seasoned force of sailors from the royal navy and soldiers from the regular army. They were commanded by Captain Robert Barclay, a veteran who had fought with Nelson at Trafalgar.

Perry had the greatest difficulty getting men of any sort to man his ships. Time after time he wrote to his superior officers and to the secretary of the navy: "Give me men, sir, and I will acquire both for you and myself honor and glory on this lake or perish in the attempt." And again he wrote: "For God's sake and your own and mine, send me men and officers, and I will have the enemy in a day or two." But only a few men could be sent to him, and they gave little appearance of being good fighting material—"a motley set, blacks, soldiers and boys."

The men were drilled, however, and exercised in seamanship and gunnery, and late in August the little fleet left Erie and sailed in search of the British squadron. At sunrise on the morning of September the tenth, while cruising off Put-in-Bay at the western end of Lake Erie, the lookout at the flagship *Lawrence's* masthead sighted the English ships. Perry immediately ordered the squadron to set all sail and close with the enemy.

As the ships moved slowly over the glassy waters of the lake, driven by the merest whisper of a breeze, Master-Commandant Perry called his men aft and unfolded a large blue flag bearing in white muslin letters the stirring words of the dying Lawrence, commander of the *Cheasapeake*: "Don't give up the ship!"

"Men," said Perry, "this flag bears the last words of Captain Lawrence. Shall I hoist it?" With one voice the men shouted, "Ay, ay, sir!" As the flag was run up to the masthead and fluttered out over

the ship like the guardian spirit of the departed captain, cheer upon cheer sounded from the other vessels of the squadron.

The English vessels, drawing gradually closer, presented a brave appearance on this morning of battle. "Newly painted, gaily bedecked with flags and under easy sail," says one account, "throwing their shadows ahead, glancing along the sunlit waves, as they came down in line of battle under the cloudless sky. The *Detroit* was especially noticeable for the tautness of her rigging, the dazzling whiteness of her canvas and the handsome style in which she was handled. About half-past ten o'clock a bugle was heard from the flagship, which was followed by a succession of cheers from the different vessels, and at the same time the strains of 'Rule Britannia' from a band in the *Detroit* were carried by the faint breeze to the ears of the Americans. In the *Lawrence* nothing served to break the silence except a few short orders which, followed by the shrill piping of the boatswain's whistle, broke over the waters with startling clearness; then another silence, the more oppressive by the contrast, would follow."

Perry now arranged his ships in line-ahead formation, led by the *Lawrence* and *Niagara,* which were to concentrate their fire on the English flagship *Detroit* at the head of the British line. At the same time he designated which of the English ships the other American vessels were to engage. As these orders were being given, the *Detroit,* at 11:45 A.M., fired one of her 24-pounders to test the distance. The squadrons were still a mile apart, but the shot ricocheted along the water and passed beyond the *Lawrence.* Five minutes later the *Detroit* fired a second shot, and this one crashed through the *Lawrence's* starboard bulwarks and sent a cloud of splinters flying over the men stationed at the batteries. The *Scorpion* and *Ariel* were the first American ships to return the fire and were soon followed by the *Lawrence* and *Niagara.*

Captain Barclay had evidently given orders for the English fire to be concentrated on the *Lawrence,* for the leading British ships poured a heavy and devastating hail of shot at the American flagship. Cannon balls fired by the *Queen Charlotte* crashed through the *Lawrence's* mainmast and through her starboard side at the water line, and she was hit in other spots by other British ships. Perry closed in to bring his short-range guns into play, and was followed by the *Scorpion* and *Ariel,* but the other vessels of the squadron were unable to keep up due to lack of wind and in a few minutes the three ships in the van were receiving the concentrated and destructive fire of almost all the English fleet.

For nearly an hour the *Lawrence* dueled with the *Detroit* and the *Hunter,* and then was still further battered by the broadsides of the *Queen Charlotte* and the *Lady Prevost.* No ship could stand up for long under so heavy a fire at short range and the condition of the *Lawrence* at the end of an hour of this unequal contest was appalling. Her guns had been disabled, one by one, until only one on her engaged side could be worked. Her rigging was badly cut up; her spars were shattered beyond description; her sails were torn into shreds; out of her complement of one hundred and three men on active duty, eighty-three had been killed or wounded. Perry and his thirteen-year old brother James were among the handful not seriously wounded or killed, and their escape seemed truly a miracle, for both had been constantly on deck exposed to the full blast of the English fire.

At half-past two o'clock the *Lawrence,* the *Ariel* and the *Scorpion* had borne the brunt of the battle for an agonizing two hours and forty-five minutes. At this time, as the battered *Lawrence* was drifting almost helplessly away from the enemy, a breeze ruffled the smooth waters of the lake. It was very light, but it can truly be said that it changed the course of history, for it enabled the *Niagara* to come to the relief of the shattered American flagship. Perry seized the miraculously proffered opportunity, put off in a small boat with his brother James and four seamen and transferred his flag to the comparatively uninjured *Niagara.* "The American commander," Captain Barclay wrote in his official report, "seeing that as yet the day was against him, made a noble effort to regain it." Just as Perry was shoving off from the side of the *Lawrence,* a seaman hauled down the flag bearing the motto "Don't give up the ship!" rolled it up and tossed it to his commander.

A survivor of the action, a gunner on the *Queen Charlotte,* described the passage of Perry's boat from the *Lawrence* to the *Niagara* as follows:

"The *Lawrence* being disabled, Perry took advantage of the settling smoke to go from her to the *Niagara*. We did not see him until he had nearly effected his purpose, but the wind causing the smoke to lift, I saw the boat and aimed a shot at her, and saw the shot strike the boat. I then saw Perry strip off his coat and plug the hole with it, which prevented the boat from filling before it reached the *Niagara*."

Clambering up the side of the *Niagara*, Perry quickly rehoisted his broad pennant and the flag bearing the words of Captain Lawrence, and then made his plans for continuing the battle. An officer was sent in a small boat to order the other ships to close up for an immediate attack at close quarters. The *Niagara* then drove ahead toward the leading English ships, passed between the *Detroit* and *Queen Charlotte* and raked them fore and aft, firing two broadsides simultaneously. The effect of this fire at such close quarters was devastating. The rushing cannon balls swept along the English ships' decks, bringing death and destruction as they tore through the crowds of officers and men.

Now everything seemed to favor the gallant *Niagara*. She ran astern of the *Lady Prevost* and delivered another terrific raking broadside; then she bore down on the *Hunter* and settled down to the work of hammering her into surrender. The other American vessels, aided by the freshening breeze, followed the *Niagara* in to close quarters and grimly set about avenging their comrades. For the first time the entire American squadron was engaged at close quarters and the gunners were firing like men possessed. The roar of the American cannon rose to a furious crescendo; their orange-red flashes seemed to hem the British in from every side; between the thundering of the cannon the resounding crashes of the American shot could be heard, bursting through the bulwarks and sides of the English ships.

Under this appalling rain of metal, the English were driven from their guns, and officers and men were killed or wounded by the score. In a few minutes, incredible though it seems, all was over. Only fifteen minutes from the time the breeze enabled the Americans to close in, the *Hunter* struck her colors and the other English ships followed her example. Seldom in naval history have the fortunes of battle changed so swiftly and decisively from near-victory to complete defeat.

Perry received the formal surrender of the English officers on the deck of the battle-scarred *Lawrence*. She and her men had suffered terribly. "When Master-Commandant Perry stepped aboard, it was a time of conflicting emotions," her doctor wrote. "Not a cheer was heard; the handful of men that was left of the gallant crew silently greeted their commander."

As each English officer came aboard and presented his sword to Perry, the American commander quietly bade him to retain it. He was too moved to speak, but immediately on completing the formalities of surrender, he wrote with a pencil on the back of an old letter, using his cap as a support, his famous dispatch:

"We have met the enemy and they are ours—two ships, two brigs, one schooner and one sloop."

The consequences of this American victory, won against heavy odds by a twenty-six-year-old youth, were tremendous. The British, deprived of their naval power on the Great Lakes, were compelled to evacuate Detroit and Michigan, and the vast Michigan Territory which might have become a British possession was regained for the United States.

19

The Dreadnought

Fastest of the American Packet Ships

ONE of the most glorious epochs in the history of American sailing vessels was the era of the "flash" Yankee packet ships—the hard-driving, fast-sailing vessels which for nearly half a century carried on the important north Atlantic passenger and mail service. The greatest of these ships, and the one that made the fastest packet-ship passage across the Atlantic, was the Red Cross liner *Dreadnought*.

Starting in 1816 with the founding of the famous Black Ball Line, the packet ships were the only regular means of communication between the Old World and the New. They not only established new records for speed and comfort on the Western Ocean, but played an important part in the development of the United States, for hundreds of thousands of immigrants came to America on them, from the overcrowded shores of England, Ireland and the Continent of Europe. The Yankee packet ships were the forerunners of the great trans-Atlantic passenger liners of today and, until the coming of steam, these vessels bearing the Stars and Stripes showed their heels to all rivals and completely dominated the stormy highway of the north Atlantic Ocean.

After the Declaration of Independence in 1776, and until the termination of the War of 1812 and the long-drawn-out Napoleonic wars, there was no regular service between the United States and Europe. Both France and England did their utmost to eliminate the export and import trade of all their adversaries and, as a consequence, it was almost impossible for Yankee vessels to trade peaceably and profitably. For these reasons, many of the vessels in the American merchant fleet were dismantled and laid up pending the outcome of the wars. For the most part, only the privateers still kept the seas.

Finally, in 1814, peace was signed with Great Britain. In the following year the battle of Waterloo brought about Napoleon's downfall and brought peace to the world. The Yankees immediately commenced to re-establish themselves on the high seas.

While American ships were sailing on trading voyages to all the ports of the world shortly after the close of hostilities, it was considered most essential to have regular, dependable sailings between Europe and the United States. It was for the carrying out of this purpose that the famous packet lines were established. The word "packet" was used to describe a ship which, instead of making irregular voyages here, there and everywhere as cargo offered, plied on regular schedules between definite ports, carrying passengers and mails as well as cargo.

The early packets, though considered perfectly adequate in those days, were scarcely larger than one of the lifeboats on the giant passenger liners of today. The service was started with four vessels of about four hundred tons each—the *Amity, Courier, Pacific* and *James Monroe.* They sailed from New York for Liverpool regularly—no matter what the weather—on the first and sixteenth of each month, and for many years everybody in the United States knew that these were the two "mail days" for letters and parcels going to Europe. On sailing days great crowds would flock to the waterside of New York to see the fleet and handsome packet ships get underway for the trans-Atlantic passage.

Black Ball skippers—most of whom were trained to handle sail in the speedy privateersmen which stayed out in all weathers—had no fear of the fogs and ice or the furious winter gales of the dreaded north Atlantic. Even today, these storms hold up the great passenger liners and frequently batter them mercilessly. But a hundred years ago, it was:

> "Whatever the weather, blow high or blow low;
> With a way, aye, blow the man down,
> Its the Liverpool packet; oh Lord, let her go—
> Give me some time to blow the man down."

So popular was the regular service provided by the first four ships of the Black Ball Line that within six months four additional vessels, the *New York, William Thompson, Orbit* and *James Trotter,* were added to the fleet. Soon after, the increase in the demands for passage made it necessary to put the *Albion, Canada, Nestor, Britannia* and *Columbia* into service.

All these ships were of three hundred to five hundred tons register and were, of course, very primitive as compared with the standards of today. They were only about one hundred and fifty feet long, and had a flush deck which, much of the time, was flooded with water. For the emigrant passengers who filled them on their westward voyages, the accommodations were simple in the extreme. They were packed like sardines into the between-decks amidships, from which,

in times of bad weather, they were often unable to escape for days at a time. The company provided water, but no food, and everyone, consequently, brought his own food and cooked it at the ship's galley on the main deck between the fore and main masts.

The cabin passengers who lived aft fared considerably better. They had separate cabins and a large dining saloon or "cuddy," furnished with upholstered seats.

The long-boat which housed most of the fresh food was lashed on top of the galley. These delicacies were intended only for the cabin passengers. The inside of the long-boat was a regular farm yard—pigs, sheep, ducks, geese, hens and chickens—all messing together and sometimes, in heavy weather, all were washed overboard together. Over the main hatch was lashed a small house containing one or two cows upon which the ship's company depended for milk.

All the Black Ball Liners were full-rigged ships and had black hulls, this color being relieved by the bright green used for the rails, boats, deck-houses and the inner side of the bulwarks. They could be distinguished at a distance by the large black ball painted on their foretopsails. When closer to, one could make out their famous house-flag—a red swallow-tail pennant with a black ball in its center.

The speed of these vessels on the eastward voyage, which was always the faster owing to the prevailing westerly winds, was very good, the average trip being twenty-three days. On the westward voyage, however, the average time was forty days. The fastest eastward voyage of the early days was made by the Black Baller *Canada,* which went from New York to Liverpool in fifteen days, eighteen hours, and her average passages—nineteen days eastward and thirty-six days westward—made her the fastest packet ship on the north Atlantic run.

So great was the success of the Black Ball Line that others soon entered the field to take part in the increasing emigrant trade and in the growing commerce between the New World and the Old. The principal new lines were John Griswold's "London Line," the Red Star, the Swallow Tail, the Red Cross and the Dramatic Lines from New York, Cope's and Girard's ships from Philadelphia, and Enoch Train's service from Boston.

These were the most famous of the great packet lines, which provided a faster and more dependable service between the New World and the Old than had ever before existed. They gave the United States a dominant position in the Western Ocean trade for nearly half a century. Their names and those of their ships were household words all through the United States and Europe. The captains, too, were well known to everybody, as were the house-flags and other distinguishing marks of the different lines and, in some instances, of individual vessels.

The *Dreadnought*

To match the big black ball on the foretopsails of the swift Black Ballers, the Dramatic Line painted a great black X from corner to corner of their vessels' foretopsails, while Enoch Train's Liverpool ships carried a giant black T. The famous packet ship *Dreadnought,* as a member of the Red Cross Line, had an upright red cross boldly painted on her foretopsail.

Every owner took great pride in his house-flag, and their designs and coloring were a matter of common knowledge, the boys of the time learning them just as today they learn the distinguishing marks of the different makes of automobiles and airplanes. The Dramatic Line's Liverpool ships carried a blue and white flag (in two bands, the blue being uppermost). A large L was in the center, the upper half colored white and the lower half black. For the ships in the Line's New Orleans service, the flag was a red swallow-tail with a white ball and a black L in the center. The flag of John Griswold's London Line was a red swallow-tail with a black X in the center; that of the Swallow Tail Line a red and white swallow-tail for the London ships and a blue and white swallow-tail for the Liverpool ships. All these flags, famous in their day, and those of the other great packet lines, vanished from the north Atlantic many years ago, and with their passing went the dashing packet ships and their hard-driving, sail-carrying Yankee captains, the most famous group of mariners of their day.

Probably the most famous of all the company of packet ship masters was Captain Samuel Samuels of the Red Cross Line's great packet ship *Dreadnought.* This vessel was the most famous, as well as one of the largest and fastest of all the packet ships and, since she was not built until 1853, her design embodied all the refinements and improvements that had been developed since the first days of the packet ship trade. The *Dreadnought* was two hundred and ten feet long, had a beam of forty feet, and measured more than fourteen hundred tons. One of the last sailing vessels to be built for the north Atlantic packet trade, she was the supreme achievement of the packet ship builders' art, and the ship which most vividly calls to mind the vanished glories of the packet-ship era.

> 'Tis of a flash packet,
>   A packet of fame;
> She is bound to New York,
>   And the *Dreadnought's* her name.
> She is bound to the west'ard
>   Where the stormy winds blow.
> Bound away to the west'ard
>   Good Lord! let her go!

Captain Samuels commanded the *Dreadnought* for ten years, and during that time she made many fast passages which established her as one of the swiftest of the entire north Atlantic packet fleet. She crossed the Atlantic eastward, in 1859, in faster time than any packet ship before her—thirteen days, eight hours. Her many fast voyages were due in large measure to the fact that she could be driven mercilessly in the heaviest weather. This was possible not only because of her powerful build, but also because her standing and running rigging and all other gear were of the best material available and were always kept in the very best condition. Even with these qualities, however, she would not have been able to maintain her marvelous record for speed and reliability had it not been for the great skill and unremitting vigilance of her commander who would, and did, go without sleep for days on end if, by so doing, he could squeeze another knot out of the vibrant, eager vessel entrusted to his care.

Captain Samuels recorded many of his experiences while in command of the *Dreadnought* in his memoirs, *From the Forecastle to the Cabin:*

"She was never passed in anything over a four-knot breeze. She was what might be termed a semi-clipper, and possessed the merit of being able to stand driving as long as her sails and spars would stand. By the sailors she was nicknamed the 'Wild Boat of the Atlantic,' while others called her the 'Flying Dutchman.' Twice she carried the latest news to Europe, slipping in between the steamers. The Collins, Cunard, and Inman Liners were the only ones at that time. There are merchants still (in 1887) doing business in New York who shipped goods by us which we guaranteed to deliver within a certain time or forfeit freight charges. For this guarantee we commanded freight rates midway between those of the steamers and the sailing packets."

Even on her first voyage, before she was properly broken in, the *Dreadnought* demonstrated her extraordinary sailing qualities, as her captain wrote: "We crossed Sandy Hook bar with the then crack packet ship *Washington,* Captain Page. We landed in Liverpool, and took on a cargo and two hundred immigrants, and met her off the Northwest Lightship bound in as we were running out. On our way home we crossed the bar the day after the steamer *Canada* sailed for

Boston, and when the news of her arrival reached New York, we were reported off the Highlands."

Like all the other packet ship commanders, Captain Samuels had to deal with crews made up of the toughest, wildest sailormen afloat on any ocean. "Liverpool Irishmen," they were called. Because of their depravity and coarseness and the fact that they preferred the north Atlantic trade to all others, they were generally referred to as "packet rats."

Despite their wild ways, these "packet rats" had certain rules of conduct to which they adhered with the strictest fidelity. They would not steal from each other, for example, although it was their greatest delight to plunder sailors of other nationalities and to make away with the ship's stores to sell for money with which to buy rum. Nor would they fight each other with knives. These weapons were far too dangerous for their tender skins! But there was nothing to keep them from settling their differences—and these occurred very frequently—with bare fists and beating each other into unconsciousness by this means. Their peculiar code of honor, however, did not prevent them from knifing and stabbing officers and sailors not of their particular gang.

On one occasion Captain Samuels shipped a crew of these beauties, members of a case-hardened gang known in Liverpool as the "Bloody Forties." When they came aboard, they were searched and all their weapons were removed. This so infuriated them that a few days after leaving port they mutinied and refused to work the ship until one of their comrades, in irons for insubordination, was released. Captain Samuels quite properly refused to do this. While the men skulked and threatened dire things, the officers and boys handled the sails. The mood of the men was so dangerous, however, that Captain Samuels enlisted the aid of some of the stronger passengers to beat the "Bloody Forties" into submission. It is interesting to note that when the *Dreadnought* arrived in New York, the Liverpool "rats," realizing the justice and necessity of Captain Samuels's actions, cheered him over and over again.

Tough and depraved as the "packet rats" undoubtedly were, they were great sailormen when they put their minds to the job in hand. They were at home on the wild, storm-driven north Atlantic. Heavy weather held no terrors for them and they scorned to go aloft, even in the coldest weather, wearing a coat or a monkey jacket to keep themselves warm. Their hairy, tattooed chests and their bright red shirts were all the protection they needed against the iciest gales of winter.

When the rigging was sheathed in ice and the great sails, coated with snow and sleet, were thundering wildly before a gale that made the packet leap to the heavens and then plunge her bowsprit into the giant rollers and take tons of green water aboard, these beauties were most at home. Laying out on the dizzily swaying yards, they proved themselves real sailors as they fought, inch by inch, to claw up and reef the sails which struggled beneath them like wild things.

When a race was on—and there were many desperate contests between the rival packets—the "rats" gave their best. Sometimes, to be sure, this was because they were offered extra wages if their ship won; but many and many a time they worked their ship for all that was in her only for the thrill of being the first to surge flying across the bar at the end of the voyage.

After serving for a little over ten years in the north Atlantic packet service, the increasing competition of steamships drove the *Dreadnought* from this trade, and forced her into general tramping service, which took her to all parts of the globe. She met her end, in 1869, in a howling blizzard off Cape Horn. Her crew was rescued after being adrift for fourteen days in the boats. But the noble old packet ship was beaten to pieces by the roaring breakers that hurled her upon the menacing crags of the dreaded Cape.

20

The Britannia

First of the Cunarders

WHILE the American shipping lines were busy despatching their famous "flash" packet ships across the north Atlantic, apparently with little or no realization that the era of the sailing vessel was soon to come to an end, some of the more forward-looking British shipping men were becoming increasingly interested in the possibility of building steamships that would be able to make the trans-Atlantic voyage. Several steamships crossed the Atlantic in the early 1800's, and two British companies attempted to establish regular services during the 1830's. It was not until the year 1840, when the *Britannia* inaugurated the Cunard Line service, that the steamship really proved its ability to compete with the white-sailed, hard-driven packet vessels.

The honor of being the first steamship to make the Atlantic crossing has been claimed for the American ship *Savannah,* a sailing vessel fitted with an auxiliary steam engine, which made a voyage from Savannah to Liverpool in 1819. While the *Savannah* unquestionably did cross the Atlantic, she used her sails for the greater part of the voyage, bringing her engines into play only when entering and leaving port. Her voyage took twenty-nine days, eleven hours, and during it her engines were run only for a total of eighty hours. For this reason, many have held, and with considerable justice, that her trip cannot be regarded as a real steamship passage.

It seems probable that the ship to whom the honor rightfully belongs was the little Dutch steamer *Curacao*. She was built at Bristol, England, but was sold to the Netherlands navy soon after completion. Converted into a warship, she sailed for South America in 1827, making the voyage continuously under steam, and during the next two years she made several passages across the Atlantic, carrying mails, passengers and freight. With this record to her credit, the *Curacao,* though seldom mentioned in the histories of steam navigation, seems fully entitled to be recognized as the first steamship to cross the Atlantic, using her engines as the only means of propulsion.

The distinction which rightfully belongs to the *Curacao* is generally given to the *Royal William,* a Canadian steamship which crossed from Quebec to London in 1833. In her case, as in that of the *Savannah,* it is doubtful if the voyage was made entirely under steam. It seems probable, from all the available evidence, that the *Royal William* did not use her engines continuously, but that the intervals when she used sails alone were relatively short.

The *Royal William's* voyage gave rise to a great deal of enthusiasm for steamships in Canada, and to some extent in England. She was described by one writer as "the first ship to cross the ocean by continuous steam power," and another called her "the Herald of the Canadian Confederation and the pioneer of the Cunard fleet and of Ocean steam navigation." Although these claims are high-flown in the extreme, there is no doubt that the *Royal William's* voyage did convince

a large number of people that steamships would soon be able to cross the Atlantic as regularly as sailing vessels.

Among those who were most deeply interested in the *Royal William's* passage was Samuel Cunard, a ship owner of Halifax, Nova Scotia, and the agent at that port for the Honourable East India Company. He had been one of the principal shareholders in the company that built the *Royal William* and had taken every opportunity to study her sea qualities, speed and fuel consumption—particularly the latter, since one of the greatest difficulties in connection with starting a trans-Atlantic steamship service was to build ships that could carry enough coal to make the voyage and still leave sufficient room for passengers and cargo. Cunard had studied all the early experiments in steam navigation and had satisfied himself that regular trans-Atlantic voyages by steamships were entirely practicable. His imagination enabled him to look beyond the "tea-kettle" steam engines of the day to a time when steamships would make their ocean passages with the punctuality of railway trains.

After the *Royal William* had successfully made her crossing and with coal to spare, Cunard was still further convinced that steamships fit in every way for the Atlantic service could be built. This belief was further confirmed in 1838, when several British steamships, the *Sirius, Great Western, Liverpool* and *British Queen* made the passage from England to New York and back. The passages made by these ships were considerably faster than those of the sailing packets, the *Great Western* making the eastward run in twelve days, ten hours, and the westward crossing in thirteen days, three hours.

As a result of the steamships' success, the British Government asked for tenders for an Atlantic steam-packet service to carry the mails. When this news came to the ear of Samuel Cunard, he lost no time in sailing for England to make an attempt to obtain the contract. There were many difficulties to be overcome. He encountered very determined opposition on the part of the powerful sailing-ship owners, who realized that they would be faced with ruin if steamships were successful. To complicate matters still further, many prominent scientists still maintained that steamships could not carry enough coal to make the Atlantic voyage with a reasonable degree of safety.

These difficulties made Cunard more determined than ever. He journeyed to Glasgow with a letter of introduction to Robert Napier, at that time the greatest of the Clyde shipbuilders and marine engineers. Napier introduced him to two of Glasgow's leading ship owners, George Burns and David MacIver, each of whom had had considerable experience in operating steamships in the coastwise services around the British Isles. The two Scotsmen were so thoroughly acquainted with the steamship business that they were able to vision the possibilities of a trans-Atlantic service more readily than many others, and the result was the formation of a partnership between Cunard and his two Scottish friends under the name of the British and North American Royal Mail Steam Packet Company. A seven-years' contract was then obtained from the British Government for the carriage of the Royal mails between Liverpool, Halifax and Boston. The original company lasted until 1878, when it became the Cunard Steamship Company.

The *Britannia* was the first and most famous of the four sister ships with which the Cunard Line service was started. The other three were the *Acadia, Caledonia* and *Columbia*.

The *Britannia* was built at Glasgow, and, though described at the time as a "mammoth" ship, she was but two hundred and seven feet in length and thirty-four feet in beam, and measured gross a little more than eleven hundred tons. She was built of wood and was driven through the water by thrashing paddle wheels propelled by engines that developed seven hundred and forty horsepower. These were capable of giving her a speed of eight and a half knots on a coal consumption of thirty-eight tons a day. Since there was always a possibility of the engines breaking down, the *Britannia* was given three masts rigged to carry fore and aft sails, while the fore and main masts could carry great bellying square sails as well. Accommodations were provided for one hundred and fifteen cabin passengers. Her smoke-stack was given the same color as that used on a fleet of coastwise steamers owned by Robert Napier, a red color produced by a mixture of bright ochre and buttermilk. This distinctive color has ever since been used on the funnels of Cunard Line ships.

The *Britannia* sailed from Liverpool on her maiden voyage to Halifax and Boston on July the fourth, 1840. Her departure on the American "Independence Day" was thought to be a good omen for the future of the service to the United States.

Although she encountered strong head winds most of the way, the *Britannia* reached Halifax on July the seventeenth after a passage of thirteen days. After a stop of a few hours, she continued to Boston, where she arrived at ten o'clock on Saturday evening, July the eighteenth. Although it was a late hour for staid old Boston, she was greeted by hundreds of people, crowded at the waterfront to cheer her arrival. Cannon were fired in welcome and the band on a frigate in the harbor played *God Save the Queen* over and over again.

A few days later there was a public procession of thousands of New England citizens, marching eight abreast and led by the mayors of the principal New England cities, the foreign consuls and the leading men of Massachusetts. They had gathered to honor the *Britannia* and Mr. Cunard and "to show to their fellow countrymen and to the world, that they knew how to appreciate the magnitude and importance of the undertaking which was so successfully commenced by that gentleman who, it is well known, is one of the most enterprising and public spirited merchants of today."

Two years after her maiden voyage, by which time her name and fame were known around the world, the *Britannia* carried the famous novelist, Charles Dickens across the Atlantic. His description of the voyage, contained in his *American Notes,* gives us a vivid account of what a winter crossing was like on the most "magnificent" steamship then plying on the north Atlantic. Of his first impressions upon passing through the main saloon, Dickens wrote: "Before descending into the bowels of the ship, we had passed from the deck into a long narrow apartment, not unlike a gigantic hearse with windows in the sides; having at the upper end a melancholy stove, at which three or four chilly stewards were warming their hands; while on either side, extending down its whole dreary length, was a long, long table, over each of which a rack, fixed to the low roof, and stuck full of drinking-glasses and cruet-stands hinted dismally of rolling seas and heavy weather."

After inspecting the saloon and his stateroom, Dickens returned to the deck to see Captain Hewitt coming out to the ship. He wrote:

"What have we here? The captain's boat! and yonder the Captain himself. Now, by all our hopes and wishes, the very man he ought to be! A well-made, tight-built, dapper little fellow; with a ruddy face, which is a letter of invitation to shake him by both hands at once; and with a clear blue, honest eye, that it does one good to see one's sparkling image in!"

And now the moment of departure has arrived . . .

"Away the *Britannia* sailed, down through the Irish Sea, and St. George's Channel to the heaving rollers of the Atlantic Ocean. For a few days the skies were bright and the weather moderately calm. But then a storm came up and the little *Britannia,* though battling against it valiantly, was tossed and thrown about as though she were an eggshell. Her movements are atrocious; all the passengers are miserably seasick; and still the wind continues to howl down from the west and the *Britannia's* yacht-like bow first points high aloft to the low-hanging sullen storm clouds and then directs itself toward the bottom of the sea as the little craft mounts and descends the vast hill-like waves of the Western Ocean. . . ."

The passage made by Dickens must have been far stormier than usual, for he was deeply impressed by the valiant struggle that the *Britannia* was forced to make and, after the gale had run its course, he wrote that "the life-boat had been crushed by one blow of the sea like a walnut shell; and there it hung dangling in the air, like a mere faggot of crazy boards. The planking of the paddle-boxes had been torn sheer away. The wheels were exposed and bare; and they whirled and dashed their spray about the decks at random. Chimney, white and crusted with salt; topmasts struck; storm-sails set; rigging all knotted, tangled, wet, and drooping: a gloomier picture it would be hard to look upon."

But blow high or blow low, the *Britannia* and her three sister-ships stuck to their schedules and thrashed their way across the Atlantic, passing the sailing packets on the way and establishing firmly the supremacy of steam on one of the world's greatest ocean highways. The Cunard Line quickly gained the favor of the public, and during the first ten years of its existence eight ships had to be added to the fleet to deal with the steadily increasing traffic. The last of the wooden Cunarders, the *Arabia,* was built in 1852. In the following year the company began to build iron ships, the first of these being the *Persia.*

Throughout the years, the *Britannia's* successors have established enviable records for safety, speed and reliability of service. It was a Cunarder which carried to Europe the first American exports of manufactured goods, and Cunarders brought many thousands of immigrants from Europe to help in the building of the United States. Throughout its existence the Line has followed the policies laid down by Samuel Cunard and his partners—to make safety at all times the first consideration, to order ships from the best builders, to be made of the strongest materials, and to apply every proved advance in engineering science. While other lines have come into being, run their course, then disappeared from the seas, the Cunard Line has gone steadily forward, maintaining year in and year out its high position, driving onward through good times and bad, through peace and war, as the *Britannia* and her sisters drove resolutely through the north Atlantic gales of a century ago.

21

The Arctic, Baltic, Atlantic and Pacific

The American Steamers That Captured the Blue Ribband of the North Atlantic

FEW people today, impressed by the wonders of the foreign-owned super-liners that hold all the available ocean speed records, remember that there was once a time when American steamers captured and held the blue ribband of the north Atlantic—the semi-mythical emblem awarded to the fastest vessel plying this greatest of all ocean highways. Much has been written about the speedy voyages of the American clipper ships, and many have heard of crack sailing packets like the *Dreadnought*. But little or nothing has been said in recent years to recall the great adventure of the Collins Line. This, at the time when American sailing ships were the fastest in the world, was America's bid for world leadership in steam.

For a brief period the crack steamers of this company—the *Arctic, Baltic, Atlantic* and *Pacific*—were the wonders of the maritime world, the fastest and most luxuriously appointed vessels afloat. Then came a series of disasters and reverses, almost unprecedented in maritime history, and with them ended the hopes of those who wished to establish the supremacy of American steam-propelled vessels on the north Atlantic.

216

The *Arctic, Baltic, Atlantic* and *Pacific*

While the American ship *Savannah* was the first vessel to cross the Atlantic with the aid of steam, her voyage being made in the year 1819, American ship owners were little interested at trying to develop other, more efficient steamships for the ocean services. Instead, they turned their attention to the building of better and faster sailing packets. Meanwhile, the British commenced to experiment with steamships, and, in 1840, the famous Cunard Line inaugurated regular sailings between Boston and Liverpool. Despite this portent, the Americans kept on with wooden sailing vessels, and this, all things considered, was only natural, for the skill and aptitude of their shipwrights and their vast supply of magnificent timber gave them a great advantage over other countries in the building of this type of ship.

The Americans, nevertheless, watched the British steamers with the keenest interest, and, although their chief enthusiasm continued to be centered upon the packet ships, they little by little commenced to experiment with steamers. Finally, in 1847, an American firm, the Ocean Steam Navigation Company, put two wooden paddle-wheel steamers into service between New York and Bremen, and in 1849, the New York and Havre Steam Navigation Company started operations with two steamers that carried the mails between New York and Havre.

Thus, by 1849, there were four American-flag ocean steamers making regular crossings of the Atlantic. Competing against them was the Cunard Line, which had been steadily improving its service. More and more Americans were now coming to believe that steam had come to stay, and to feel that it was high time to develop a steamship company to compete on all counts with the Cunarders.

This sentiment was finally brought to a focus by Mr. E. K. Collins, the owner of the famous Dramatic Line of sailing packets. In 1849 he approached the government and suggested to it the building of four first class steamers designed to surpass the existing Cunarders in every particular. They were to be of about two thousand tons each and speedy enough to make twenty round voyages a year. The government was to provide a subsidy of $19,250 per voyage. All this was agreed to and a company, officially called the New York & Liverpool United States Mail Steamship Company, was organized. Despite its high sounding title, the company was always known as the "Collins Line," and as such it became the outstanding contender for supremacy on the north Atlantic.

Four ships were designed and built—the *Arctic, Baltic, Atlantic* and *Pacific*. While the original plans had called for vessels of two thousand tons, enthusiasm for the new project was so great and the determination to produce the finest steamships afloat to uphold the prestige of the Stars and Stripes became so overwhelming, that their size was increased to nearly three thousand tons. This increased the cost of the ships to such an extent that the government agreed to increase its mail payment to $33,000 a voyage, with a maximum of $858,000 a year.

These ships were two hundred and eighty-two feet long, with a beam of forty-five feet, and a depth of twenty-four feet. They were propelled by paddle wheels and built of wood, as was the American practice, although the British had commenced to go over to iron.

Unlike the sailing vessels of the time, with their clipper bows, the Collins Line steamers had straight stems. These appeared to the people of that day very novel and also very ungraceful. To obtain high

speed they were fitted with engines which, as subsequent events proved, were far too powerful even for their strongly constructed hulls. After the ships had been in operation for a short while, one of the company's greatest troubles was that the engines racked and twisted the hulls alarmingly, thus necessitating heavy and continuous repairs. But despite this drawback, Mr. Collins and the United States Government had achieved their objective and produced the finest passenger steamers on the north Atlantic, or, for that matter, in the entire world.

"To our English cousins these ships were at first as much of a curiosity as our ventilated trains were a few years since," said one writer. "When the *Atlantic* first reached Liverpool in 1849, the townspeople by the thousands came down to the dock to examine a ship with a barber shop, fitted with the curious American barber chairs enabling the customer to recline while being shaved. The provision of a special deck house for smokers was another innovation, while the saloon, sixty by twenty, the rich fittings of rosewood and satinwood, marble-topped tables, expensive upholstery, and stained-glass windows, decorated with patriotic designs, were for a long time the subject of admiring comment in the English press."

The success and popularity of the Collins Line alarmed the British very greatly and, in an effort to meet this new and almost overwhelming competition, the British Post Office insisted that the Cunard Line inaugurate a better service with larger and speedier vessels. The Cunard Line, however, required some time to lay its plans and, meanwhile, the Collins liners held all the records for the Atlantic crossing. On both sides of the Atlantic there was intense public interest in the hard-fought struggle between the two lines. To the public, who judged the rival ships chiefly by their speed, it seemed evident that the Collins liners were beating the Cunarders hands down. But in the end there was a different story to tell.

Of the four Collins ships, the *Pacific* proved to be the one with the greatest turn of speed. In May, 1851, she made the eastward voyage of 3,078 miles, in nine days, twenty hours, twenty-six minutes, at an average speed of thirteen knots. This greatly surpassed the best achievement of the Cunard Line's *Acadia,* which for ten years had held the record for the eastward voyage. On her fastest passage she had averaged no more than ten and three-quarter knots.

Then, in August, 1851, the Collins liner *Baltic* broke the record for the westward run, doing the crossing in nine days, eighteen hours, at an average speed of thirteen knots. The previous record had been held by the Cunarder *Europa* which, in 1848, had made the passage at an average speed of eleven and one-quarter knots, the trip requiring eleven days, three hours. The *Baltic's* record stood for thirteen years, or until 1864, when it was finally eclipsed by the Cunard liner *Scotia.*

The *Arctic, Baltic, Atlantic* and *Pacific*

The *Pacific's* record did not stand for long, for it was broken in February, 1852, by her running mate, the *Arctic,* which made the eastward run at an average speed of thirteen and one-quarter knots.

With the setting of these records, which made the Collins Line the most spectacular enterprise on the north Atlantic, it seemed as though the Stars and Stripes were destined to be a lasting and important factor on this much-traveled ocean highway. But no one in America was able to see the disasters, which lay ahead and were soon to put an end to this magnificent and dashing American trans-Atlantic service.

The first blow fell in 1854, when the *Arctic* was run down by the steamer, *Vesta,* off Cape Race. The *Vesta* was a much smaller vessel than the crack passenger liner, and those on board the *Arctic,* believing that the smaller ship must be seriously damaged, rushed to save her passengers and crew. They did not believe it possible that their own great ship could be vitally hurt. In this, however, they were wrong, for the *Arctic* was mortally wounded below the water line and commenced to fill with alarming rapidity. Soon it became apparent that she was foundering, and a desperate rush was made across the sloping decks to clamber into the boats. A violent storm was raging and most of the boats were broken or overturned before they could get clear of the ship.

All told, three hundred and twenty-two lives were lost in this terrible disaster, including those of Mr. Collins' wife and children. Only two boats were picked up, and these held but fourteen passengers and thirty-four members of the crew. Later, a vessel passing the scene of the tragedy, picked up a raft, launched in desperation after the lifeboats had been destroyed by the raging seas. Of the seventy-six people on it, however, only one was still alive when the hour of rescue came.

The Collins Line carried on in spite of this appalling catastrophe. It replaced the *Arctic* with the wooden paddle steamer *Nashville,* previously running in the coastal trade between New York and Charleston. Nor were they the only line to suffer during 1854, for in the same year, the *City of Glasgow,* of the newly founded British-owned Inman Line, disappeared at sea. The same company's *City of Philadelphia* was wrecked off Cape Race, though fortunately without loss of life.

For two years the Collins Line ran its ships without further accident. Then, in January, 1856, the *Pacific* started out from Liverpool with the eyes of the world focussed upon her, for she was racing the Cunarder *Persia,* which sailed at the same time. A little more than two weeks passed; the *Persia* came limping into New York, her bow bent and buckled from having collided heavily with an iceberg.

"When did the *Pacific* get in?" was the first eager question asked by those on board.

"She has not yet been reported," was the ominous reply. Nor was she ever heard from again. What had happened to her, no one could say, though it was believed that she must have come to grief in the same ice field through which the *Persia* had passed.

The loss of the *Pacific,* following relatively so soon after the wreck of the *Arctic,* was a bitter blow to Mr. Collins and to all who were interested in seeing the American flag kept in a prominent position on the north Atlantic. The company, however, never thought of giving up and immediately ordered a new ship, the *Adriatic,* which was completed in 1856. She was, by all odds, the most magnificent passenger liner yet to be built and was much larger than the earlier Collins liners, having a tonnage of 5888, and engines that developed 1350 horsepower. She was also a much handsomer ship than her predecessors, as she had a very finely shaped hull and two widely spaced funnels which gave an impression of great power and speed.

Although the owners of the line thus paved the way for continued progress in the future, their efforts were suddenly and unexpectedly brought to nought and the existence of the enterprise was irrevocably doomed—not because of further disasters on the high seas, but because of the policies which were adopted by the government. Practically without warning, the mail payments were reduced in 1856 from the $858,000 originally agreed upon to $385,000. It was obvious, even to those who knew little about the matter, that such crack fliers as the great Collins liners could not possibly be operated with so small a subsidy. The directors of the company strove to maintain the service under the new conditions, but it was an impossible task and, with the sailing of the *Baltic* from Liverpool on February the third, 1858, the glorious Collins Line came to an end.

It had done much for the American flag, for it had brought it the highest prestige on the north Atlantic. Furthermore, the magnificent qualities of its ships, their speed, splendid accommodations and seaworthiness had stimulated ship owners and shipbuilders in Great Britain and other countries to improve upon their existing vessels and had thereby caused enormous improvements in steamship safety and design. The Collins liners fired the imagination of every one and the news of their fast passages created a world-wide interest in steam-propelled ships. By awakening this interest, the *Arctic* and her sisters did much to help the Cunard and other British lines that were just beginning to radiate out from England to the farthest corners of the globe. Thus, though a failure as a business venture, the Collins Line played an enormously important and far-reaching role in establishing steamships on the world's great ocean routes and did much to advance the development of the fast, seaworthy and luxurious ocean passenger liner of today.

22

The Monitor and the Merrimac

EARLY in the year 1862, while Admiral Farragut was making his preparations for the great attack upon New Orleans, two naval vessels —one from the south and one from the north—waged a battle that is among the most famous in the world's naval history. This was the fight between the *Monitor* and the *Merrimac*—the first encounter ever to take place between two ironclad ships.

The *Merrimac,* flying the "stars and bars" of the Southern Confederacy, was originally built as a 40-gun steam frigate. When the Union or Northern forces fired the Norfolk navy yard early in the Civil War, the *Merrimac* burned down to the water's edge, but sank before the flames had seriously damaged her lower hull. Her masts were gone, but her hull, according to Confederate opinion, could serve admirably as a foundation for armor-plating, and work was started at once to convert her into an ironclad.

Along her berth deck, for one hundred and seventy feet amidships, bulwarks were built, consisting of twenty inches of pitch pine covered with four inches of oak, and sloping at an angle of thirty-five degrees. Outside of this twenty-four inches of solid wood backing were laid two layers of rolled-iron plates two inches thick. This formidable craft was pierced for ten guns, one at each end, and four on each side.

While the Confederates were hurrying the construction of the

Merrimac through the autumn months of 1861, another ironclad was in the making at a shipyard on Long Island, far to the north. Here, on the twenty-fifth of October, the keel of the *Monitor* was laid. Her design was novel in the extreme and her appearance has been best described by an unknown observer who called her "the Yankee cheese box on a raft." She was an iron-plated raft one hundred and seventy-two feet long, forty-one feet wide, and eleven feet deep. On this substructure was mounted a revolving iron turret containing two 11-inch guns. Forward of the turret there was a small pilot house made of massive bars of iron and covered by a heavy iron plate. As less than two feet of the hull was to appear above water, the target surface was reduced to a minimum; and, as a further security, this surface was plated with five layers of iron, each of which was one inch thick.

The *Merrimac* was finally completed early in March, 1862, and on the eighth of that month she cast loose from her moorings in Norfolk and steamed north toward Hampton Roads, where a number of the largest Union men-of-war lay unsuspectingly at anchor. A little before one o'clock, the *Merrimac,* looking like "the roof of a large barn belching forth smoke from a chimney," came in full view of the Union ships and opened fire on the sloop-of-war *Cumberland.* Despite a heavy return fire, the *Merrimac* pressed steadily on under a full head of steam and, with a terrific impact, drove her ram into the *Cumberland's* side.

Then, for several hours, the *Merrimac* bombarded the Union ships, finally sinking the *Cumberland,* forcing the *Congress* to surrender and damaging several other ships. The news of this "most disastrous day in the career of the United States navy" spread unalloyed fear through-

out the North. The President called a special meeting of the Cabinet, and the belief was freely expressed that the whole character of the war was changed. Nothing, now, in the opinion of the Northern statesmen, could prevent the "terrible monster" from destroying all the ships in Hampton Roads, making her way up the Potomac and reducing Washington to a heap of burning ruins. After raising the blockade of other Southern ports, she would steam northward and attack New York and Philadelphia. Nothing but a miracle could save the situation. And that miracle was at hand.

On the very night of the *Merrimac's* attack, while the waters of Hampton Roads and the skies above them were illuminated by the flames of the still-burning *Congress,* the *Monitor,* newly arrived from New York, slipped unnoticed into the Roads and came to anchor. Surely it was one of the strangest coincidences in all history, that this craft—the only other ship in existence that could offer resistance to the *Merrimac*—should have arrived at the spot where she was needed on the precise day, hour and almost minute when she could play her part.

The *Monitor* had had a stormy passage from New York and several times had nearly foundered. The waves, breaking completely over the pilot house, had knocked the helmsman from the wheel and poured down the smoke-stack into the fires, filling the engine room with suffocating gas. Two of the engineer officers had been rescued in the nick of time, more dead than alive. Water had surged into the turret and entered the hull through the hawse holes and, since the steam pumps could not be made to work, all hands had had to form a bucket line and bail for their lives. Destruction stared the heroic crew in the face, and undoubtedly the *Monitor* would have foundered in a few hours had not the wind lessened in force and the waves subsided.

When the *Monitor* at last reached Hampton Roads, her crew was completely exhausted, but they immediately set to work pumping out water and making repairs. Word was brought to her commander, Lieutenant John Worden, of the damage inflicted by the *Merrimac,* and he gave orders that work be continued throughout the night, so that the *Monitor* would be ready to grapple with the enemy at daybreak.

At eight o'clock in the morning, volumes of black smoke could be seen pouring from the *Merrimac's* smoke-stack, as she confidently prepared to continue her awful work of destruction. Shortly afterwards she steamed slowly toward the Union men-of-war. Now was the time for the *Monitor* to enter the scene. As the thousands on board the Northern vessels waited in suspense, their defender moved slowly and silently out into the stream and headed for her antagonist.

The *Merrimac* checked her speed, hesitated for a few moments as though appraising this strange creature of the deep, and then, belching forth dense clouds of smoke as though furious at this interruption to her work of violence, turned toward the quietly waiting *Monitor*.

When at short range both ironclads opened fire. The *Monitor* had only two guns, but they were big ones hurling a massive eleven-inch solid shot. She had no difficulty in hitting her slab-sided opponent, but the shots at first bounced harmlessly off the armor plate. The *Merrimac*, firing broadsides as fast as she could, found it difficult to hit the small target presented by her opponent's "cheese-box" revolving turret. A number of her shells struck the turret, however, though without penetrating the armor plate.

After firing broadside after broadside with no apparent injury to his antagonist, Lieutenant Worden searched for some weakly armored place where he could ram the *Merrimac*. At length he picked out the stern and made a dash for it, in the hope of disabling the propeller or the rudder. The lunge was well aimed, but missed its mark by three feet, so that the *Monitor* ranged forward along the Merrimac's side.

At this moment, at point-blank range, the *Monitor* discharged both her guns at the same time. The two shots struck together, bashing in the iron plates two or three inches. The concussion was terrific and knocked most of the *Merrimac's* men off their feet, causing many of them to bleed from the nose and ears.

By now, Lieutenant Jones, the commander of the *Merrimac*, had given up all hope of being able to injure the elusive and strongly-armored *Monitor*. Giving the order for "Full Speed," he made off toward the Union steam frigate *Minnesota;* but after proceeding a short distance his vessel ran aground. In a short time, however, she was afloat again and heading directly for the *Minnesota*. This ship, as the *Merrimac* approached, delivered full broadsides, but with no effect, although fifty solid shot were fired. The ironclad responded with shells from her bow gun, one of which exploded inside the frigate and set her on fire.

By the time the *Merrimac* had fired her third shell at the *Minnesota* the *Monitor* was again within range, and the duel between the ironclads was renewed. Lieutenant Jones now decided to try to ram his opponent, since his shells seemed useless against her armor plate. For some time he maneuvered for position, and an opportunity at last presented itself. The ironclad surged forward at full speed, but the *Monitor* quickly turned away, receiving only a slanting blow which did no damage.

One of the men in the *Merrimac* wrote: "Nearly two hours passed, and many a shot and shell were exchanged at close quarters, with no perceptible damage to either side. The *Merrimac* is discouragingly cumbrous and unwieldy. To wind her for each broadside fifteen minutes were lost, while during all this time the *Monitor* is whirling around and about like a top, and the easy working of her turret and her precise and rapid movements elicit the wondering admiration of all. She is evidently invulnerable to our shell. Our next movement is to run her down. We ram her with all our force. But she is so flat and broad that she merely slides away from under our hull, as a floating door would slip away from under the cutwater of a barge. All that we could do was to push her.

"Lieutenant Jones now determined to board her, choke her turret in some way and lash her to the *Merrimac*. The blood is rushing through our veins, the shrill pipe and hoarse roar of the boatswain,

'Boarders away!' are heard, but lo, our enemy has hauled off into shoal water, where she is safe from our ship as if she was on the topmost peak of the Blue Ridge."

When the *Monitor* once again drew near, the *Merrimac* shifted her fire from her enemy's turret to the little armored pilot house on the forward deck. Almost immediately she drove home a shot that exploded just outside the sight-hole through which Lieutenant Worden was looking, cutting and burning his face and eyes with powder. Lieutenant Greene, the *Monitor's* second in command, hurried forward and found his commander, dazed and bleeding, clinging to the ladder that led to the pilot house. Lieutenant Greene led Worden to his cabin and then hastened to the pilot house to continue the battle. To his great surprise, however, he saw the *Merrimac* steaming rapidly away in the direction of Norfolk. Her commander had discovered that she was leaking seriously and, despairing of doing any damage to the *Monitor,* had decided to withdraw without renewing the battle.

Thus, the action itself was a draw; but because of its ultimate results it must be considered a victory for the *Monitor.* The vessels of the Union navy were saved from destruction, and the *Merrimac* was forced to stay in Norfolk for a number of weeks undergoing repairs. Shortly after she was made ready for action, Norfolk was abandoned by the Confederates and the *Merrimac* was set on fire. After her destruction, the Union navy was left unchallenged in control of the sea, and was free to blockade the Southern ports and carry out the great attacks on New Orleans and Mobile which played an important part in bringing final victory to the forces of the North.

23

The Hartford

Admiral Farragut's Flagship at the Battles of New Orleans and Mobile Bay

DURING the Civil War the Mississippi River was known as the "Backbone of the Rebellion," and there was good reason for its being so named. Possession of the Mississippi and its tributary streams gave the Confederacy access to a vast territory, from which much of the food for their armies was brought by fleets of river steamers. The barrier of the river kept the Union armies from gaining Texas, from which immense supplies of beef were obtained long after the supplies in the southern seaboard states had been exhausted. Cotton, in hundreds of thousands of bales, came down the Mississippi to New Orleans. Here it was loaded and carried to England on swift blockade runners that returned with arms, munitions of war and many other vitally needed supplies. In New Orleans, the gateway to the river, the Confederacy had important plants for building ironclads, casting cannon and making small arms. In short, control of the river and the farms, plantations and factories on or near its banks was one of the chief sources of the Confederacy's strength.

All this was well known to the leaders of the Union or Northern cause, and plans for gaining possession of the Mississippi were formulated during the first year of the conflict. Due to a lack of sufficient warships and to other delays, however, it was not until 1862 that the major attack on the river—an assault against New Orleans—could be carried out.

The commander chosen to lead the Union attack was Captain David Glasgow Farragut. He had started his naval career as a midshipman on the *Essex* and had been aboard her during her famous cruise to the South Pacific under Captain David Porter. Later, he had served in the Mediterranean in the frigate *Washington,* and, after the close of the wars with the Barbary pirates, had commanded several United States naval craft. For the assault on New Orleans, his flagship was the new steam-propelled sloop-of-war *Hartford.*

This ship was one of the most powerful warships in any of the world's navies. Built in 1858 and described as a "screw sloop," her unarmored wooden hull was two hundred and twenty-five feet in length and had a beam of forty-four feet. Her engines developed a speed of eight knots, but she was equipped with a full set of sails and, under sail and steam combined, could make a speed of eleven knots. Her main battery consisted of twenty-two 9-inch smooth-bore guns. In addition to the *Hartford,* Farragut had some forty other men-of-war. Eight of these were nearly as heavily armed as the flagship and the rest were small gunboats and mortar schooners, the latter towed by steamers.

Farragut arrived off the mouth of the Mississippi in the *Hartford* on the twentieth of February, 1862, and from that time on until the actual attack was carried out in April, the officers and men of the Union fleet were kept feverishly busy preparing for the formidable task ahead. Gun-crews were drilled unceasingly; coal-passers and deck hands were engaged in taking aboard coal, provisions and ammunition. When this work was completed, all hands set to work to protect the engine-rooms of the ships with piles of sand bags and heavy chain cable. Farragut was constantly active, overseeing everything. As an officer on one of the ships wrote, he "was about the fleet from early dawn until dark, and if any officer had not spontaneous enthusiasm, he certainly infused it into him. I have been on the morning watch from four to eight o'clock, when he would row alongside the ship at six o'clock, either hailing to ask how we were getting along, or perhaps climbing over the side to see for himself."

While these preparations were under way among the vessels of the Union fleet, the Confederates were losing no time in strengthening their means of defense. The two most formidable obstacles to Farragut's advance were Fort Jackson and Fort St. Philip which stood, one on each side of the river, about ninety miles below New Orleans. Ready for battle near the forts, was a powerful fleet of gunboats and ironclads, the most dangerous of which were the ironclad *Louisiana* and the ram *Manassas*. In addition, the Confederates were rushing to completion three "floating batteries," the *Mississippi, Memphis* and *New Orleans,* of sixteen, eighteen and twenty guns. Downstream from the fleet, under the guns of the forts, the Confederates threw across the river a heavy boom of cypress logs held together by strong iron cables. There was also made ready a great number of long flatboats filled with pine knots ready to be set on fire and sent down the current into the midst of the hostile fleet.

Farragut's preparations were finally completed by April twenty-

third, and the order went through the Union fleet that the attempt to pass the forts and break through the Confederate's squadrons of rams and ironclads would be made that night. During the afternoon, Farragut visited every ship in the fleet to make certain that his orders for the night were perfectly understood. At two the following morning the fleet got underway.

With all lights darkened and in utter silence, the long line of ships steamed up-river toward the forts. Their presence was not detected until they reached a point just below the forts. Then sentinels made out the dim shapes of the darkened craft, and with thunderous reports the guns of the forts opened fire. The warships' cannon roared in reply, and the flashes from hundreds of guns stabbed through the darkness, producing a weird illumination over the water.

Now, from upstream, came scores of wildly flaming fire rafts, making the night as bright as day. One of these drifted alongside the *Hartford* and set her rigging on fire. To escape the flames, the flagship was turned to one side; the swift current caught her and drove her hard and fast on the muddy bank. Here she was so close to the guns of Fort St. Philip that those on board could hear the Confederate gunners talking. The *Hartford* was soon discovered and the fort began firing on her with great rapidity.

"It seemed to be breathing a flame," said Farragut after the action. "On the deck of the ship it was bright as noonday, but out over the majestic river, where the smoke of many guns was intensified by that of the pine knots of the fire rafts, it was dark as the blackest midnight." It seemed a miracle that the *Hartford* was not smashed into a shambles, but in their excitement the Confederates aimed too high so that most of their shot passed over the ship. With guns blazing in reply, the *Hartford* reversed her engines and, after what seemed an eternity to those on board but was in reality less than half an hour, she freed herself from the bank and once again headed upstream.

The Confederate's rams, gunboats, ironclads and armed steamers now came roaring downstream, under forced draft, hurrying to throw themselves against the hostile fleet. One large steamer filled with troops made a dash for the *Hartford,* with the intention of getting alongside and boarding, but a broadside crippled her and sent her drifting down the stream. The ironclad *Louisiana,* much dreaded by the Union officers who had heard rumors of her tremendous striking power, plunged past the *Hartford* and fired a heavy shell that struck the *Brooklyn.* Troop-laden steamers followed and made attempts to board the Union ships, only to be beaten off by savage broadsides. The ram *Manassas* came out of the night and struck the *Brooklyn,* making a gaping hole that would have sunk the Union ship, had it not been that her bunkers were full of coal which prevented the water from pouring in.

The *Hartford*

Despite these encounters, and many others that took place as the Confederate warships drove through the Union fleet, the latter forged steadily upstream. One ship after another passed the forts; one attacker after another was beaten off. As daybreak commenced to lighten the skies, the last of the Union ships passed through the danger zone. Many of the Confederate ships had been demolished, and, unopposed, the *Hartford* led the way upstream to New Orleans which, shorn of its defenses, was compelled to surrender.

Two years later, the *Hartford* was again to lead the Union naval forces to victory. And again, she was commanded by David Farragut, who had been made a Rear Admiral as a result of his success in capturing New Orleans and opening up the Mississippi.

When New Orleans fell, the Confederates knew that the Union navy's next major attack would be launched against Mobile. This port was now of supreme importance to them, for it was the principal remaining rendezvous of the blockade-runners that brought the Confederacy supplies from the outside world. Everything possible was done, therefore, to make the harbor impregnable. The guardian forts were rebuilt and strengthened; the entrance channel was filled with torpedoes, or mines, as they would be called today; and work was hurried forward on a number of rams and gunboats. Among these craft was included the ram *Tennessee,* the most powerful armored vessel yet completed by the South.

Farragut, in the *Hartford,* arrived off the entrance to Mobile Bay late in July, 1864. In addition to the flagship, he had in his squadron twenty other unarmored wooden vessels and four ironclads, the *Tecumseh, Manhattan, Winnebago* and *Chickasaw.* The task that lay

237

ahead of these ships was a formidable one, for Mobile was situated at the inner end of a bay some thirty miles long, every foot of which was covered by the guns of the three harbor forts. To these defenses were added the menace of hundreds of submerged torpedoes and the powerful rams and gunboats of the enemy.

Farragut's plan was to pass up the channel close under the guns of Fort Morgan. Since it was on the right-hand side of the entrance to the bay, he gave orders that each ship should protect its starboard side as thoroughly as possible. Chains were hung over the sides; the starboard boats were taken from their davits; barricades of sand bags were piled up, and many of the commanders filled their vacant gun-ports on the starboard side with guns from the port batteries.

These preparations were completed by the afternoon of August the fourth. At six o'clock on the following morning, the fleet started toward its trial by fire, the four grim ironclads in the van and the twenty-one black and menacing unarmored vessels following close behind in an imposing line of battle. As the vessels forged steadily on toward the entrance, the thousands of men on their decks nerved themselves for the terrible ordeal ahead. In almost complete silence, they stood beside their huge guns, waiting for the moment of action and battle.

The long-drawn-out period of suspense was broken when, a few minutes before seven o'clock, the *Tecumseh,* leader of the ironclads, commenced firing upon Fort Morgan. Soon afterwards a puff of white smoke and a long tongue of flame leaped from the fort's parapets, and a heavy shell splashed the water near the *Brooklyn,* the first of the unarmored ships. The firing then increased rapidly, concentrating on the *Brooklyn* and the *Hartford,* while at the same time the Confederate gunboats and the dreaded ram, the *Tennessee,* steamed out from behind Fort Morgan and commenced to fire on the leading Union ships.

Captain Craven, the commander of the Union ram *Tecumseh* now ordered "Full Speed Ahead" and drove his ship straight toward the *Tennessee,* intent upon destroying this most formidable of the enemy's vessels. Soon only a hundred yards separated the two ships. But just as Captain Craven gave the order to "Fire," there was a sudden muffled explosion, and at the same instant a great column of water sprang up from the bay alongside of the *Tecumseh.* She had struck a torpedo! The ironclad gave a deep lurch to port, a heavy roll to starboard and then her bow sank out of sight. The next instant, or in thirty seconds from the time the explosion occurred, the ironclad plunged bow-foremost to the bottom.

All the ships were now surrounded by the smoke of battle, and Farragut, in order to see above the swirling, sulphur-laden clouds, climbed up the *Hartford's* rigging and was lashed in place. As the *Tecumseh* sank, the ships ahead of the *Hartford* were thrown into the direst confusion. The *Brooklyn* and *Octorara,* afraid of striking the torpedoes, had reversed their engines and swung around so as to lie across the channel and block the progress of the other ships. To avoid a collision, the *Hartford* and *Metacomet,* which were next in line, also went astern, and were almost run down by the *Richmond* and *Port Royal.*

While the ships strove to get clear of each other, the guns of Fort Morgan opened a terrific cannonade, during which the fleet suffered the heaviest losses of the battle. "The whole fleet," said an eye-witness, "seemed to be enveloped in flame. Looking aloft from the deck of the *Winnebago* while the hulls of our ships were obscured by the smoke of battle, I could distinctly see, by the flags flying from the different vessels, the confusion in the order of the fleet, which seemed to be all tangled up, as was in reality the fact, and but for Farragut's genius for war, which enabled him at once to grasp the situation and apply the remedy, the most complete and crushing disaster would have followed!"

During this critical period Fort Morgan hurled eight shells a minute into the fleet, and the Confederate gunboats, seizing their opportunity, worked their batteries at top speed.

When Farragut saw that the *Brooklyn* did not at once straighten on her course and go ahead, he turned to his pilot and asked, "What is the matter with the *Brooklyn*? She must have plenty of water there."

"Plenty and to spare, Admiral," replied the pilot.

Farragut ordered the *Brooklyn* to be signaled, "What is the trouble?"

"Torpedoes!" was the reply.

This was the critical moment of the battle. To retreat meant an inglorious defeat. To advance might mean the wholesale destruction by torpedoes of the Union navy's finest ships and the death of thousands. The tremendous cheering and renewed firing of the Confederates showed that they already regarded the victory as theirs.

Again the *Brooklyn* signaled, "Tell the Admiral that there is a heavy line of torpedoes ahead." Farragut read the message and resolved upon victory, no matter what the cost.

"Damn the torpedoes! Damn the torpedoes!" he roared. "Go ahead, Captain Drayton! Four bells!"

The hull of the *Hartford* shook as her powerful engines drove her forward at full speed and she took the head of the battle-line. The ironclad *Tennessee* roared a broadside at her and tried to ram, but the flagship turned to one side and escaped destruction. After the *Hartford* came the other ships, straightened out on their courses at last, and pouring such a deadly fire into Fort Morgan that its guns were scarcely able to reply. The *Tennessee*, having missed the *Hartford*, steamed grimly down channel to attack the remaining vessels. She fired at the *Brooklyn*, doing considerable damage, and then plunged toward the *Richmond*, but was driven off by three thunderous broadsides and a hail of musket fire played into the ironclad's gun-ports. Each one of the remaining Union ships was attacked in turn, as the *Tennessee*, like a mad dog, ran down the line; but one and all succeeded in eluding or beating off the "terrible ram."

Meanwhile, the Confederate gunboats had closed in on the Union van, and were delivering a harassing fire on the leading ships. "Gun-boats chase enemy gunboats!" ordered Farragut. The Union ships dashed off in hot pursuit and, after a number of spirited individual engagements, succeeded in driving off or sinking the enemy's light forces.

Now, with the successful passage of Fort Morgan and the dangerous fields of torpedoes, the dispersion of the Confederate gunboats, and the retreat of the *Tennessee*, which had been driven to seek refuge near Fort Morgan, Farragut was left in undisputed possession of Mobile Bay. For several weeks the Union vessels were occupied in chasing down and capturing the remaining enemy gunboats and in silencing completely the harbor forts. Fort Morgan surrendered on August twenty-third and its downfall marked the end of Mobile as a port of entry for the blockade-runners.

Once again, the *Hartford,* flagship of as gallant an Admiral as ever trod a quarter-deck, had led the Union fleet to victory. Now, with the Mississippi and Mobile both in possession of the Union forces, the Confederate cause was seen to be without hope. Wilmington, the very last of the Southern ports open to blockade-runners, was captured in December 1864, cutting the Confederacy completely off from contact with the outside world. Within a few months, on May tenth, 1865, the formal surrender of the South took place.

24

The Flying Cloud

The Fastest Long-Voyage American Clipper Ship

On the morning of June the third, 1851, Battery Park, at the lower end of the island of Manhattan, was filled to capacity by an excited, jostling crowd of people. Many were pushing forward, trying to get closer to the water's edge, in order to get a closer view of the sight which had brought them to the harbor on this sunny morning. This was the *Flying Cloud,* the newest of Donald McKay's lofty-sparred clipper ships. She had finished loading at her East River pier the night before and now, as was customary, had anchored off Battery Park to make final preparations for her voyage to San Francisco.

The sailing of a California clipper was an exciting and important event in those days, and everyone who could came down at the Battery whenever one of the beautiful ships was to get under way. The rush to California, started by the discovery of gold in 1849, was in full swing. Fortune-hunters were crowding on board any and every vessel that could make the voyage around Cape Horn, and the clippers were making enormous profits carrying supplies and food for the miners and the new settlements springing up in California.

While the crowd moves to and fro, studying every detail of the new clipper and excitedly discussing her fine points, boatmen scull out to the ship and back, putting the crew and their dunnage on board. On the *Flying Cloud's* deck, the mate is watching everything, for it is his responsibility to get the ship under way. As the men come aboard, he studies each face intently, considering those on whom he can rely.

Soon the crew is all on board. The pilot stands aft near the wheel, deep in conversation with the master, Captain Josiah Creesy. Everything is in readiness for the beginning of the voyage, and the mate walks rapidly to the topgallant forecastle, and musters the crew. The first job is to weigh anchor.

"Now, then, boys," sings out the mate, "man the windlass breaks and heave away. Chantyman, there, strike a light. Let's see what you can do."

The chantyman fetches a deep breath and breaks into song.

> "In eighteen hundred and forty-eight,
> I found myself bound for the Golden Gate,
> A-working on the railway, the railway.
> Oh, poor Paddy works on the railway, the railway."

Verse follows verse until the anchor comes into sight, when the mate orders "Vast heaving," and reports to the captain: "Anchor's apeak, sir."

"Very good, sir. Loose sails fore and aft," orders Captain Creesy.

"Aye, aye, sir. Aloft there, some of you men, and loose sails," bellows the mate. "You there, and you, and you, lay out and loose the head sails."

Some of the men clamber aloft like monkeys, while others lay out along the bowsprit. Soon the sails are loose and straining against their

244

gear. Next the three topsail yards must be mastheaded. All hands are warmed up by now, and as they walk away with the topsail halliards, they sing out with:

"Away, way, way, yah,
We'll pay Paddy Doyle for his boots."

The topsail yards go aloft, and then, one after another, topsails, topgallantsails, royals and skysails are set and the *Flying Cloud* looks like a great white-winged bird poised for instant flight. Her mainmast towers eighty-eight feet above the deck, and her mainyard is eighty-two feet long, with other spars in proportion. There are many in the crowd watching from the Battery, who marvel that any ship can carry such an enormous mass of canvas and not capsize.

Now the anchor is brought to the rail to the roaring of another chanty, the foreyard is squared, and the ship gathers headway and glides forward. The spectators cheer her again and again, until their throats are hoarse. Captain Creesy orders the ensign to be dipped in

245

acknowledgement. The *Flying Cloud,* her white sails gleaming in the bright June sunshine, slips more and more swiftly through the blue waters of the bay. She is on her way to Cape Horn and the Golden Gate.

*   *   *   *   *   *   *

The *Flying Cloud's* commander, Captain Josiah Creesy, was out to drive his ship to the utmost. At that time, a fast passage from New York to San Francisco was one made in one hundred and ten days. This time had been bettered by several ships, however, and only the year before the clipper ship *Sea Witch* had astonished the world by making the voyage in ninety-seven days. It was Captain Creesy's supreme desire to beat the *Sea Witch's* record.

Late in the afternoon of her sailing day she cleared Sandy Hook and, under a cloud of billowing white sails, sped swiftly away to the south'ard. The wind was fair and she roared steadily along, trampling the green seas into snow, her taut rigging humming and every sail including royals and studding sails set and drawing. Captain Creesy, well trained in the China trade, was a thorough clipper ship commander, who never allowed his ship to suffer for want of canvas.

All went well until the third day out from port, when the wind freshened and blew hard from the northwest. Captain Creesy stumped the quarter-deck, eyeing the lofty spars and sails to gauge the strain that was being put upon them. One thing was certain. He would never take in sail until the last minute. But this time he was caught without warning by a sudden vicious squall that drove down fast on the swift-moving ship. Suddenly there was a crack aloft, swiftly followed by another crash of splintering timbers. That had done it. The main and mizzen topgallantmasts had both been snapped off. Relieved of the pressure, the *Flying Cloud* straightened momentarily. Then, with a louder and more ominous crash, the great 60-foot-long maintopsail yard carried away.

Here was a fine beginning for a record-breaking passage. The ship virtually stopped, two masts crippled, and the deck cluttered with a confused mass of canvas, rigging, blocks, tackles and all manner of other gear brought down by the failure of the maintopsail yard.

But Captain Creesy was imperturbable.

"Clear away the mess," he ordered, "and shape up the spare spars ready to replace the topgallantmasts."

As did all the other clipper ships, the *Flying Cloud* carried a plentiful supply of extra spars to take the place of those broken by the strain of continuous "cracking on." Under the direction of the ship's carpenter, two of these were trimmed to the right size, and on the following day were slipped in place at the summits of the main and mizzen topmasts. The ship drew ahead more swiftly through the water. On the next day, June eighth, a new maintopsail yard was sent aloft. Now, with her full suit of canvas once more spread to the wind, the *Flying Cloud* gathered speed and sprang forward through the water like a thing possessed.

With fair winds she slanted southeastward to clear Cape St. Roque, in Brazil, the easternmost point of South America, and then straightened on a southerly course for her run down to Cape Horn. It soon became apparent that the stormy weather that had carried away her spars had also weakened her mainmast. On June fourteenth, Captain

Creesy wrote in the ship's log: "Discovered mainmast badly sprung about a foot from the hounds, and fished it."

This temporary repair held up well while the *Flying Cloud* passed through the doldrums, crossed the equator and breezed south before the trade winds of the South Atlantic. As she reached into the lower latitudes, however, and encountered the savage pamperos that volleyed out from the Argentine coast, the weakened mainmast was a source of constant worry. On July eleventh, she plunged forward through a tormented sea, lashed into a boiling cauldron by a pampero. Thunder crashed and rumbled overhead and jagged flashes of lightning ripped continuously across the black-clouded sky. The *Flying Cloud,* under double-reefed topsails and staysails, cut through the water as though pursued by demons, her masts bending like willow whips, her fine-drawn bow rising and falling amid cascades of flying spray.

Under her reduced canvas she was riding well, but Captain Creesy still had more sail on her than would be carried by any but a clipper ship commander. Suddenly, as the wind came down with momentary terrific violence, the fore and maintopmast staysails split. A few moments later the mate, returning from a round of the main deck, reported that the mainmast had sprung.

This called for immediate action. If the mainmast should go by the board, the ship would be a cripple indeed. Men were sent aloft through the driving rain and spray, and, while the ship bucked and plunged beneath them like a frantic, untamed pony, they sent down the royal and topgallant yards and studdingsail booms. This relieved the strain on the mast and the clipper, riding more easily, tore on to the southward, her next test the rigors of the Horn.

Forty-nine days out from New York, on July the twenty-second, the lookout who had been sent aloft at daybreak saw a faint gray streak on the horizon ahead.

"Land ho!" he hailed the deck.

"Where away?" came the voice of Captain Creesy.

"A point on the lee bow, sir!"

"Very well! Lay down!" shouted the captain.

It was Staten Island, to the northeast of Cape Horn. The *Flying Cloud* closed in rapidly with the land and at noon it was visible from the deck. By eight bells in the afternoon watch, she was sailing past the bold, rocky shores and drawing the island well abeam. Running south for a good offing, she hauled her wind to the starboard quarter with the coming of darkness and headed boldly for Cape Horn.

On the following morning, Captain Creesy recorded in the ship's log:

"Cape Horn north five miles. The whole coast covered with snow."

It was the middle of the Antarctic winter, the most perilous season to attempt the passage of "Cape Stiff." As the day wore on, the wind veered round to west-nor'-west, blowing directly off the land and with increasing force. The light sails were taken in during the afternoon. The *Flying Cloud* rode the Cape Horn rollers, sweeping up to the crest of one with her forefoot riding clear of the water and, then, with bowsprit pointed downward at a forty-five degree angle, plunging into the hollow separating the first wave from the next. With the starboard tacks aboard, she sailed southwestward, slowly making her westing.

During the night the wind increased in violence and at four bells in the morning, the watch below was called on deck to help in shortening down. Topgallantsails, mainsail and jib were taken in, and these were followed in quick succession by other canvas, as the wind continued to increase in force and the seas, sweeping down from the west, rose to mammoth proportions.

The sails that remained set were soon stiff with ice, and all the rigging was coated with frozen rain and spray. At nightfall the *Flying Cloud* was hove to. Even Captain Creesy dared not drive her through the menacing, swift-moving, forty-foot rollers that bore down on her in continuous succession like moving mountains of water. During the night, when the wind during squalls rose to hurricane force, the *Flying Cloud* lay over on her beam ends. A hissing smother of white phosphorescent water lit up her tall swaying masts and rigging as the seas broke over her deck, intensifying the blackness of the sky overhead. The roar of the crashing waves, the clanging of the freeing ports and the steady shrill screaming of the wind drowned all attempts to shout orders from the poop.

But all things have an end and toward noon of the following day the weather abated somewhat, the topsails were set and the *Flying Cloud* rode more easily over the troubled waters. The dreaded Horn was safely passed. Now there lay ahead the long beat northward through the Pacific.

Captain Creesy lost no time in setting every thread of canvas possible and giving the clipper her head. The *Flying Cloud* responded like a thing alive to his masterly handling, and, a week after leaving the Horn behind, reeled off the fastest day's run ever made by a sailing vessel up to that time. Captain Creesy recorded this great achievement as follows in the log:

The *Flying Cloud*

"July 31st—Fresh breezes, fine weather, all sail set. At 2 P.M. wind southeast. At 6 squally; in lower and topgallant studdingsails; 7, in royals; at 2 A.M. in foretopmast studdingsail. Latter part, strong gales and high sea running. Ship very wet fore and aft. Distance run this day by observation is 374 miles. During the squalls 18 knots of line was not sufficient to measure the rate of speed. Topgallantsails set."

This was the fastest day's run, under steam or sail, that had ever been made up to that time, and exceeded by forty-two miles the best day's run that had ever been made by a mail steamship on the Atlantic. If sustained, this speed would have carried the *Flying Cloud* from New York to Queenstown in less than seven and one-half days.

What a magnificent sight the great clipper must have presented as, leaning far over beneath the steady blowing of the wind, she set the record that few other sailing ships ever equaled. In the morning, with all sails set, she evidently was carrying all her studdingsails, these being sails extending on special booms out to each side of the regular sails. It was not until six in the afternoon that a few of these were taken in, and not until an hour later that the royals, the highest of all the sails, were furled. Then, still with more sail than any but a clipper ship captain would carry, the *Flying Cloud* drove on at breath-taking speed through the hours of darkness.

The fair winds held and the *Flying Cloud* sped without faltering to the northward. Her luck had been good, and now, with the goal almost in sight, Captain Creesy knew that he had a good chance of beating the 97-day record of the *Sea Witch*. But there was always the danger of being becalmed while passing through the doldrums of the equatorial belt. There could be no slackening in vigilance, no let-up in driving the clipper as hard as she could go.

Light airs were met with in the doldrums, but the *Flying Cloud* ghosted along before them as handsomely as she had driven at express speed before the killing southerly gales. Then the steady-blowing trade winds were picked up and she made swiftly toward the Golden Gate. When within two days of the end of her voyage, heavy weather blew up. Captain Creesy, as usual, held onto everything aloft, trusting his ship to stand the strain. But once again, he carried on a little too long. On August twenty-ninth, when within sight of the coast, the fore topgallantmast carried away, bringing down the fore royal and fore topgallantsail. Another spar was sent aloft, and new sails bellied out. The clipper's keen bow tossed the seas aside, and she closed in rapidly with the coast. On the following day, Captain Creesy made his final entry for the voyage in the log:

"August 30th—Night strong and squally. Six A.M. made South Farallones bearing northeast ½ east, took a pilot at 7; anchored in San Francisco harbor at 11:30 A.M. after a passage of 89 days, 21 hours."

The *Flying Cloud* had beaten the *Sea Witch's* record! She had made the fastest passage ever recorded between New York and San Francisco. What is more, no other clipper ship ever surpassed her achievement, and it was only once equaled when, in 1860, the medium clipper *Andrew Jackson* made the voyage in the same number of days.

In San Francisco the beautiful ship's achievement was celebrated for days on end. All the thousands who had come from the East to seek their fortunes now felt nearer their former homes and their old friends. The voyage took only three months! It was scarcely believable. In every settled part of the country the *Flying Cloud's* exploit was regarded as a magnificent proof of the skill of America's shipbuilders, captains and seamen. There was nothing on the seven seas that could compare with her. One of the New York papers (New York Commercial, October 8, 1851) expressed the general enthusiasm:

"Such a passage as this is more than a local triumph, and inures to the reputation not alone of the builder of the ship and her enterprising owners, but of the United States. It is truly a national triumph, and points clearly and unmistakably to the pre-eminence upon the ocean which awaits the United States of America. The log of the *Flying Cloud* is now before us. It is the most wonderful record that pen ever indited, for rapid as was the passage, it was performed under circumstances by no means the most favorable."

After discharging their cargoes at San Francisco, the California clippers frequently sailed to the westward across the Pacific and loaded tea or other cargo at Chinese or East Indian ports. This was the route followed by the *Flying Cloud*. She made a good passage to China and, after loading a cargo of tea, sailed the two thousand miles between Canton and Java Head in six days, reducing by almost half the best previous record. Again the world sang her praises and toasted Captain Creesy and his marvelous clipper ship.

Like the other clippers, the *Flying Cloud* continued in the California and China trades during the fevered years of the gold-rush period, when freights were high and passengers bound for the Golden Gate to make their fortunes were plentiful. The California trade remained a profitable one for about ten years, or until 1860, and it was during these years that the American clippers with their long, lean hulls, lofty spars and towering clouds of white canvas were undisputed masters of the ocean routes. Then, as the rush to the gold fields diminished and freight rates began to decline, it became impossible to operate the clippers at a profit in the California trade. Then, with yards cut down and carrying fewer sails and a smaller crew, they traded round the world as ordinary cargo ships, tramping to Australia, China, the Mediterranean, or wherever cargoes offered that would pay their way. The *Flying Cloud,* notwithstanding her former glory, went the way of all the rest. After some years of general trading, she was sold in 1863 to James Baines, of Liverpool, and in 1874 she was destroyed by fire at St. John, New Brunswick.

But her name is still reve.ed by those who love the sea and ships, and so long as the American clippers and their brilliant exploits hold a place in the memory of man, the names of Josiah Creesy and the *Flying Cloud* will be remembered with pride.

25

The British Tea Clippers

WHILE the extremely fast clipper type of vessel was developed in the United States and the first ships of this description flew the American flag, the British were quick to follow the American lead.

As has already been told, many of the California clippers, after unloading their cargoes at San Francisco, crossed the Pacific and loaded tea for Great Britain at one of the Chinese ports. The first American ship to enter the tea trade was the clipper *Oriental,* which arrived in London in 1850. She was soon followed by the *Argonaut, Challenge, Surprise, Nightingale, White Squall, Sea Serpent* and other clippers built for the California trade. These American vessels were so much faster than the British ships in the tea trade that they received much higher freights and for a short period gave their British rivals a very bad time of it indeed.

British ship owners, realizing the danger of their position, set the best of the English designers to work on plans for ships that would equal the Yankee clippers in speed and sailing qualities. The first of the British clippers—the *Stornoway*—was launched toward the end of the year 1850. On her first voyage to the East this ship made Hong-Kong in one hundred and two days, and returned from Hong-

Kong to London in one hundred and three days, these being at that time the fastest passages between these ports ever made by a British ship.

The *Stornoway* was soon followed by other British clipper ships, among them the *Chrysolite, Abergeldie, Challenger, Cairngorm, Crest of the Wave, Flying Dragon* and *Lord of the Isles*. These vessels all made very fast passages between London and China and competed on equal terms with the American clippers, receiving the same high freights, and oftentimes beating their Yankee rivals home. Their building, and the excellence of their design, brought British ships once more to the fore in the tea trade, a position they never thereafter relinquished.

Many efforts were made to arrange for races between the British and American clippers, but very few voyages of this nature ever occurred, for the rival ships rarely left China at the same time or close enough together to make a real race possible. One very closely contested race did occur in 1856, however, between the British *Lord of the Isles* and the American clipper bark *Maury*. The *Lord of the Isles* was the only tea clipper built of iron at that time and in addition had very fine, sharp lines, a combination which made her a very wet ship. For this reason, she was frequently referred to as the "Diving Bell," and it was said that her commander, Captain Maxton, drove her into one side of a wave and out the other.

On the voyage on which she raced the *Maury,* the *Lord of the Isles* finished loading her tea and sailed from Foo-chow four days ahead of her rival. She was the first ship to leave for home and Captain Maxton went all-out to make a good passage, not only to beat the competing

American, but also to win a premium of one pound per ton on the freight which had been offered for the first ship to dock in London. Both ships made good time, but the *Maury* was able to overhaul the Britisher. The two ships arrived in the Downs on the same morning and, after taking tugs, passed Gravesend within ten minutes of each other, with the *Maury* in the lead. The *Lord of the Isles* had the faster tug, however, and so was able to reach her dock ahead of the Yankee, thus winning the premium money.

Gradually the British refined the lines of their tea clippers and developed a new and distinctive type of ship, admirably suited for the China trade and different in many ways from the American California clippers. The first of these was the *Falcon,* launched in 1859, and others of the same type which were built during the following ten years included the most celebrated clipper ships ever turned out by the British builders, such famous flyers as the *Fiery Cross, Serica, Ariel, Taeping, Titania, Sir Launcelot, Lahloo, Duke of Abercorn, Thermopylae* and *Cutty Sark.* These were the great ships of the China tea trade, whose races aroused the interest of all the world. As the term went in those days, they were out-and-out "full bloods."

These clippers were smaller than their American sisters, and did not carry as heavy spars or as much canvas. Owing to the fineness of their lines and their comparatively small breadth, they did not require much canvas to make them turn out their best speed. Particular skill was exercised in designing them so they could sail well to windward, since they invariably had to beat against the southwest monsoon when leaving China with new teas and, later in the voyage, had to make good time through the northeast trade winds in the Atlantic. These ships could ride fast and dry before the blast of an out-and-out gale. At the same time they could develop amazing speed in light and moderate winds. All in all, they were one of the finest sailing-ship types ever designed and built.

The tea clippers were like yachts in the way that their fittings were made and tended. Their deckhouses were of teak, as were their bulwarks and hatch-coamings and the decks themselves, which were always holystoned to a gleaming whiteness. Sparkling brasswork shone on the rails and stanchions, and the belaying pins in the fife rails at each mast were either of solid brass or capped with brass, which was always kept highly polished. They were beautiful little ships in every detail, and their masters and men were rightfully proud of them.

There were many exciting races between these new-style clippers, one of the first real contests being that between the *Fiery Cross* and the *Serica* in 1865. The two ships left Foo-chow on the same tide on May the twenty-eighth, both bound for London. Several times during the voyage they parted company, only to meet again, and, after beating up through the north Atlantic, both ships made their reporting signals off the Isle of Wight within a few minutes of each other. Neck and neck, they raced on up the Channel. Slowly the *Serica* forged ahead so that, when they reached Beachy Head where tugs were waiting, she was leading the *Fiery Cross* by about two miles. To everyone's way of thinking, the race belonged to the *Serica;* but, as luck would have it, the *Fiery Cross* had the fastest tug and was the first to dock, thus winning the premium for the first ship to arrive and be in position to discharge her cargo.

This race was followed by others, the most famous of which took place in the year 1866. It had been arranged that nine clippers should sail from Foo-chow as near the same date as possible—the *Ada, Black Prince, Chinaman, Fiery Cross, Flying Spur, Serica, Ariel, Taeping,* and *Taitsing.* The *Fiery Cross* was the first ship to be ready; next the *Ariel* was ready and she was followed by the *Serica, Taeping* and *Taitsing.* These five became the competing ships.

Throughout the long voyage, the five contending clippers were frequently within sight of each other. Good winds favored them all to the Straits of Sunda and from there onward to the southwest across the Indian Ocean. It was on this lap of the passage that each ship made her best twenty-four hours' run—the *Fiery Cross* 328; *Taeping* 319; *Taitsing* 318; *Ariel* 317; and *Serica* 291. At the Cape of Good Hope three of the ships had managed to get fairly well in the lead. The *Fiery Cross* rounded the Cape on July the fourteenth, forty-six days from Foo-chow, followed by the *Ariel,* also forty-six days, the *Taeping* forty-seven days, *Serica* fifty days and *Taitsing* fifty-four days.

On the long passage to the northward, the clippers changed their relative positions several times, as first one and then another obtained the most favorable wind. At the Azores, the *Ariel* was in the lead, but closely followed by the *Taitsing* which had come up handsomely from the rear position.

"Then," says Captain Clark,* "at daybreak on the morning of September 5th, two of the clippers sighted each other running in for the Lizard; they were about five miles apart, beam and beam, steering on slightly converging courses. There was a strong southerly wind with smooth sea, and both ships were being driven at their utmost speed —a good fifteen knots—their lee scuppers smothered in foam, with the wind well abaft the starboard beam; both were under the same canvas, main skysail, topmast, topgallant, royal, and square lower studdingsails. Neither captain required the example of the other to send his ship along at her best speed—they had been doing that for ninety-eight days and nights. When their signals could be made out these ships proved to be the *Ariel* and the *Taeping*."

These two ships had left the port of Foo-chow but twenty minutes apart, and now, after covering sixteen thousand miles through calm and storm, they were again in the same relative position as at the beginning of the hard-fought contest. They raced up the Channel side by side, now one and then the other gaining a slight advantage, each making the most desperate efforts to draw decisively ahead. As they approached the finish-line, which was Deal, the *Ariel* swept past the mark eight minutes ahead of the *Taeping*. In the final reckoning,

* *The Clipper Ship Era,* Capt. Arthur H. Clark, G. P. Putnam's Sons, New York, 1910.

however, the victory was awarded to the *Taeping*, for she had left the port twenty minutes after the *Ariel*, and so had covered the total distance in twelve minutes less time than her rival.

The *Thermopylae*, launched in 1868, and the *Cutty Sark*, launched in 1869, were two of the later tea clippers, but two of the most famous and best remembered. The *Thermopylae* made some extraordinarily fast passages and she has been judged by many to have been the best of all the tea clippers. In heavy weather she was a flyer and, when driving to the eastward in the roaring forties, she more than once passed other ships snugged down to lower topsails or lying hove to. The *Thermopylae* could also make good progress in light breezes and could, as the saying went, maintain steerage way by the flap of her sails; but she was perhaps not quite so fast in smooth water as was the famous *Ariel*.

On her first voyage the *Thermopylae* astonished the shipping world by breaking three records—London to Melbourne in sixty-three days; Newcastle, New South Wales, to Shanghai, pilot to pilot in twenty-eight days; and Foo-chow to Gravesend in ninety-one days. This last record was held only for about a fortnight, for the clipper *Sir Launcelot* then arrived at Gravesend after a passage in eighty-nine days.

The *Thermopylae's* great rival was the *Cutty Sark*, built in 1869, of almost the same dimensions. It was said that the *Cutty Sark* was built expressly to outclass the *Thermopylae*, but if this is so the object was not achieved, despite the unquestioned speed of the former vessel. In the first year in which the two ships were matched against each other—1870—the *Cutty Sark* made the passage from China to London in one hundred and ten days, while the *Thermopylae* covered the course in one hundred and five days, and in succeeding years it was the same story, with the single exception of 1876, when the *Cutty Sark* made the homeward passage in one hundred and eight days against one hundred and fifteen for the *Thermopylae*.

It is probable that the *Cutty Sark's* commanders had something to do with her showing on homeward passages, for during her early days she was never commanded by a man who deliberately set out to drive her at the utmost possible speed. This was in many respects unfortunate, for everyone interested in the great tea clippers of other days would like to know what the *Cutty Sark* could have done on the China passage against the *Thermopylae* and such other ships as the *Serica, Ariel, Fiery Cross* and *Taeping* if properly handled by a hard-driving master.

The *Thermopylae* and *Cutty Sark,* together with a handful of the other famous tea clippers, continued in the China trade until about the year 1880. Some drifted into the jute and sugar trade of the Philippines; others went into the so-called "Country" trades of the Coromandel Coast of India, the Gulf of Martaban, and the Java Sea; while a few, among them the *Thermopylae* and *Cutty Sark,* entered the wool trade between Australia and England.

With the closing of the tea trade to sailing vessels, the clipper ship era came to an end. From its inception, with the building of the first American clippers in 1850, to its end, it lasted some thirty years. The ships and the voyages that have made the era a glorious memory were the work of shipbuilders and seamen of the United States and

Great Britain, for the flag of no other nation was represented in these epoch-making ocean contests. No sailing vessels to equal the clippers in beauty or speed were built before or have since been built; they stand alone as the supreme achievement of the minds and hearts of the master sailing-ship builders of England and America.

26

The Oregon

ALTHOUGH war between the United States and Spain was not declared formally until April the twenty-fifth, 1898, relations between the two countries had for several months been so strained that it was known open warfare would be inevitable. The United States Navy Department, realizing that Spain's strongest battle squadron would probably be encountered in the West Indies, decided early in March to re-enforce the fleet in those waters with the battleship *Oregon,* then on the Pacific coast.

The *Oregon* was designed primarily as a coast defense battleship and, though a splendid vessel, was not intended for long-distance cruising in stormy seas. The great difficulties of sending her on the long voyage round South America by way of tempestuous Cape Horn were apparent to all naval men and involved no little responsibility and risk. If the ship should be lost, the blame would necessarily fall upon those ordering her dangerous voyage. Such a run by a ship of the *Oregon's* type had never before been attempted, and many freely expressed their doubt of her ability to perform the feat.

Fully conscious of the responsibility he was assuming, secretary of the navy Long telegraphed the commander of the *Oregon,* then in Puget Sound, Washington, on March the seventh saying: "The situation is getting worse. You should go to San Francisco as soon as possible and get ammunition." The *Oregon* sailed at once and five days later in San Francisco, her commander received his further orders: "When in all respects ready for sea, proceed with the vessel under your command to Callao, Peru, and await further orders. In view of the present critical condition of affairs the *Oregon* should leave San Francisco at the earliest possible date and arrive at Callao as soon as practicable. The crew is to be constantly drilled, the passage of the ship not to be delayed thereby."

These were the orders that started the *Oregon* on her famous "dash" round South America, a voyage that thrilled the entire English-speaking world. A last-minute change of commanders was made—Captain Charles Edgar Clark taking over because of the previous commander's ill health. On March the nineteenth the *Oregon* steamed proudly through the Golden Gate and, under forced draft with billows of black smoke pouring from her two buff-painted funnels, she raced away to the south.

As she ran down toward the Equator, the thought uppermost in the minds of her men and officers was: "Will we get there in time to fight the Spaniards?" No one knew how soon war would be declared or how soon the Spanish fleet would be encountered. But every man on board the *Oregon* hoped that the expected battle would not take place before their ship arrived to add her guns to the strength of the American battle-line.

Callao was reached on April the fourth; the engines and boilers received the usual repairs after a long run and the ship was coaled, the men working round the clock. In three days all was ready and the great battleship resumed her headlong race against time. Her next stop for coal was to be at Sandy Point, Patagonia.

The weather was not good after leaving Callao and grew steadily stormier as the *Oregon* worked to the south. By the time she reached the entrance to Magellan Straits, the wind was howling with the force of a heavy gale and beating up vicious steep-sided cross seas. The ponderous battleship pitched heavily, even dangerously, "the jackstaff sometimes disappearing altogether under the solid seas that swept all but the superstructure," according to one of her officers. As her bows plunged downwards and sank beneath the swirling waters, her propellers came clear of the water and whirled around at terrific speed, shaking the ship like a quivering leaf. The strain on both hull and machinery was enormous, but Captain Clark shouldered the risks and plunged ahead, for his orders were to take the *Oregon* to West Indian waters with the utmost possible speed.

The quieter waters of Magellan Straits were reached at last and coal was taken on board, as planned, at Sandy Point. Then, entering the south Atlantic, the bow of the *Oregon* was pointed to the north. Driving furiously, with high white-foamed bow waves clearing away from her sharp stem and with engines laboring day and night at their highest speed, she came to Rio de Janeiro on April the thirtieth. Here Captain Clark received a dispatch from Washington stating that war between the United States and Spain had been formally declared, and that Admiral Dewey, on May first, had defeated the Spanish Pacific squadron at the battle of Manila Bay.

"All hands were very anxious for news," wrote Lieutenant Eberle, of the *Oregon*, "and memorable were the cheers that greeted the news

that war had been declared. In a few moments our band was on deck, and between the rounds of cheers the strains of 'The Star-spangled Banner' and 'Hail Columbia' floated over the Brazilian fleet and the crowds that lined the wharves. The crew uncovered and stood at attention during the playing of the national anthem, and then followed more cheers and the inspiring battle cry 'Remember the Maine,' a watchword often heard about the decks as the men turned to the coal barges and worked as they had never worked before. The intense heat and the long and trying working hours of those days and nights were borne without a murmur."

And now began the last passage of the record-breaking dash. The eyes of the world were fixed upon the *Oregon*. Could she do it? Would she get there in time? These were the questions uppermost in the minds of all. The Spanish fleet had not yet been reported; but it was believed to have left Spain and to be nearing the West Indies to protect the Spanish islands of Cuba and Puerto Rico. On the morning of April the twenty-second, Rear Admiral Sampson had led the north Atlantic fleet out of Key West harbor to search for the Spaniards. Commodore Schley, with the "Flying Squadron" composed of the *Brooklyn, Massachusetts, Texas* and *Scorpion,* was at Newport News ready to sail at a moment's notice should Spanish battleships or cruisers appear off the American coast. Five thousand miles to the south, the *Oregon* bent anew to her task and roared to the northward to join her sister men-of-war.

On May the eighteenth she reached Bridgetown, Barbados, to take on the coal needed to bring her to a home port. Still there was no news of the Spanish fleet's position. Good! The *Oregon* might still be in time. She slipped out of the harbor after nightfall and, with all lights extinguished, swept on to the north. On the morning of May the twenty-sixth, she arrived safely at Key West, having completed her fourteen thousand mile voyage around the continent in sixty-eight days. And, to the inexpressible joy of her officers and men, she had arrived in time!

The precise location of the Spanish fleet had not yet been determined, but it was believed to be in some harbor of Cuba or Puerto Rico. On May the fifteenth reports had been received that the Spanish warcraft, under Admiral Cervera, had put in at the Dutch island of Curacao for fuel and supplies. On leaving here his fleet had vanished, but it was certain that he would have to make for some port in the Spanish-owned West Indian islands. Commodore Schley with the "Flying Squadron" was ordered to sail at once and search along the southern coast of Cuba, while Sampson patroled the northern coast. The *Oregon* was detailed to go with Rear Admiral Sampson, and sailed a few hours after her triumphant arrival at Key West.

The *Oregon*

Commodore Schley soon obtained news of the whereabouts of the elusive Spanish fleet, the captains of several merchant vessels reporting that Cervera's squadron had been seen near Santiago, a port near the eastern end of Cuba. Schley at once steamed at full speed for Santiago and arrived off the harbor on the night of May the twenty-seventh. At dawn the next morning he saw the masts of the Spanish men-of-war projecting above the hills that rose between the harbor and the sea. On June the first Rear Admiral Sampson arrived with his squadron and, as the ranking officer, took command of the entire American force.

The narrow winding entrance to Santiago harbor guarded by powerful shore batteries made it impossible for Sampson to force his way in to attack. His greatest concern was to prevent the Spaniards from escaping under the cover of darkness and, to guard against this possibility, he decided to block the channel by sinking the collier *Merrimac* across it. Lieutenant Richmond Pearson Hobson volunteered for the dangerous task of taking the *Merrimac* in under the Spanish batteries and blowing her up by exploding torpedoes placed inside her hull. Hobson made his attempt early in the morning of June the fourth, but was discovered by a Spanish picket boat which shot away the *Merrimac's* rudder chains and made it impossible to turn her across the channel. Nevertheless, the torpedoes were exploded and the ship was sunk lengthwise in the harbor entrance. Hobson and those with him jumped for their lives. They were taken from the water by the picket boat and held as prisoners until an arrangement could be made to exchange them for Spanish captives in the hands of the Americans.

Admiral Cervera was by now in an exceptionally difficult position. An American army had been landed, which was closing in on the city. Should it capture Santiago, the Spanish fleet would be forced to surrender without a fight. Yet the admiral was by no means anxious to attempt to run through the blockading squadron of the navy. In the end, his hand was forced, for he received peremptory orders from Madrid to leave Santiago immediately and proceed to the Philippines.

Cervera made all necessary preparations and ordered his ships to be ready to get under way at midnight of July the second. His squadron consisted of four fast and powerful armored cruisers, the *Cristobal Colon, Almirante Oquendo, Infanta Maria Teresa* and *Viscaya,* and three torpedo boats, the *Furor, Pluton* and *Terror.* To check the flight of these vessels and if possible destroy them, the Americans had on station on the day of Cervera's attempt to escape the battleships *Iowa, Indiana, Oregon* and *Texas,* the armored cruisers *New York* and *Brooklyn,* the torpedo boat *Ericsson,* and the armed yachts *Gloucester* and *Vixen.*

For some inexplicable reason Cervera delayed his start and thus lost the chance of making good his escape under cover of darkness. It was not until the morning of July the third that the Spanish ships were ready. At about half-past nine the Americans saw dense clouds of black smoke pouring from the Spanish cruisers' funnels, and soon the first of the enemy ships, the *Infanta Maria Teresa,* appeared.

"They're coming out! They're coming out!" roared the American sailors, exultant that at last action was at hand. "Battle Stations" was sounded by gong and bugle on every ship and the men hurried to their guns. "Hoist two-fifty," Sampson ordered and the flags, meaning

"Close in toward the harbor entrance and attack vessels," fluttered to the yardarm of the flagship *New York*.

Now the Spanish ships, piling up enormous white bow waves and belching clouds of smoke, came one by one into view. Clearing the harbor entrance, they turned sharply to the west and rushed along at full speed close to the shore. After them, gradually working up speed, came the Americans, led by Captain "Fighting Bob" Evans in the *Iowa*. Nine minutes after the Spanish ships had first been sighted, her starboard battery opened fire as she steamed on a course parallel to that of the enemy. Behind the *Iowa*, came the *Brooklyn, Texas, Indiana* and *Oregon,* which soon added the weight of their broadsides to the attack.

In the first twenty minutes of the engagement, these ships poured in the heaviest and most effective fire of the battle. At the end of this short period, both the *Infanta Maria Teresa,* the leading ship, and the *Almirante Oquendo,* the rearmost ship, were in flames. Shortly afterwards, the *Maria Teresa* was in such a damaged condition that Admiral Cervera gave orders to run her ashore and haul down the flag. The *Texas* had at first concentrated her wrath on the *Almirante Oquendo,* and in all probability would have compelled her to surrender or run ashore, had not the magnificent *Oregon,* charging at full speed through the water, closed in on the fleeing Spanish ship and subjected her to a terrific and merciless battering. The damage done by the *Oregon,* added to that inflicted by the *Iowa* and *Texas,* sealed the *Oquendo's* fate. Afire from stem to stern, she had been mortally wounded, and, turning toward the beach, she ran ashore and displayed the white flag.

The Viscaya and *Cristobal Colon* were now the only Spanish cruisers left. At this stage of the battle the *Oregon* and *Brooklyn* had drawn considerably ahead of their consorts, and the combined fire of these two ships drove most of the *Viscaya's* men from their guns and set her on fire fore and aft. At eleven o'clock her commander saw that she was doomed, and gave the order to haul down the ensign and run the ship ashore. This was done and all day the *Viscaya* burned furiously, finally blowing up when the flames reached her magazine during the night.

There now remained only the *Cristobal Colon*. She was the swiftest vessel of the squadron and, at the time the *Viscaya* was beached, had gained a lead of eight or ten miles over the leading American ships, the *Brooklyn* and *Oregon*. These vessels now started in full pursuit and were soon joined by the *Texas* and *New York*.

The four American ships presented a magnificent spectacle as they raced through the blue Cuban sea under a cloudless sky. The roaring of their great guns had abruptly ceased, but stains of burned powder bore witness to the terrific cannonading they had just been engaged in. Far out on the horizon, barely discernible save for a trail of smoke, was the *Cristobal Colon,* the quarry upon which the four American warships were now doing their best to close in. "At the bows of each ship," wrote an officer, "a snow-white wave rose high on the cutwater, at times spilling over and onto the forecastle. So great was the momentum that the forward part of the vessels rose a foot or two higher than their normal level, while their sterns sank correspondingly as they settled in the trough the ships had dug in the sea. Mighty columns of black smoke rushed up to the tops of their funnels and . . . scurried off toward the horizon."

The *Oregon*

Despite the supposedly greater speed of the *Cristobal Colon,* the American ships gradually overtook her and, after the pursuit had continued for two hours, the *Oregon* and *Brooklyn* opened fire with their forward turret guns. The shells fell near the *Cristobal Colon,* those from the *Oregon's* 13-inch guns landing beyond her. Again and again the American ships hurled their missiles at the target and, as the tornado of steel and high explosive threatened to rend his vessel to pieces, the Spanish commander realized the futility of further resistance. The *Oregon* was drawing closer and closer and, with every minute that passed, her fire was becoming more deadly. Shortly after one o'clock, the *Colon's* commander followed the example of the other three Spanish captains and ran his ship ashore.

And so the last of the four proud Spanish cruisers—vessels which all had believed to be among the most deadly fighting ships afloat— was destroyed. The chase had been one of the most dramatic running battles in the history of naval warfare, and, like the Battle of Manila Bay, had been exceptionally one-sided, the American gunnery being far superior to that of the Spaniards. About three hundred and fifty Spaniards were killed and one hundred and sixty wounded, while the American loss was one man killed and two wounded. The destruction of Cervera's squadron led to the surrender of Santiago by the Spanish land forces and the war was soon afterwards brought to an end. Seapower had once again shown its power of bringing victory to the country possessing a superior and well-trained navy.

27

The Lion

Admiral Beatty's Flagship in the First World War

FEW ships of the World War Royal Navy saw more action or played a more telling part in defeating the German High Seas Fleet than the battle cruiser *Lion*, flagship of Admiral Sir David Beatty throughout the whole period of the conflict.

Beatty and the *Lion!* A gallant admiral and a gallant ship—true successors to Blake and the *Triumph*, Hawke and the *Royal George*, Rodney and the *Formidable*, Nelson and the *Victory*.

Beatty, who had entered the navy at the age of thirteen and had seen an exceptionally large amount of fighting service in Egypt, the Sudan and China, was appointed to command the First Battle Cruiser Squadron in 1913. On March the first he hoisted his flag on the *Lion*. The other ships in the squadron were the *Princess Royal, Invincible, Indomitable* and *Indefatigable,* a group of battle cruisers well described as "the fastest and most powerful scouting force ever launched."

The command of this squadron was given to Beatty by Winston Churchill, then First Lord of the Admiralty, even though the admiral was the youngest on the navy list, and the last to be entitled to the position by the laws of seniority. "I had no doubt whatever," said Churchill, "when the command of the Battle Cruiser Squadron fell vacant in the spring of 1913, in appointing him over the heads of all to this incomparable command."

The battle cruiser was then a relatively new type of fighting ship, which had been designed largely as a result of the conviction of Lord Fisher (First Sea Lord, 1904-1910) that "speed is armor." In accordance with this principle, the *Lion* had a speed of thirty knots as compared with about twenty-one knots for the battleships of the period. Though much more lightly armored than a battleship, the *Lion* had a powerful main battery of eight 13.5-inch guns, the British battleships of the period having chiefly 12-inch guns and the German battleships 11.5-inch guns. Thus, it was planned that the *Lion* and her sisters could overtake any enemy battleship afloat, keep out of range and yet punish her severely with her more powerful guns. At the same time, with her tremendous burst of speed, she could escape from any overwhelming enemy force that might come through the mists at close range.

It became Beatty's task and responsibility to determine the most effective uses to be made of this new and formidable type of fighting craft in war time, and to test his plans and ships under the ordeal of battle. Drawn by his own nature to the swift and heavy-hitting battle cruisers, he had already given much study to the problem of directing them under war-time conditions and, shortly after he took command, he laid down the following main duties for his squadron: "To provide on occasion an independent scouting force, and to act as a provocative or decoy force to engage the enemy's heavy ships and, by the use of superior speed, bring them within reach of the main fleet and so force them to action; . . . while in general action they would form a fast division of the Battle Fleet." His strategy and tactics might be summed up in his own phrases, "to get at the enemy; to destroy him or to lead him to destruction."

Beatty did not have long to wait to put his plans and his fighting ships to the test. At six o'clock on the morning of August the fourth, 1914, when news came that the Germans were planning an immediate invasion of Belgium, the Grand Fleet steamed out to sea. The ultimatum to Germany expired at midnight; Great Britain was at war. The long grim struggle between the two most powerful navies the world had ever known had begun.

For three weeks the rival fleets felt their way cautiously, scouting to find out possible weak spots in the enemy's defense. The British Grand Fleet, under Admiral Jellicoe, was kept constantly moving about the North Sea, searching for enemy ships. But the Germans were afraid at this time to let their big ships venture out. A few minelayers and submarines were dispatched to the English coast; but the German battleships, battle cruisers, cruisers and destroyers stayed safely in or near their harbors.

Meanwhile, British submarines, sent out to reconnoiter, had returned with reports that German light cruisers and destroyers were patroling in an exposed position in the Heligoland Bight. This was the stretch of shallow water between the island of Heligoland and the great naval harbor of Wilhelmshaven. Toward the end of August, the British decided to raid these outposts, both to attempt to deal a body blow at the German navy and to keep the patroling vessels busy while British troops were being landed at Ostend.

A force of thirty-one destroyers and six submarines, led by two light cruisers, all from the Harwich Force kept in the south for the

protection of the English Channel, were told off for the attack. Supporting these craft, ready to rush in if German battleships should steam out from Wilhelmshaven, were Beatty's five battle cruisers and Commodore Goodenough's First Light Cruiser Squadron. Off to the north in the distant background, lay Jellicoe with the whole Grand Fleet.

At dawn on August the twenty-eighth, the attacking force came out of the mists surrounding Heligoland and took the German outpost destroyers completely by surprise. As the Germans turned and ran for shelter toward the island, the British pursued, firing whenever they could sight a target. One German destroyer was overtaken and destroyed.

Meanwhile, German light cruisers, summoned by wireless, were steaming at full speed to the aid of their harassed and frightened destroyers. On they came, with funnels belching enormous clouds of smoke, tearing through the early morning mists, with gun crews at their stations, tense and alert, ready for instant battle. They soon sighted the British force and pounded into action, firing with great

277

accuracy, and maneuvering at the highest speed of which they were capable. It was a brilliant display of aggressiveness and at the first it drove the British back. One of the fiercest actions was between the German cruiser *Frauenlob* and the British light cruiser *Arethusa,* the latter being seriously damaged.

As the British light forces rallied to stem the German onslaught, the supporting forces came to their aid. Out of the mist came the *Lion* and Beatty's four other huge battle cruisers. Thundering with their turret guns at the German light cruisers, they blasted the enemy ships and drove them back in headlong flight. Two cruisers were ripped to pieces and sunk by the *Lion,* while a third cruiser was destroyed by the other British ships. In these three cruisers alone the Germans lost an admiral and over one thousand officers and men; while the British losses amounted to but thirty-two men killed and fifty-five wounded.

The victory was hailed with great rejoicing in Britain, the first really good news of the war. Admiral Beatty and his flagship *Lion* were acclaimed throughout the nation. The Royal Navy was once again sweeping the enemy before it as it had so often done before.

Following the Heligoland Bight battle, the battle cruisers were comparatively inactive for a period of about three months, although they made several sweeps through the North Sea.

On December the sixteenth, however, they very nearly got their teeth into their opposite numbers, the battle cruiser squadron of Germany. This force, under Admiral Hipper, had made a night run across the North Sea and at dawn of the sixteenth began a heavy bombardment of the English coastal towns of Hartlepool, Scarborough and Whitby.

The Admiralty had intercepted the enemy's wireless messages, and Beatty, with the battle cruisers *Lion, Queen Mary, Tiger* and *New Zealand,* was sent into the North Sea to cut off the German retreat.

Hipper finished his bombardment and started for home. There was a thick fog, and the huge gray German battle cruisers drove into mountainous seas, throwing up clouds of spray as they pushed forward at high speed, striving to make good their escape. Beatty, meanwhile, steamed through the fog and storm, keeping his ships across the enemy's probable line of retreat. Two British light cruisers sighted the German ships and signaled to Beatty, who, half blinded by the fog, started in pursuit. But, though contact was made, the fog swallowed up the speeding enemy ships before the British guns could fire. Cursing his luck, Beatty was at last forced to give up the chase, and turn the *Lion* toward home.

In his next encounter with the enemy, he was to have better luck. On January the twenty-fourth, 1915, the Germans attempted another raid, Hipper steaming again through the night with the three battle cruisers *Seydlitz, Derfflinger* and *Moltke,* the armored cruiser *Blücher* and a screening force of four light cruisers and nineteen destroyers. Beatty, warned by the British wireless interception service, put to sea from Rosyth in the Firth of Forth, where the Battle Cruiser Fleet was now based, while Commodore Tyrwhitt's Harwich flotillas steamed north to meet him. Forty-seven ships comprised the British force, which was led by the battle cruisers *Lion, Tiger, Princess Royal, New Zealand,* and *Indomitable.* At the same time Jellicoe and the Grand Fleet left Scapa Flow and moved down the North Sea.

The January day dawned sullen and gray, and in the half-light the lookouts searched the eastward horizon for signs of the enemy. The ships were now off the Dogger Bank, about two hundred miles east of the mouth of the Tyne. Beatty and Tyrwhitt joined forces a little before eight o'clock and, a few minutes later, British light cruisers out ahead of the big ships contacted the German destroyers. Signals were flashed to both Beatty and Hipper. The latter wheeled to a reverse course and sped for home. On board the *Lion*, Beatty ordered full speed ahead, and the battle cruisers drove furiously ahead in wild pursuit.

By nine o'clock the British were within gun range of the four big German ships, and both sides commenced to fire with their huge turret guns. Almost at once the *Blücher*, rear ship of the German column, was hit. One shell after another plunged through her armor and exploded in her interior. Her engines were soon damaged, and she began to drop behind, her guns still blazing defiantly.

The *Lion* now concentrated on Hipper's flagship, the *Seydlitz*, churning along at nearly thirty knots at the head of the German column. Two hits were made, the second of which burst against the after turret with terrible results. Red hot armor plating and shell fragments set fire to a powder charge, and a flaming sheet of powder-gas killed every man in the turret. Shooting through an open door into the next turret, the flames ignited another charge of powder. There was another thunderous detonation, and a column of flame flashed upward, higher than the masthead. By the heroic action of three crew members, who turned the red hot wheels controlling the flood valves to the magazines, while the flesh was burned from their hands, the ship was saved at the last moment from destruction. Six hundred tons of water poured in, and the *Seydlitz* tore on toward home.

At half-past ten the *Blücher* was hit by a 13.5-inch shell which set her afire amidships, and damaged her steering gear and engines. Hipper left her to her fate, and Beatty detailed the *Indomitable* to finish her off. Until the very last, this German ship continued to fire her guns; and, though hit by more than a hundred shells and twice torpedoed by British destroyers, she did not sink until 12.13 P.M. As she rolled over, scores of her crew appeared, sliding down her side and dropping into the water. Many of them were rescued by the British light craft.

Meanwhile, the *Lion,* in an exposed position at the head of the British line, had been hit several times. Water had come in through one hole in her side, giving her a list to port; one turret had been put out of action, and a final hit damaged her port condenser and stopped her port engine. The great ship slowed down, and the five other British battle cruisers thundered past her. As they went by, Beatty hoisted the signals: "Attack the enemy's rear" and "Keep closer to the enemy."

Rear Admiral Moore of the *New Zealand,* who now automatically assumed command as the second ranking officer present, believed that by "the enemy's rear" Beatty meant the disabled *Blücher.* Accordingly, he turned aside and led the other British ships to help make an end of the armored cruiser. Hipper, delivered by this mistake, rushed headlong on to the southeast and made good his escape. Beatty was furious; but it was too late to think of overtaking the fleeing Germans and the British ships perforce gave up the pursuit.

During the remainder of the year 1915 and, indeed, until March, 1916, when Admiral von Scheer assumed command of the High Seas Fleet, the Germans kept their ships in port. Their two brushes with the British battle cruisers had convinced them that the danger of annihilation was ever present in the mists and storms of the gray North Sea, where, during this period, the British Grand Fleet made constant "sweeps" in an effort to draw the Germans out to fight.

Early in March, 1916, the German battle cruisers cooperating with Zeppelins once again came out to make a flying raid on the English coast, and, under cover of darkness, were able to elude the Grand Fleet, which came down to intercept them. Another raid took place in April, when Lowestoft and Yarmouth were bombarded, and again the Germans had the good fortune to elude the British and speed safely back to their bases. Elated by his success, Scheer planned another dash across the North Sea. This time he did not escape.

On the evening of May the thirtieth, the Grand Fleet, led by Admiral Jellicoe in the *Iron Duke,* left Scapa Flow and steamed eastward in the general direction of the Skagerrack, between Denmark and Norway. At the same time, Beatty in the *Lion* set out from Rosyth. With him were five other battle cruisers, the *Princess Royal, Queen Mary, Tiger, Indefatigable* and *New Zealand,* and also the famous Fifth Battle Squadron, composed of the four new battleships *Barham, Valiant, Malaya* and *Warspite,* under the command of Rear-Admiral Evan-Thomas, as well as a number of light cruisers and destroyers.

The Admiralty had discovered, from intercepted wireless messages, that the German fleet intended to leave port at some time on the following day. Very well. The British Grand Fleet, if all went well, would be on hand in full strength to intercept it and force it to battle.

Admiral Jellicoe had with him twenty-four battleships and three battle cruisers, under Rear-Admiral Hood, a descendant of Admiral

Hood who commanded the van at the Battle of the Saints. These ships were screened by the armored and light cruisers attached to the Grand Fleet. All told, the British force, including Beatty's squadrons, comprised one hundred and fifty-one ships—twenty-eight battleships, nine battle cruisers, eight armored cruisers, twenty-six light cruisers, seventy-eight destroyers, one seaplane carrier and one minelaying vessel.

The Germans had twenty-two battleships, under Admiral Scheer; five battle cruisers, led by Vice-Admiral Hipper in the *Lutzow;* eleven light cruisers and sixty-one destroyers, a total of ninety-nine ships. The German battle cruisers were the *Lutzow, Seydlitz, Von der Tann, Derfflinger,* and *Moltke.* These ships were protected with heavier armor than the British battle cruisers and were subdivided internally into numerous small compartments separated by water-tight bulkheads. As the fleet steamed north toward the Skagerrack, the battle cruisers, screened by light cruisers and destroyers, formed the van. Some fifty miles behind were the battleships with their attendant lighter ships.

At 2:20 in the afternoon of May the thirty-first, the British light cruisers *Galatea* and *Phaeton,* steaming to the east of Beatty's forces, sighted two German destroyers which had stopped a Danish tramp steamer. The *Galatea* at once wirelessed the *Lion,* "Urgent! Enemy in sight!" and dashed after the enemy destroyers. A few minutes later the German light cruiser *Elbing* came over the horizon under forced draft, responding to calls for help from the destroyers. Sighting the British cruisers, she signaled Admiral Hipper, "Enemy armored cruisers in view to the northwest!"

Each fleet now knew that the enemy was close at hand, and preparations were made forthwith for battle. On the British battle cruisers the bugles blared "Action stations," while on the German ships the rapid ruffling of the drums beat all hands to quarters. On every ship the tension increased, and the decks were alive with hurrying men running to their battle station in turrets, ammunition passages, conning towers and gun-casemates. Water-tight doors were closed and dogged, hospital parties laid out their instruments. The turret guns were swung about to point over the side, and, one by one, were reported "Ready!"

At this time the British and German battle cruiser squadrons were about forty miles apart, Beatty steering east, and Hipper north. Both forces were to the west of the Jutland Bank, off the northwest coast of Denmark and some seventy miles off the coast. Jellicoe, with the Grand Fleet, was seventy miles away to the north, and Scheer, with the German High Seas Fleet, about fifty miles distant to the south.

On board the *Lion,* Beatty hoisted the signal "Change course! Follow the *Lion!*" The flagship swung to the southeast, and the remaining battle-cruisers followed in her wake. Five miles astern, the slower Fifth Battle Squadron took up the chase.

At about 3:30 the opposing squadrons sighted each other. Two minutes later Hipper turned his flagship *Lutzow* in a complete semicircle, to a course exactly the opposite of that which he had been steering. The other German ships turned after him, and all sped to the southeast toward the High Seas Fleet. Hipper's plan was to draw Beatty under the guns of the German battleships and then destroy him.

Both sides held their fire, waiting until the range was short enough to ensure hits. It was the Germans who opened fire first, a broadside thundering from the *Lutzow* at 3:48. A moment later the *Lion* replied. Then all the ships came into action, their turret guns rearing and belching flame. As the shells fell into the sea, they sent up huge columns of water which rose a hundred feet into the air, hiding the speeding ships from sight. Yellow powder smoke drifted between the two columns. Men worked tensely and grimly at their posts, range-finding, training the guns, spotting the fall of the shells and correcting the range and deflection.

The greatest of all sea battles had begun.

From the very beginning the German fire was accurate, fast and effective. Three minutes after fire was opened, the *Lion,* at the head of the British column, was straddled by enemy shells, which sent up towering pillars of water on either side. A moment later with devastating force, two shells struck the *Lion,* exploding with an ear-splitting crash of rending metal. Then, in rapid succession, the *Tiger, Princess Royal* and *Indefatigable* were struck. Under the rapid firing the British line was hidden from view in spray and smoke.

Then the British began to find their targets. Seven minutes after the firing opened, the *Queen Mary,* third in the British line, sent a salvo into the *Seydlitz,* which set her on fire. Four minutes later the *Lion* drove home a salvo on the *Lutzow.*

The German battle-cruisers now put forth a supreme effort. Nine salvos a minute thundered from each ship. The side of each vessel flamed with the gun-flashes; within the turrets the noise was stupendous, annihilating the senses. The gunners worked at utmost speed, bathed in sweat, loading and firing with incredible rapidity. Their ships trembled and shook like leaves as they tore southward.

Under this demoniac onslaught, the British ships began to suffer severely. One shell struck the *Lion,* burst within a turret and forced the flooding of her magazines. A few minutes later came disaster. The *Indefatigable,* last ship in the British line, was hit by three shells, which injured her steering gear. As she turned out of line, with a list to port, two more shells struck her. One burst in a forward turret, and set powder on fire. In a few seconds she became one enormous explosion. As her magazines blew up, sheets of orange flame and black columns of smoke shot upwards from her hull. A deafening roar drowning out even the thunder of the turret guns, filled the air as she was burst asunder. In a few moments she sank, taking with her over a thousand officers and men.

Little by little, the two lines had drawn apart. By 4:10 the range had opened to twenty thousand yards, too great for effective firing. As the guns quieted down, Beatty saw an opportunity for a different kind of attack. He signaled his destroyer force, "Attack the enemy with torpedoes." Smoke poured from the destroyers' funnels as they gathered speed and plunged toward the German ships. As they swept forward, German destroyers moved to ward them off. The two flotillas met half-way between the battle cruiser formations and, as they dashed past each other, fired as rapidly as possible. Two German destroyers were sunk, and the remainder were forced to wheel and retreat. Two British destroyers were damaged and were afterwards sunk by the battleships of the High Seas Fleet.

Soon the British and German heavy ships drew together again and, for nearly half an hour, a tremendous fire was exchanged. By this time Evan-Thomas's 15-inch gun battleships of the Fifth Battle Squadron had come within range and commenced to hurl their 1,900-

pound shells at the enemy. The *Barham* hit the *Von der Tann.* Then the *Moltke* was struck. Both ships began to zigzag to escape the accurate fire, and the effectiveness of their fire was at once diminished. The range closed and the British battle cruisers obtained a number of hits. But the more heavily-armored German ships could take more punishment than the British. Salvos that should have destroyed them were landed and did heavy damage; but did not send them to the bottom.

At about 4:30 the British suffered their second major loss. Surging forward at express speed, the *Queen Mary,* third ship in the British line, came under a tremendous fire from the German *Derfflinger* and *Seydlitz.* Two of the German salvos landed. The *Queen Mary* shuddered in a tremendous convulsion. One or more of the shells penetrated to the magazines and, with a terrific explosion, the huge ship blew up. To those in the nearby vessels, the sight was so staggering they could hardly believe what they saw. One moment a gallant ship; the next a column of smoke and flame shooting up more than a thousand feet, with parts of the ship's equipment circling and wheeling by the hundreds high aloft in the sky. In a few seconds the *Queen Mary* vanished. The *Tiger* and *New Zealand,* which had been astern of her, closed up on the *Princess Royal* and the *Lion,* and the four ships rushed on, their turret guns thundering as before.

Ten minutes later Beatty received a wireless signal from the *Southampton,* a light cruiser sent ahead on a scouting mission: "Have sighted enemy battle fleet bearing approximately southeast, course of enemy north. Time 4:38 P. M."

This gave Beatty the information he needed. Jellicoe was now only fifty miles away to the north, and coming south at full speed with the entire weight of Britain's naval strength. With luck, Beatty knew that he could decoy the German fleet north and force it into a general fleet engagement.

At 4:43 signal flags streamed from the *Lion's* yard-arm, "Alter course in succession 16 points (180 degrees) to starboard." The flagship's helm was put over and the *Lion* swept around in a great curve to starboard, reversing her course and heading northwest. The *Princess Royal, Tiger* and *New Zealand* followed her. At the same time Beatty wirelessed Jellicoe his position and that of the enemy fleet. Hipper, the records show, did not realize that Beatty was setting a trap. To the contrary, he believed that the British ships, afraid of the oncoming High Seas Fleet, were running away. He turned his ships about and pursued the British battle cruisers at top speed. Three miles astern of him, the German battleships increased their speed and plunged on to the north.

On this famous "run to the north," which lasted from about a quarter to five until the Grand Fleet was sighted at six o'clock, the battle cruiser forces continued to fire at each other as often as weather conditions permitted. Haze, the forerunner of fog, was settling down over the sea.

Now, for the first time, the British Fifth Battle Squadron was able to bring its 15-inch guns into effective play. Their heavy and accurate shooting was the outstanding event of the hours between five and six o'clock. The *Warspite* and *Malaya* hit the German battleship *Grosser Kurfurst* and *Markgraf* heavily, and then concentrated on the leading battle-cruisers. The *Seydlitz, Lutzow* and *Derfflinger* were struck time

288

and again, and the *Seydlitz,* already hurt, was seriously damaged. She was set afire, four of her turret guns were put out of action and shell holes in her bow admitted so much water that she began to lose speed. Though hit repeatedly, the *Lutzow* was lucky. No vital parts were damaged, and she continued to plow furiously ahead, firing whenever the smoke and mist lifted enough to show her a target. The *Derfflinger,* struck just above the forward torpedo-room, settled by the head but still kept on. She and the *Seydlitz* were only kept afloat by the numerous internal water-tight bulkheads which localized their injuries.

At a quarter to six came the moment of Beatty's triumph, when, looking toward the northern horizon from the high upper bridge of the *Lion,* he saw half a dozen small specks trailing smoke clouds. They were the first of the light cruisers steaming south in advance of the Grand Fleet. The battle cruisers' work was nearly done. As the *Lion* swept on with guns still thundering, Beatty turned her to starboard to cross ahead of the German line. He wished to use his superior speed to turn the enemy's ships away to the eastward. This would make their shooting more difficult, would delay and confuse them and would screen the Grand Fleet until the last possible moment. Unable to see for any distance through the gathering gloom and the pall of smoke thrown out by the British ships, Hipper and Scheer, even now, were unaware that Jellicoe was at hand with the main striking force of the British fleet.

Followed by the three remaining British battle cruisers and the Fifth Battle Squadron, the *Lion* tore at top speed to the east. Haze was everywhere; darkness was fast coming on; but each ship was in full action, belching salvos at the leading German vessels. The German line turned and gave way toward the east. Then at 6:15, Jellicoe, for the first time able to make out the location of the High Seas Fleet, gave his historic signal:

"Deploy upon the left-wing column; course south-east-by-east."

The British battleships had been formed in six columns abreast, four dreadnoughts in each column. Jellicoe's signal ordered them to form in one long line-of-battle, the four ships in the left-hand column going out ahead, the other columns falling in behind them.

It was a masterly decision. It deployed the Grand Fleet across the head of the approaching enemy—the maneuver called "Crossing the T"—the position desired above all others in fleet action because it opposes maximum strength to the enemy's weakest point.

The *Lion* had now accomplished its major task. Through nearly three hours of firing more terrific than in any previous naval battle, she had doggedly fought her way. And at the last she had delivered the German fleet to the guns of the British battleships.

Beatty led his furiously steaming ships to the head of the British line, now straightening out and steering a southeasterly course. He had been joined by three other battle-cruisers, which had come down with the Grand Fleet, the *Invincible, Inflexible* and *Indomitable*. At about 6:30, shells from the German battle cruisers struck the *Invincible* and she was suddenly enveloped in a sheet of flame from a magazine explosion such as had destroyed the *Queen Mary* and *Indefatigable*. Torn in two, the *Invincible* went down. The battleships were beginning to open fire, their gun-flashes flaming out through the deepening gloom, though the ships themselves were barely visible.

The German battleships replied, but soon Admiral Scheer was able to see that, the British line was crossing his T—passing ahead of his own battle-line. At the same time more of the British battleships were able to open fire. To continue meant certain destruction. He ordered a maneuver which his fleet had often practised. This was a simultaneous 180-degree turn of every vessel in the line, so the rearmost ship became the leading one, and the whole fleet steamed away in the opposite direction to its previous course. This movement was executed at 6:36, under cover of smoke screens and a destroyer attack against the British line, and the German battleships fled away to the westward.

Hipper, meanwhile, had been hard pressed by the British battle-cruisers. His flagship *Lutzow* was hit repeatedly and at seven o'clock Hipper was forced to abandon her in a sinking condition and transfer his flag to the *Moltke*. As Scheer moved off to the west, the German battle cruisers followed, all of them seriously damaged.

Uncertain as to the course the Germans had taken, Jellicoe altered his course to south, with the intention of intercepting the enemy vessels if they made for port. At 6:55 Scheer reversed his course again, by another simultaneous turn of every ship, and ordered a full-speed all-out attack on the British line.

Suddenly the German ships appeared. They were seen first from the rear of the British line and then by almost all the British dreadnoughts—first the four furiously firing battle cruisers, surrounded by destroyers, then the sinister shapes of German dreadnoughts. The Grand Fleet's broadsides roared, the deep, thunderous rumble of the guns rising and falling like the booming of enormous surf, a roar that voiced the might of sea-power, the wrath of embattled nations and the fate of man. Above the tremendous fury of the turret guns sounded the crackling staccato of the secondary batteries spitting destruction at the German torpedo-craft.

The fire from the British ships was more than could be faced. Scheer once more was forced to reverse his course and once more the High Seas Fleet fled to escape destruction. This was the last engagement between the two main forces of the opposing navies. Jellicoe continued to the south and then to the west, searching everywhere for the enemy, but by the greatest good fortune Scheer's course toward Wilhelmshaven was one that enabled him to reach port without again encountering the British dreadnoughts.

Altogether the British lost three battle cruisers, three armored cruisers and eight destroyers, while the German losses were one battleship, one battle cruiser, four light cruisers and five destroyers—a total of eleven ships to the British fourteen. Many of the remaining German ships were more seriously damaged than the British, however, and the injuries to the entire German fleet were so serious that further fighting would have been difficult.

After the battle of Jutland the High Sea Fleet never again sought action, and made only three half-hearted sorties into the North Sea during the entire remainder of the war—one in August and one in October, 1916, and then for the last time in April, 1918. The spirit of the German fleet was broken by the experience at Jutland, and its officers and men were filled with a never-to-be-forgotten fear of the enormous striking power of the British navy. Command of the North Sea and of all the seas still rested with the British fleet, and, for this reason, the battle of Jutland has rightly been proclaimed a British victory.

28

The Jervis Bay

To the whole world the naval warfare of the second World War has shown that the British seamen of today are true sons of the indomitable sea heroes of old. The courage, the daring and the grim endurance of Drake, Hawke, Rodney, Nelson and a host of others have been reproduced before our very eyes by the officers and men of Britain's present-day naval and merchant ships.

These men have fought their way to victory against desperate odds, as in the battle between the *Ajax, Achilles* and *Exeter* and the far more heavily-armed *Graf Spee*. They have dashed their ships at the enemy's craft whenever the latter have appeared. Gladly and bravely, they have incurred the most terrible risks in order to do their part in winning the war at sea.

Many fiercely stirring naval battles have been fought in the second World War, and there have been many British victories. The *Jervis Bay* did not win her passage at arms against an overwhelming foe; but she did win a battle of the human spirit. Doomed to defeat, her captain and crew fought an unequal battle to the last and gave their lives to save those of the men on the ships the *Jervis Bay* had been charged to protect.

One could look far to find another such sea encounter. Its closest parallel, perhaps, is the battle of the *Revenge* against the massed might of the Spanish fleet—the immortal fight of "the one against fifty-three." But one is reminded too, of the three small British cruisers harrying the pocket battleship *Graf Spee* to her doom and of the ballad written after that occasion by one Charlie Holmes, a stoker on the *Exeter.*

"You've heard of British heroes, bold in air, on land or sea,
  But here's a tale will e'er be told, the fate of the "Admiral Spee."
Thirteenth of December was her unlucky date,
Was then she met the "Exeter" hard by the River Plate.
And though she was the stronger in armaments, indeed,
We'd speed aboard the "Exeter" and men of bulldog breed.
We met as dawn was breaking; she raked us with her shell,
But we put our trust in the turbine's thrust and our faith in Captain Bell."

There were men of bulldog breed on board the *Jervis Bay* when she sailed from a Canadian port on a day late in October, 1940. Before the war she had been a combination freight and passenger liner plying between England and Australia. Upon the outbreak of hostilities she was fitted with five 6-inch guns and manned by a Royal navy crew. The British navy, desperately short of regular cruisers to protect the convoys carrying food and war supplies from overseas, needed as many auxiliary cruisers of the *Jervis Bay* type as it could secure. To be sure, such ships were totally incapable of taking on enemy battleships or heavy cruisers, but they did provide a good measure of defense against submarines, and anti-submarine work was their principal job.

Under the protection of the *Jervis Bay,* as she steamed eastward across the Atlantic, was a convoy of thirty-eight merchant ships. Among them were tankers loaded with oil and gasoline, cargo vessels carry-

ing beef and other foodstuffs and other freighters deep with cargoes of airplanes, army trucks, ammunition and other urgently needed war supplies for Britain. The value of these cargoes ran into the millions of dollars, but even greater than their monetary worth was their value to the support and defense of the United Kingdom, fighting for its life.

For a week or more the convoy proceeded on its way without any untoward occurrence. Out in front, surging heavily through the long north Atlantic swells, the *Jervis Bay* served as a spearhead for the following ships. Since the first day out, her lookouts had kept a constant and vigilant watch for enemy craft of any kind. Their orders were ironclad and were given to them directly by the *Jervis Bay's* commander, Captain Fogarty Fegen, himself the son of a British rear-admiral and a distinguished destroyer commander in the first World War. No one knew better than he the need for a constant watch against surprises when fighting the Hun, and the crew of his ship was thoroughly trained and disciplined in its various wartime duties. Captain Fegen, it is interesting to know, had been specially com-

295

mended, while commanding the cruiser *Suffolk* a few years before the war, for rescuing the crew of the German motorship *Hedwig* after the vessel grounded in a storm in the China Seas.

The afternoon of November the fifth passed quietly, as had all the previous days of the voyage. The short autumn day was drawing to an early close, and all arrangements for steaming through the coming night were being completed, when a distant noise, as of an explosion, was heard by those aboard the *Jervis Bay*. It was to the northward and all eyes turned in that direction. Captain Fegen was just raising his binoculars to his eyes when he heard the whine of shells whistling through the air. The next moment three huge spouts of water rose in the air as the shells plunged into the sea. They fell close beside the big two-funneled *Rangitiki,* a passenger liner previously on the Canada-Australia run.

At once the *Rangitiki* wireless operator sent out his message *"Rangitiki* being shelled," giving the latitude and longitude. The convoy was then in mid-Atlantic and it was possible that some British battleship or cruiser might be within reach. The wireless sets of the other ships went into action, too. "Convoy being shelled by German raider. Convoy being shelled." Listeners in all parts of the world grew tense, as they picked up the ominous messages, telling of danger to Britain's life-line.

Captain Fegen sized up the situation rapidly. Far to the north he could see through his binoculars the fighting-top of the raider, lit by the rays of the setting sun. Her hull was obscured by the gathering darkness, but at regular intervals there glowed through the gloom the white-hot flames of her turret guns. She was a big ship; there was no doubt of that. More than a match for the *Jervis Bay*. The geysers thrown aloft by her shells showed that her guns were 11-inch or longer. She could be one of the two remaining pocket-battleships, the *Admiral Scheer* or *Lützow;* or she might be one of the two recently completed German battleships *Scharnhorst* or *Gneisenau.* Formidable craft, all four of them, armed with 11-inch guns and well protected by armor plate. The *Jervis Bay* could do them little harm, and her own unarmored sides offered no protection against the raider's heavy guns.

Within a few moments Captain Fegen had planned his course of action. The *Jervis Bay's* wireless crackled shrilly as he ordered the convoy: "Scatter and get away in the darkness. I will engage the enemy!"

Great clouds of smoke poured from the *Jervis Bay's* funnel as she gathered speed. At the same time she dropped dozens of smoke floats to hide the merchantmen from the enemy. The *Rangitiki* was now in flames, and shells were falling all around the other ships. Suddenly the *Jervis Bay,* now plunging ahead at her utmost speed, turned sharply to the left and raced toward the attacking raider.

"I think everybody aboard was proud as our ship turned to the enemy," said one of her surviving officers. "Our captain knew just what we were going to get, but it didn't matter."

The *Jervis Bay's* guns now came into play and repeated the flashes of the enemy, lighting up the darkness with red-orange tongues of flame. The raider's fire control officers studied this unexpected antagonist through their glasses and shifted the range. One of the 11-inch salvos crashed aboard the British ship with terrible effect. She shuddered under the impact, righted herself and plunged doggedly on. Then she was hit again.

"I saw the *Jervis Bay* flaming after the first few shots," said one of the merchant ship captains.

And, as Lieutenant Sargeant, a survivor, reported: "The German fired two salvos which missed us but the third hit a bit for'ard, carrying away one gun. I was told the bridge had been blown away. Then the *Jervis Bay* took a direct hit, completely destroying the control room. Within the first fifteen minutes we were completely disabled and for another half hour we were being hit. It was just firing practice for them."

With her main stearing gear wrecked, her boats shot away, her bridge and deckhouses a shambles of twisted steel and afire in a dozen places, the old ship staggered on, firing whatever guns could be brought to bear on the raider. A shell carried away her White Ensign, but a seaman clambered aloft and lashed another to her mainmast. Early in the battle Captain Fegen's right arm was carried away by a shell splinter. Despite this, he made his way aft to the hand steering wheel to con the ship and handle her so that as many guns as possible could be kept directed toward the enemy. Wishing to see how things were faring in other parts of the ship, he started forward along the blazing deck. No one recalled seeing him after that.

Soon it was evident that the ship would shortly be a blazing inferno from stem to stern, and the stokers were ordered to come on deck. "When I went up," said Stoker Beaman after his rescue, "the forward part of the ship was a chambles. Dead and wounded were lying around and the ship was afire. There was not a sign of panic."

The *Jervis Bay*

Badly holed below the water-line and filling rapidly, it was evident that the *Jervis Bay* would have to be abandoned. While the water poured in below and the hot flames raged ever more fiercely, the British gunners kept on firing. Soon the decks were awash. Only one gun, on the forecastle, was still able to fire and barked defiance. As the water washed about the feet of its crew, an officer gave the command to abandon ship. Sixty-one men, all that were left of a crew of some four hundred, responded to the order. The one remaining boat and four life rafts were put over the side, as another salvo crashed aboard, ripping and tearing the *Jervis Bay's* remaining steelwork. Just before she took her final plunge, with her colors still lashed to the mast and illuminated by the flames, the boats and rafts got clear and drifted away into the darkness.

"After we abandoned ship I did see figures on the bridge," said one survivor. "I guess they were dead. When the ship started her last plunge I could see some of them dropping off into the sea. I was on the boat deck. I jumped from there, about 40 feet. So long as we have men like the captain and the brave lads that went down, Jerry can never lick us."

Stoker Stevens, swimming resolutely, was overlooked by those in the life boat, but found a wooden hatch cover to which he clung for ten hours. "The old *Jervis Bay*," he said, "went down while I was only 100 yards away. Gosh, I was proud of her!"

As the cold north Atlantic waves swirled over the sinking ship, extinguishing her fires, the raider hastened to search for the other ships of the convoy, sending up star shells to help discover them. But by that time they had scattered far and wide. The *Jervis Bay* had done her work well. Only four of the merchantmen were sunk. Thirty-four reached port safely together with their precious cargoes. One of these, the Swedish vessel *Stureholm,* came in later than the others, after she had been given up as lost. Deeply moved by the heroism of those on board the *Jervis Bay,* her master, Captain Sven Olander, had turned back and, creeping along beneath the raider's star shells, had found and rescued the *Jervis Bay's* survivors. "They did so well for us, I did not like to leave them," said Captain Olander. "I'll never forget it. It was glorious."

So runs the story of a British captain and crew who doomed themselves to die to save the ships they guarded. Those in the *Jervis Bay* knew they had no chance. Their first thought was for the others. They accomplished their mission and died in sacrificial glory amidst the flames of a defeat that was a victory. Such losses are England's gain. Each one strengthens a tradition which becomes invincible.

29

The British Navy in Battle

THE British navy is today the world's largest and most powerful. But it also has the world's greatest responsibilities—the protection of the far-flung British Empire, the guarding of the convoys taking supplies to Britain and the responsibility of destroying the naval forces of the enemy powers. The navy must play its part in defending England against invasion; it must maintain the sea blockade against the Axis powers to keep them from getting foodstuffs and strategic raw materials from abroad, and it must overcome the menace of the submarine and the surface raider. In addition, it must cooperate whenever and wherever possible with the Empire's armies.

All this adds up to an enormous task. The British navy has been equal to it.

The moment war was declared, the navy went into action. Merchant vessels bound for the British Isles were formed into convoys at such rendezvous as Cape Town, Gibraltar and Halifax, and were guarded against U-boat attack by cruisers and destroyers. Minelayers mined the entrances of German harbors and naval bases. Enemy merchant ships were seized by British cruisers or chased into neutral harbors. Heavy cruisers and destroyers patroled the North Sea and the English Channel, searching for enemy surface craft and subma-

301

rines. In November, 1939, Winston Churchill, then First Lord of the Admiralty, was able to report that the navy was sinking from two to four German submarines a week. In the background, veiled in the mists of Scapa Flow, the battleships lay with steam up ready to put to sea at an instant's notice, should the enemy's heavy craft attempt a raid on North Sea shipping or the English coast.

It was during the early months of the war that the navy suffered its most serious losses in large first-line ships. The aircraft carrier *Courageous* was torpedoed off the coast of Ireland, and the battleship *Royal Oak* was sunk while at anchor in Scapa Flow by a submarine that penetrated the nets and other defenses under cover of darkness.

While the world was still shocked by these reverses, there came the glorious news of the defeat of the pocket-battleship *Graf Spee* by the three British cruisers *Exeter, Ajax* and *Achilles.* The *Spee,* under the command of Captain Hans Langsdorff, had slipped out of Wilhelmshaven in August, nearly a month before the German attack on Poland and Britain's entry into the war. On Wednesday, December the thirteenth, she arrived off the Uruguayan coast after a raiding cruise in the south Atlantic and off the east coast of Africa, during which she had sunk or captured nine British and neutral merchant ships.

The British, needing their cruisers in every part of the world at once, had only a light force off the South American coast. A little after dawn on the morning of December the thirteenth, three ships of the British squadron were steaming in toward the River Plate. They were the two light cruisers *Ajax* and *Achilles,* each armed with eight 6-inch guns, and the heavy cruiser *Exeter* whose main battery consisted of

six 8-inch guns. No one of these ships was a match for the *Graf Spee* with her 11-inch turret guns. Well handled, the raider, by keeping out of range of the British cruisers' guns, could hammer all three of them to pieces without being scratched herself.

At about half-past six, the lookouts on the German ship sighted the masts of the *Exeter* over the horizon to the southeast. Langsdorff undoubtedly was confident of an easy victory. The raider's sirens screamed, ordering her men to their battle stations. Officers hurried to the conning tower, to range finders and to the inside of the turrets. Deep below in the engine room the telegraph clanged "Full speed ahead." The ammunition hoists were set in motion, and the six great turret guns were loaded and swung out over the port side.

Now the lookouts saw smoke on the eastern horizon, and soon were able to make out the low, lean hulls and broad funnels of the *Ajax* and *Achilles*. Six-inch gun cruisers. Well, they too should be easy to batter to pieces. Captain Langsdorff and his officers were not disturbed. At her full speed of twenty-six knots, the *Spee* tore on to the south to close in on the *Exeter*. At the same time her fire-control officers kept a close watch on the *Ajax* and *Achilles,* now plunging along on a roughly parallel course some twelve miles off the *Spee's* port beam.

At 6:18 A. M., four minutes after sighting the enemy, the *Spee's* forward turret guns thundered a salyo at the *Exeter*. The range was twenty thousand yards, ten sea miles. Three minutes later the *Exeter* roared a reply, and then the *Ajax* and *Achilles,* rapidly closing the range, attacked with their starboard broadsides.

The first German salvo fell short of the *Exeter,* the next was over. The third straddled the target, and splinters from the shells tore through the funnels, and damaged the fire control communication system. Again the *Spee* thundered and two of her 700-pound shells crashed into the *Exeter,* smashing her bridge and killing almost every-one on it. But the *Exeter* was now finding the target and shooting magnificently. One of her shells ripped through the *Spee's* control tower, the nerve center of her fire-control system. Others tore holes in her sides and exploded inside her hull, filling the ship with acrid fumes.

Meanwhile, the *Ajax* and *Achilles* were firing their broadsides as fast as the guns could be loaded. Their shells were hitting the mark, some of them driving through the raider's armor, others exploding against her sides. Langsdorff was getting more than he had bargained for. While his turret guns concentrated on the *Exeter,* he ordered his secondary battery to reply to the smaller cruisers. Again the *Spee's* forward guns thundered, and two more of her shells hit the *Exeter* squarely, the impact shaking her like a leaf. These shells crashed into her forward turrets and put four of her six big guns out of action. Fires were started inside the turrets, and the gun crews struggled to smother them before they could reach the magazines. The *Exeter's* decks were now a shambles. All voice tubes and electric signals were smashed. Her captain was sending his orders by messengers who groped their way through blinding smoke and clambered over the twisted wreckage of her deckhouses.

The battle had now lasted for fifteen minutes. Seeing that the *Exeter* was badly damaged, Langsdorff ordered one 11-inch turret to fire at the *Ajax* and *Achilles* alternately. But the fire control was poor, and the two cruisers traveling at thirty-two knots were not hit. Eight minutes later the German ship laid her first smoke screen and disappeared behind it, showing the British that their fire had been effective. This first phase of the battle concluded at 6:38 A. M. and left the *Exeter* considerably damaged, the *Ajax* and *Achilles* unharmed.

Plunging through the smoke, the British cruisers once again sighted the fleeing *Spee*. The *Exeter* closed in and blazed away with her remaining guns. But the Germans once more concentrated a terrific fire on her from their main battery, which tore open her hull, slowed her speed, and finally silenced her two remaining guns. The gallant ship dropped slowly astern, while her crew struggled with the fires on board and shored up her many weakened bulkheads.

Commodore Harwood, commander of the *Ajax,* now made the decision to close in, despite the danger of total destruction, should a German salvo strike his ship. The two cruisers dashed on to within five miles of the *Spee,* at which distance they brought all their guns to bear. It was then that the *Achilles* outdid herself in accurate shooting. An officer on the *Ajax* reported that "the *Achilles* was making magnificent shooting. She was straddling continuously, her spread was very small, and she was scoring hit after hit."

However, after five minutes the *Ajax* was hit by an 11-inch shell which put both her rear turrets out of action. Only three of her eight guns were now in action, and after another fifteen minutes, with the range approaching four miles—point-blank range for an 11-inch gun— Commodore Harwood determined to withdraw to a safer distance. The two British cruisers retired behind smoke screens and then settled down to shadow the *Spee.* The German ship still tore on at full speed, laying smoke screens from time to time and occasionally thundering at her pursuers with her after-turret guns. Through the rest of the morning and through the long afternoon, the *Spee* ran for Montevideo, a neutral port of refuge. Toward evening the *Ajax* and *Achilles* ran to shoreward of the raider and closed the range. Those on the *Spee* could not see them against the dark outline of the coast, but the battleship was clearly visible in the rays of the setting sun. Once again the cruisers fired and hit the target. Then they worked to seaward in order to force the *Spee* into the River Plate.

At ten o'clock the *Spee* ran into the river and shortly after anchored off Montevideo. Outside, the weary British sailors took up their watch and prepared their ships for a renewal of the battle. The *Spee* would be allowed two or three days to make repairs, according to international law. Then she would have to leave port and the two British cruisers would have to take up the unequal fight again. Fortunately, however, they were reenforced the next day by the 8-inch gun cruiser

Cumberland, which had come up under forced draft from the Falkland Islands.

The next day, Thursday, passed, and Friday and Saturday. While shipyard workers were repairing the raider's damaged plates, Captain Langsdorff talked several times with Berlin by telephone. On Sunday afternoon he transferred most of his crew to the *Tacoma,* a German merchant vessel, and at five-thirty weighed anchor. Word of her departure was brought to the British cruisers, and Commodore Harwood signalled the *Achilles* and *Cumberland*: "My object—destruction." Tensely those aboard the cruisers waited for their antagonist to come in sight. But, to their astonishment and that of the entire world, Langsdorff blew up his ship as soon as he had cleared the river mouth. And so, with the ignominious scuttling of the pocket-battleship *Graf Spee,* ended the Battle of the River Plate. Even now, say British naval officers, they cannot figure out why the Germans did it.

A sequel to the battle took place two months later when the German tanker *Altmark,* which had repeatedly fueled the *Spee* during her raiding cruise, crept down the Norwegian coast bound for a German port. On board her were some three hundred British merchant marine officers and sailors taken by the *Spee* from the vessels she had sunk. One night, while the *Altmark* was sheltering in Josing Fjord, a darkened British destroyer crept up to her side. It was the *Cossack.* She had come to rescue the prisoners. A landing platform was thrown over the *Altmark's* rail and thirty of the *Cossack's* men, armed to the teeth, rushed to her deck. No quarter was asked or given in the short, fierce fight that followed. The *Altmark's* crew was driven to bay; the hatches were thrown open, and the three hundred prisoners streamed up to the deck and were taken aboard the *Cossack*. It was as dramatic a rescue as any in the annals of naval history, and a glorious demonstration of the navy's courage and daring.

Soon after this encounter, in early April, 1940, the Germans commenced their invasion of Norway, and Britain countered by sending an expeditionary force across the North Sea convoyed by the navy. Under terrific attacks by the German air force, the British and allied troops were landed, only to be forced to evacuate a month later, as the Germans threw increasing thousands of soldiers into the campaign.

During the early days of the battle for Norway, the navy saw furious action, as it sought to interrupt the flow of German troops and supplies to Norwegian ports and to destroy the German warships on the coast. The story starts on Sunday night, April the seventh. The main British fleet was at anchor in Scapa Flow, but three minelaying squadrons, composed chiefly of destroyers, were steaming through the darkness to lay mine fields in Norwegian waters. Somewhere to the north of them lay a strong British covering force, sent out to protect the minelayers until their work was completed.

During Sunday night reconnaissance aircraft of the Royal Air Force reported that German battleships with a number of cruisers, destroyers and other craft were at sea. Blinker signals winked from the *Rodney* and Admiral Sir Charles Forbes, commander of the Home Fleet, took the Grand Fleet out into the North Sea. South and east they swept throughout the night, with the object of getting between the German ships and their bases.

The *Glowworm,* one of the British minelaying destroyers, made the first contact with the German fleet. She had lost a man overboard on Sunday afternoon and had stopped to pick him up, letting the other ships go on ahead. Hurrying to rejoin her squadron, she sighted at 8 A.M. Monday first one, then two German destroyers. Wheeling to a parallel course, she opened fire, at the same time reporting the action to the admiralty in London. Minute by minute she described her progress. Suddenly she reported an unknown German ship ahead. Her last message ended in mid-sentence. No more was heard from her and it is believed that she was overwhelmed by a vastly superior enemy force.

Meanwhile, the Grand Fleet was sweeping up the Norwegian coast from the south. It was blowing a gale, and heavy seas combined with mist reduced the visibility to a very small area around the ships. No German vessels were sighted throughout the morning and afternoon of Monday. Early Tuesday morning, when the fleet was off the harbor of Bergen, the Germans launched a furious dive-bombing attack. Scores of planes screamed down to within a few feet of the British battleships, and were met with an inferno of anti-aircraft shells from the warships' multiple pom-poms. The attack was a failure. One 1,000-pound bomb hit the *Rodney,* but her heavy deck plating stood the test and she was undamaged. Two cruisers were slightly damaged by bomb splinters.

There was one other British casualty. Five air attacks were pressed home against the cruiser *Aurora.* All were beaten off by heavy anti-aircraft fire, but the Tribal class destroyer *Ghurka,* fighting alongside the *Aurora,* was heavily hit and sank in four and a half hours. She fired her anti-aircraft guns until her deck was awash. All but fourteen of her crew were saved.

Meanwhile, on Tuesday, other actions were being carried out. In the afternoon the *Zulu,* a sister-ship of the *Ghurka,* sank a German submarine near the Orkneys. And early that morning the battle cruiser *Renown,* pounding through heavy seas and snow squalls, sighted two German ships—the *Scharnhorst,* one of Germany's two 26,000-ton battleships, and a 10,000-ton Admiral Hipper class cruiser. The *Renown,* laboring in the violent seas and with snow blurring her sights, opened fire at 18,000 yards. For three minutes her great 15-inch guns thundered, and then the *Scharnhorst* replied and simultaneously turned away. After six minutes more firing, those on the *Renown* saw their shells strike the enemy's control tower. The *Scharnhorst* then stopped firing, but a minute or two later resumed again with her after-turret, presumably under local control.

At top speed the *Scharnhorst* fled, while after her at twenty-four knots plunged the *Renown,* leaving her escorting destroyers far behind pitching into the steep seas. During this chase a German shell passed clear through the *Renown's* hull above the water-line without exploding. A few moments later a tall column of smoke rose from the *Scharnhorst,* leading the *Renown's* crew to believe they had scored another hit. A German cruiser now steamed at high speed across the wake of the flying battleship and laid a smoke screen. The *Renown* continued firing, but the swifter enemy craft were able to draw ahead and finally disappeared in the murk to the westward.

On the following day, Wednesday, April tenth, five British destroyers raided Narvik, the northern Norwegian port at which German ships loaded iron ore, needed for munitions. Within the port were six heavy German destroyers and a number of supply ships. German marines had been landed the day before. Captain B. A. W. Warburton-Lee, in command of the British flotilla, led his ships through narrow Narvik Fjord to the inner harbor and opened fire with all his batteries. One enemy destroyer was sunk, several were damaged, and all the supply ships were sent to the bottom—the real object of the raid. Two of the British destroyers, the *Hardy* and *Hunter,* were sunk. On the way out to the sea, the remaining three blew up a German ammunition ship.

Meanwhile, on the same day, bombers of the Fleet Air Arm attacked two German light cruisers lying at anchor in the harbor of Bergen, covering a landing party. One of the cruisers, the *Königsberg*, was hit squarely amidships. Smoke and flames enveloped the stricken ship, water poured in through her fractured plates, and in less than ten minutes she sank.

On April the thirteenth, three days after the first raid on Narvik, a strong British force consisting of the battleship *Warspite* and nine destroyers was sent to the port to destroy the shore batteries set up by the Germans and sink the remaining German destroyers. It was a risky task to take the big *Warspite* through the narrow fjord leading to the harbor, especially since the waiting destroyers might use their torpedoes.

With destroyers acting as a screen, the *Warspite's* planes flying out ahead and the destroyer *Icarus* leading the van, the squadron started up the fjord at noon. The first contact was made at 12:26 P. M. when a German destroyer steamed out of the mist on the south side of the fjord. The *Icarus, Bedouin, Punjabi* and *Cossack* (the same *Cossack* that rescued the *Altmark's* prisoners) opened fire, and the enemy turned away and was lost to sight.

At 12:45 another German destroyer loomed out of the mist, and five minutes later another appeared. The British destroyers engaged both, and a few minutes later the *Warspite* opened fire. As the squadron moved on, engaging the two Germans with all their strength, a British plane reported that another German destroyer was coming down the fjord. She was soon sighted, and the *Bedouin*, *Punjabi* and *Eskimo* dashed ahead to attack her. In eight minutes the rain of British shells set her afire in three places, but she kept on firing with a single gun until a salvo from the *Warspite* silenced her.

Meanwhile, more German destroyers appeared until all told there were six. As the *Warspite* swung into position close to shore to shell the land batteries and harbor works, the British destroyers engaged the enemy in a spectacular running fight. The British fire was superior and within half an hour, two of the German craft had been destroyed. The four remaining destroyers then fled up Rombaks Fjord, with the *Eskimo, Hero, Icarus, Forester* and *Bedouin* in hot pursuit. Half-way up the ten-mile long fjord, the *Eskimo* put one of the Germans out of action. Storming on, the British at last found the three others against the ice at the end of Rombaks Fjord. For a few minutes the British ships laid down a barrage of destruction. Then all was over. The German destroyers, already crippled in the encounter, were done for.

The British craft made their way back to Narvik harbor, where they found that the *Warspite* had completed her work, and was ready to depart. Every German merchant vessel and warcraft that had been in Narvik harbor had been sunk, and the shore batteries had been demolished. Three of the British destroyers had been hit, but none was lost. As the late afternoon sun sank slowly toward the western horizon, the squadron threaded its way down the fjord to the open sea and made good its return to England.

There followed the German invasion of France and the Low Countries and Italy's entry into the war. To the whole democratic world, one of the gravest possibilities resulting from the overthrow of France was that the Germans would gain control of the French navy. At that time the French navy, discouraged and uncertain, held the balance of naval power over the entire world. Added to the navies of Germany, Italy and Japan, it would have made a total naval strength superior to that of Great Britain and the United States combined. As time went on, it seemed more and more probable that, by the use of threats, harsh treatment of French prisoners or other means, the Germans would be able to force the French to hand over their navy. Finally, toward the end of June, 1940, the danger seemed imminent. The British Admiralty decided to act.

On July the third a British battle squadron of three capital ships, three cruisers and one aircraft carrier under the command of Vice Admiral Sir James Somerville, appeared off the Algerian harbor of Oran, in which the bulk of the French fleet was riding at anchor. Here were the giant battle cruisers *Dunkerque* and *Strasbourg,* the battleships *Provence* and *Bretagne,* and a number of cruisers and destroyers. From the British battle cruiser *Hood*, the flagship, a launch set out and ran speedily into the harbor, coming to rest at the accommodation ladder of the *Dunkerque*. A British officer, Captain C. S. Holland, stepped briskly up the ladder and requested to see the French senior officer present, Vice-Admiral Gensoul. To him, Captain Holland stated the British position. There was no wish to harm or attack the French ships; but they must not be delivered to the Germans. The Admiral could, therefore, take his choice of surrendering, scuttling his ships, or taking them to the French West Indies. If none of these alternatives were accepted, the British would be compelled to open fire and endeavor to destroy the French ships in battle.

Admiral Gensoul flatly rejected the British demands, but retired to discuss the situation with his officers. Shortly after noon, he asked for more time for consideration. The British gave him till three o'clock. This hour passed, and the admiral sent no word. The British waited. Surely, it seemed, he and his staff would decide to accept one of the proposals which did not involve the destruction of the fleet. But the French admiral apparently thought the British were bluffing. The afternoon wore on, and he still gave no indication of his attitude. Just before 6:00 P. M. the British opened fire.

Steaming in to close range, the battle cruiser *Hood* hurled her 15-inch broadsides at the French *Bretagne*. In a few minutes she was on fire and two great columns of smoke and flame surged upward from her blazing fuel oil. Now salvos from the other British ships screamed into the harbor. The *Dunkerque,* pride of the French fleet, got slowly under way, but was hit repeatedly and, enveloped in flames, was run aground. Fifteen-inch shells then crashed into the *Provence.* She, too, was set on fire and, an hour after firing commenced, was a gutted, smoking hulk.

Meanwhile, a group of destroyers had gotten under way and steamed toward the northeastern entrance of the harbor, laying down a dense smoke screen to hide the *Strasbourg*, sister ship of the *Dun-*

kerque. The British cruisers poured their broadsides into the smoke. Two of the destroyers were sunk. But the remainder escaped, and behind their smoke screen the *Strasbourg* and five French cruisers also were able to get away. British planes from the aircraft carrier *Ark Royal* launched torpedoes at the *Strasbourg* and reported at least one hit, but the huge ship survived and raced ahead toward the open sea. At top speed the fugitive squadron streaked northward across the Mediterranean to seek refuge in the harbor of Toulon.

Thus, of France's four capital ships at Oran, three were sunk or beached, and out of the reach of Germany's clutching hands. Three days later British planes bombed the grounded *Dunkerque*. Meanwhile, the French had voluntarily delivered to Great Britain three other battleships, the *Lorraine, Courbet* and *Paris*, and six cruisers, and more than two hundred smaller ships—torpedo boats, minesweepers, patrol vessels and submarine chasers. There remained only two French battleships, the *Richelieu* and the partly-finished *Jean Bart*. A week after the Oran battle, the British damaged the *Richelieu* at Dakar. The *Jean Bart* was reported at Casablanca, but was not attacked.

There was little rejoicing over the battle in England. It had been a matter of grim necessity, of self-defense against an unscrupulous foe. The British people were relieved, but not elated. As Prime Minister Winston Churchill said, the battle was "a melancholy action."

Two weeks after the Battle of Oran, a British ship scored the first major success against Italian surface warships. And, symbolical of the Empire's unity in the face of a common enemy, it was the Australian cruiser *Sydney* that bore the brunt of the action. Early in the morning of July the nineteenth the *Sydney,* while patroling with four destroyers north of Crete, sighted two of the Italian navy's sleek, incredibly speedy light cruisers. They proved to be the 6- inch gun cruisers *Bartolomeo Colleoni* and the *Giovanni Delle Bande Nere.* Their main armament was the same as that of the *Sydney.*

The instant that the Italian cruisers sighted the British ships, they started to speed away toward the southwest in an effort to escape action. As their maximum speed was forty knots, they were able to get off to a flying start. But the *Sydney,* working up to her full speed of thirty-two knots, hurtled after them, firing first at one and then the other.

The *Bande Nere* "turned tail in a hurry," said one of the Sydney's officers, "but the *Bartolomeo Colleoni* tarried long enough to answer our fire." Shells from the *Sydney's* forward guns struck the *Bande Nere* several times, but none of the hits were in a vital spot. Fleeing for dear life, with a long plume of black smoke trailing behind her the Italian cruiser made good her inglorious escape.

The *Colleoni* was not so fortunate. Even though her speed permitted her rapidly to open out the range, the *Sydney* continued to hit her. None of the *Colleoni's* salvos found their mark. Within a few minutes of the beginning of the chase, a huge cloud of white steam shot up from the *Colleoni's* decks. The boilers had been hit. She slowed down immediately. Her one chance of escape—the superior speed with which her builders had endowed her—was gone. She could still, however, have fought her guns and hurled a murderous fire at the oncoming *Sydney.* Instead, as one of the *Sydney's* officers reported, "the Italian commander ordered the crew to abandon ship because they had started stripping themselves of clothing and flinging themselves overboard, then crying for us to save them."

As the *Sydney* checked her speed and lowered boats to pick up the hundreds of Italian sailors struggling in the water, the British destroyers dashed on toward the wounded quarry. When at close range, they loosed torpedoes. One of these penetrated to the *Colleoni's* magazines. There was a terrific explosion and the slim grey-hulled craft commenced to settle. She was done for.

The destroyers immediately lowered boats and commenced to rescue those who had leaped overboard after the fated hit. Hundreds of them were thrashing the water and calling for help and the destroyers' boats were fully occupied.

In the midst of the rescue work, the roar of airplane motors was heard overhead. It was a flight of Italian bombers. Crossing and recrossing the British ships, they "let loose everything they had." "We carried on with our efforts to rescue the Italians," the *Sydney's* officers related upon their return to Alexandria. "The Italian planes kept up their bombardment until nightfall."

Further comment would be superfluous.

In October the *Ajax,* which played so gallant a part in the battle with the *Graf Spee,* saw lively action again. A section of the British Mediterranean fleet was making one of its periodic sweeps of "Mare Nostrum." Far out ahead of the capital ships and aircraft carriers, light cruisers were spread out to serve as the eyes of the fleet, to contact and report the position of any Italian warships that might be out.

Late one afternoon the *Ajax* sighted a flotilla of fast Italian torpedo boats. As they rushed in at full speed, the *Ajax* met them with a hail of fire that sank two of their number. The torpedo boats wheeled and darted off, with the *Ajax* in hot pursuit. On she pounded, intent on picking off more of the torpedo boats or of following them to larger Italian ships. As dusk was closing in, the shapes of enemy vessels were seen ahead. The bow guns of the *Ajax* thundered, and one of the ships was seen to be hit. Red flashes stabbed through the darkness as the other Italian ships, before retreating, poured a brief but intense fire on the British cruiser. One of the salvos struck the *Ajax,* and damaged her slightly. Her speed was slowed, and for the time being she could not resume the action.

But other British ships had been summoned by wireless, and in a short while the heavy cruiser *York* arrived on the scene. All through the night the two ships cruised to and fro near the scene of the action, hoping that at dawn there might be further contact with the enemy. At sunrise several ships were sighted. The British cruisers sped toward them, and found that they were a group of Italian destroyers towing the destroyer damaged by the *Ajax*. She proved to be the crack 1620-ton *Artigiere*. As the cruisers approached the towing destroyers cast off and hurried away, leaving the *Artigiere* to her fate.

She was finished off by the *York*. The British ship's commander gave the Italian's crew half an hour to abandon ship. Then, at short range, the *York's* 8-inch guns blasted the doomed ship, hammering her to pieces and finally exploding her magazine. As the *Artigiere* sank, the *York* radioed the position of the Italian survivors on an Italian commercial wave length, thus giving her own position to Italian bombers if any cared to attack. None appeared. Satisfied with their work, the *York* and *Ajax* steamed back to their base.

Just one month later, on November the twelfth, the navy carried out its daring attack on Taranto, the major base of the Italian fleet. An imposing squadron of British warships had first completed a 4000-mile sweep of the Mediterranean, searching for Italian craft. None had been found. Well and good. If the Italian ships would not come out, the British would carry the attack to them where they lay at anchor.

On the evening of November twelfth, the aircraft carriers *Eagle* and *Illustrious* steamed into the Bay of Taranto, shielded by darkness from possible Italian scouting planes or bombers. Behind them, the rest of the British squadron deployed in a wide semicircle. From the aircraft carriers' decks, one plane after another, each carrying a 2100-pound torpedo, took off and sped through the darkness toward Taranto harbor. Here they found the bulk of Italy's battleships and nearly a hundred lighter warships.

The British planes caught the Italians like sitting birds, their anchors down, their crews asleep or on shore. Skimming low over the water they loosed their torpedoes and the harbor was suddenly a turmoil of thunderous explosions and skyward-leaping flames. The results were disastrous for the Italian navy. Three of its six battle-ships were crippled. One 35,000-ton battleship of the *Littorio* class—of which Italy had two—was left listing heavily to starboard, with her bow so deep under water that her forecastle was covered. A 2300-ton battleship, one of the four *Cavour* class ships, lay beached, her stern submerged and her after-turret awash. Another battleship of the *Cavour* type was severely damaged, and in addition, two cruisers and two supply ships were hit and crippled.

During the remainder of the year 1940, the Mediterranean fleet was almost continually active. An Italian convoy was attacked in the Straits of Otranto, between Italy and Albania. One ship was sunk, two were set afire, and a fourth was damaged. A British submarine attacked a convoy of supply ships on its way to Libya, sent one vessel to the bottom and hit another. When General Wavell's troops commenced their victorious westward march across eastern Libya early in December, the navy followed the coastline and played an active part in driving the Italians from their strongholds. Sidi Barrani fell on December eleventh, Bardia on January fifth, and Tobruk on January twenty-first. At each of these battles, as later at Derna and Bengasi, the navy operated in closest coordination with the army and air force, hurling shells into Italian troop concentrations and gun emplacements to help prepare the ground for the attacking troops. One of the vessels that did yeoman service in this campaign was the old British monitor *Terror,* which, in the first World War, many times shelled German-held Ostend and Zeebrugge, then being used as U-boat bases.

The scene of spectacular naval activity shifted now two thousand miles to the north where, on March the fourth, 1941, the navy carried out the most successful hit-and-run invasion of German-held territory up to that date. Early in the morning of the fourth, five British destroyers and two transports steamed quietly up Norway's Vestfjord to Svolvoer, the principal fishing port of the Lofoten Islands. Picked British soldiers, with "Free Norwegian" marines as guides, climbed down the sides of the transports into specially-designed "invasion barges." These were flat-bottomed boats which carried fifty men apiece and were propelled by Diesel engines. Their bows were fitted with high steel shields perforated with holes through which automatic rifles and machine guns could be fired.

In the darkness just preceding dawn, the barges moved in to the shore and landed their soldiers. Six groups went at once to the six Svolvoer plants in which the Germans were extracting fish oil to be made into glycerine for high explosives and codfish oil for food. Within fifteen minutes the plants had been blown up with dynamite bombs. The British then systematically fired all of the port's oil-storage tanks, destroyed the German seaplane base and radio station, and sank eleven German ships that were waiting to load oil cargoes for the Reich. With the exception of a small armed German trawler, no resistance was offered.

Searching through the town, British patrols then rounded up all the Germans and a group of Norwegian "Quislings." These were taken to England as prisoners. As they were being put on board the British ships, the townspeople on the quay went wild with excitement and shouted "Hurrah! Our friends are here!" and "Drown the Nazis and Quislings!" Also on board the British ships went some three hundred Norwegian volunteers, eager to get to England where they could continue to fight against the common enemy.

Three weeks went by following the Svolvoer raid without another important naval action. Then, on March twenty-eighth there came another tremendous blow at Italy's naval strength and national prestige—a naval disaster even worse than Taranto. In the pre-dawn hours of the twenty-seventh, the Italian eastern Mediterranean fleet was steaming eastward, apparently on German orders, to attack a British convoy on its way to Greece. Shortly after daylight it was spotted by British planes and submarines. These radioed messages at once to Admiral Sir Andrew Cunningham at Alexandria, and early in the afternoon the British eastern Mediterranean fleet steamed out to sea.

The Italians, depending chiefly on land-based aircraft, were totally ignorant of the British fleet's approach. But British planes watched the Italians' every move. Late in the afternoon, they were able to report a piece of good news. The Italian fleet had split into two squadrons. One of these steered to the northeast toward Greece, while the other steamed on a course that would bring it to the island of Crete. Admiral Cunningham decided to attack the southern squadron, which was the closest. In this group, the reconnaissance planes reported, there were eight cruisers, a large battleship, probably the 35,000-ton *Vittorio Veneto,* and a number of destroyers. The British had three battleships, the *Warspite, Barham* and *Valiant,* four cruisers, the aircraft carrier *Formidable,* and a dozen destroyers.

All through the day and night of the twenty-seventh the fleets steamed toward each other at a speed of twenty knots. Early the next morning, their advanced scouting forces made contact southeast of Cape Matapan in Greece. Admiral Cunningham had sent some of his light cruisers and a few destroyers on ahead to find the Italians and, if possible, lure them to the eastward to the guns of the slower battleships. The plan worked to perfection.

A few minutes after 8 A. M. the British cruiser *Orion,* commanded by Admiral Henry D. Pridham-Whipple, sighted the enemy force. The *Orion* wheeled and sped back to the eastward. The Italians followed in hot pursuit. For nearly an hour the cruisers plunged ahead at full speed. Then, having outdistanced the enemy, they turned and once more steamed toward them, as if bent on estimating their force. For some time, the Italian cruisers seemed to hesitate. Whether they suspected a trap is not known. But as the cruisers approached again, they abruptly changed course, turning 180 degrees and steaming off to the northwest. In all probability, they had decided to return to the *Vittorio Veneto,* which it was their mission to protect.

After them steamed the British cruisers, determined to keep them interested in her activities until the British battleships, now pounding westward at their utmost speed, could reach the scene. At ten fifty-eight A. M. the *Orion* sighted the *Vittorio Veneto,* sixteen miles to the north, and immediately radioed Admiral Cunningham on the *Warspite.* For a half hour more the little cruisers raced toward the Italians. As they closed down the range, the *Vittorio Veneto* roared with her after 15-inch turret guns. Great geysers of water leaped upward where the shells struck, but the *Orion* pressed on unscathed. Again and again the huge guns thundered; but the cruisers seemed to bear charmed lives and received no hits.

Now Admiral Cunningham, seeing that the Italians were bent on escape, ordered the *Formidable* to unleash her torpedo planes. From the carrier's decks there rose a swarm of swift swordfish torpedo bombers. Straight toward the *Vittorio Veneto* they charged, drove through an inferno of anti-aircraft fire to within two hundred yards and loosed their deady missiles. Hit squarely and crippled, the huge battleship turned heavily, changing course to head for her Taranto base. Around her clustered the cruisers and destroyers, belching forth smoke screens to hide her from the planes.

After returning to the *Formidable* for more torpedoes, the planes attacked again during the afternoon. Screaming down through the smoke, the bombers harried the battleship for more than two hours. When evening came it was known that she had been struck by at least four torpedoes and had suffered serious underwater damage. Hits had also been scored on one or more of the cruisers.

Night fell, and the British course was still to the westward. Possibly contact might be made during the hours of darkness. Otherwise, the enemy might be brought to action the following morning. The men remained at their battle-stations and the fleet rushed onward beneath the star-lit Mediterranean skies.

The fleet was now steaming in close formation, the screening destroyers in the van being about two miles ahead of the battleships. At 10:30 P. M., one of the leading destroyers saw a dimly-lighted warship to port. Wary of closing in, lest she be caught in a searchlight beam and blasted by heavy guns, the destroyer wirelessed the flagship. Admiral Cunningham immediately ordered the squadron to change course toward the unknown vessel.

Suddenly other vessels were detected on the starboard bow. Quickly the destroyer *Greyhound* turned on her searchlight. There, brilliantly silhouetted against the blackness and at incredibly short range, was the Italian heavy cruiser *Fiume*. An instant later the 15-inch guns of the *Warspite, Valiant* and *Barham* dealt her a terrible blow. The *Fiume* seemed to explode in one enormous flash of flame. Her 8-inch turrets were torn from their foundations and were hurled high aloft. Her hull was riven to pieces and she lay helpless and partially submerged. The searchlight switched to the next Italian ship, the cruiser *Zara.* Again the 15-inch guns flamed in the night, and under the killing blow the *Zara* broke apart, demolished. At the same moment the British battleships' after batteries were sinking the vessel which had first been sighted. She proved to be the cruiser *Pola,* which had been crippled by torpedoes during the air attacks of the afternoon.

For a moment there was silence. Then, hurtling through the night at forty knots, came an Italian destroyer charge. Closing in, they launched a swarm of torpedoes, wheeled and dashed off into the night. Instantly, the British battleships turned away to present as small a target as possible. The maneuver succeeded, and the torpedoes churned swiftly past without finding a target. At the same time the British directed a heavy fire at the destroyers, sinking two of them.

Again the British turned to the westward to take up the pursuit. No further trace of the Italians was found, but during the night heavy gunfire was heard. No British warships were near the scene of this cannonading. It appeared probable that the damaged *Vittorio Veneto* had become engaged with her own cruiser and destroyer forces. Whether there were further casualties has not been revealed by the Italians, and will not be until the war is ended.

"It was not a battle," said an Italian survivor rescued by one of the British warships, "it was an Italian disaster." The battle was not only a material triumph for the British, but also a moral one. There had not been such an overwhelming victory since the battles of Manila Bay and Santiago. Two British planes were lost against at least three Italian cruisers and two destroyers, while one of Italy's most powerful battleships was severely punished.

Slowly but surely the British fleet has whittled down the naval power of the Empire's enemies. In addition, the blockade of Germany and Italy has deprived those countries of numerous strategic raw materials formerly obtained from overseas. It has been a tremendous task, and it has been well done.

To some, who visualize modern warfare in terms of vast numbers of marching men, with their tanks, lorries and guns, the expectation that sea-power will play a decisive part in determining the outcome of the second World War may seem unwarranted. They find it difficult to realize how enormous armies can be affected by the movements of ships hundreds or even thousands of miles away. Some of the methods used by the British navy to wear down the enemy have already been indicated. Admittedly, today the task of making the blockade effective and starving the Axis powers of raw materials is more difficult than formerly, for Germany has gained control of many regions that were unaccessible to her in the last war. Yet the blockade prevents her from obtaining many needed commodities, and in the end should be a decisive factor.

It is not always possible, of course, to judge present events by those of the past. There is, however, much to justify the belief that sea power, as represented by the British navy, will now as in the past, be a mighty aid in bringing about the collapse of the aggressor nations.

It is well to remember the words of Admiral Mahan. "Great Britain withstood Napoleon. She shut him off from the world, and by the same act prolonged her own powers of endurance beyond his power of aggression."

30

Hood--Bismarck

Two months after the Battle of Cape Matapan, or during the last week of May, 1941, came the extraordinary chase and destruction of the German battleship *Bismarck*. She was the pride of the German navy, and with her sister ship the *Tirpitz,* was hailed by the Germans as the most powerful fighting ship afloat. Her destruction was a terrific blow to German pride, self-esteem and prestige. The psychological effects on the German nation may well have been more important in deciding the course of the war than the military result of the loss of her striking power.

The *Bismarck*, accompanied by the new 8-inch gun cruiser *Prinz Eugen,* was first sighted in the harbor of Bergen, Norway, by reconnaissance planes of the British coastal command. It was evident that the two ships were intent on making their way to the Atlantic, probably by the favorite German route north of Iceland. Should they succeed, there could be no telling what havoc they would make of the north Atlantic convoys. It was imperative that they be intercepted and destroyed.

The Admiralty began at once to throw its net around the North Sea and the waters through which the German ships would have to pass. The 8-inch gun cruisers *Norfolk* and *Suffolk* were ordered at once to steam at full speed to Denmark Strait which separates Iceland from Greenland. Another signal went out ordering the battle cruiser *Hood,* largest fighting ship in the world, and the new battleship *Prince of Wales* to set out for the same destination.

Late in the evening of Friday, May twenty-third, Admiral Wake-Walker of the *Norfolk* flashed to the Admiralty the message that he had sighted the *Bismarck* and *Prinz Eugen* steaming under forced draft through Denmark Strait to the southwest. The Germans were only six miles distant when first sighted, but storms, snow, sleet and patches of fog reduced the visibility to one mile. The British cruisers closed in and followed the enemy, determined to keep in touch and guide the British battleships to their quarry.

Early the following morning lookouts on the *Hood* and *Prince of Wales* sighted the German ships. They were still plunging through heavy seas, pressing on at highest speed, seeking the safety of the wide waters of the Atlantic. Action was immediately joined, the big guns blasting at each other across miles of heaving, storm-tossed water.

The first round went to the Germans. A lucky hit from one of the *Bismarck's* 15-inch guns found one of the *Hood's* turret magazines, and the great ship blew up with heavy casualties. The *Prince of Wales,* in action for the first time, was damaged slightly. But the *Bismarck* did not escape unscathed. She also was hit, and at one time was seen to be on fire. Furthermore, her engines or fuel tanks had apparently been damaged, for her speed was reduced and reconnaissance planes reported that she was leaving a wake of oil.

Throughout the daylight hours of Saturday the chase continued. By nightfall the *Prince of Wales* had made good her damage and over-

taken the fleeing Germans again. When within range she opened fire and there was a short but inconclusive action. In the gathering dusk the German ships turned westward, and the British cruisers and the *Prince of Wales* swung around to follow. Then the German ships turned southward again.

Night fell and the pursuit became more difficult. But other British forces were now approaching the scene of action. Among them was the new aircraft carrier *Victorious*. While still many miles distant, her torpedo bombers flashed into the air. One of them, roaring through the murky darkness, found the *Bismarck* and struck her with an aerial torpedo.

Fleet Admiral Guenther Luetjens, aboard the *Bismarck,* must now have known that he was trapped and could escape only with extraordinary luck. By every device possible, he tried to shake off the three grim British bulldogs that followed in his wake. The weather aided him, for it grew steadily worse during Saturday night. The lookouts in the British ships strained their eyes, but visibility diminished steadily and at three o'clock Sunday morning contact was lost. The ships were then about three hundred and fifty miles southeast of the southern tip of Greenland.

As she steamed on to the south, the *Prince of Wales* gave her position to the other British forces that the admiralty had flung into the death-hunt to avenge the *Hood*. The home fleet, with the commander's flag of Admiral John C. Tovey on the *King George V*, had left its base and was steaming at high speed in a southwesterly direction from northern waters. Part of the western Mediterranean fleet, with Vice-Admiral Sir James F. Somerville's flag on the battle cruiser *Renown*, was heading northwest under forced draft from Gibraltar. Out in the Atlantic the battleships *Rodney* and *Ramilles*, which were escorting convoys, turned and raced toward the enemy from east and west. At the same time British submarines were moving in to cover German ports and harbors on the French coast where the wounded *Bismarck* might seek shelter.

The most important search of all, however, was in the air. Patrol planes from the British coastal command airports roared out over the sea, and other planes of the Royal Canadian Air Force thundered eastward from Newfoundland. At the same time Fleet Air Arm planes launched from aircraft carriers spread over the rolling north Atlantic in a ceaseless search.

Throughout Sunday and Sunday night these patrols met with no success. But at 10:30 A. M. on Monday, May twenty-sixth, an American-made Catalina plane sighted the *Bismarck* five hundred and fifty miles off Land's End, making for Brest. "There was a 40-knot wind blowing and a heavy sea running," said the Catalina's captain, "and the ship was digging her nose right in. At first we were not sure she was the *Bismarck* . . . the first we knew there were a couple of puffs of smoke near the cockpit window . . . then we were surrounded by brownish-black smoke as the *Bismarck* shot at us with everything she had . . . she looked just like one big flash."

Radio flashes sparked from the Catalina to the rest of the hunters. Nearby was the Mediterranean squadron with the aircraft carrier *Ark Royal,* from whose deck there rose a swarm of planes. At 11:15 A. M. one of her flights sighted the *Bismarck,* which was alone and still ploughing eastward. The *Prinz Eugen* had evidently left her in order to make good her own escape. At this time the *King George V* and the *Rodney* were approaching the scene, but were not sufficiently close to bring the enemy to action.

From now on contact was never lost. Acting upon reports received from the *Ark Royal,* Vice-Admiral Somerville ordered the cruiser *Sheffield* to race ahead and shadow the *Bismarck.* While the cruiser was steaming in pursuit, the *Ark Royal's* planes launched an aerial torpedo attack, but it was unsuccessful.

Shortly after 5:30 P. M. the *Sheffield* sighted the enemy and proceeded to shadow her. Within twenty minutes after word had been received that the *Sheffield* was in contact, the *Ark Royal* launched another flight of planes. Swiftly they thundered toward the enemy and delivered their attack. Two torpedoes found the mark. One hit the *Bismarck* amidships and the second struck her starboard quarter. The second one damaged the rudder and propellers and threw the giant ship out of control. Plunging wildly through the heavy seas, throwing up clouds of spray, she careened off her course and made two complete circles. Also, the *Bismarck's* speed was further reduced by these hits. Now, wounded but still a savage, snarling brute, she struggled on to the end, while the converging forces of British fighting ships closed in for the kill.

The destroyers were now sent in to launch torpedoes. During the early hours of the night a flotilla of Tribal class destroyers led by the *Cossack* (of *Altmark* fame) made contact. Between 1:20 A. M. and 1:50 A. M., these swift craft ran close aboard the *Bismarck*, and the *Cossack, Zulu, Sikh,* and *Maori* all delivered torpedoes at close range. The *Cossack* and *Maori* each hit with one torpedo. After the *Maori's* attack, the *Bismarck* was seen to be on fire.

An hour after these attacks the shadowing destroyers reported that the *Bismarck* had halted. She then was about four hundred miles due west of Brest and had been pursued by the British forces for more than seventeen hundred miles. She soon got under way again, but her speed was greatly reduced and her huge bulk moved forward at a speed of no more than eight miles an hour. Her great guns, however, apparently were not damaged.

Dawn broke at last on the morning that was to witness the death agony of the wounded monster. At daylight of May twenty-seventh the *Ark Royal* dispatched another flight of torpedo planes, but visibility was so poor that the attack was not carried through. Shortly after daylight the doomed ship snapped at the surrounding destroyers, barking viciously at them with her guns, but doing no damage.

By now the bulk of the British pursuing forces was drawing close in and, as it happened, it was the cruiser *Norfolk,* which had been one of the first to set out on the long chase, that first opened fire. Soon afterward, at about 9:00 A. M., the *King George V* and the *Rodney* came within range and immediately opened a merciless fire with their 14-inch and 16-inch guns. Under the terrible impact of the avenging battleships' broadsides, the *Bismarck's* turrets were silenced. Flames burst from her in a dozen places, jagged holes were torn in her sides and superstructure, and twisted steel and debris were hurled about her decks.

Still, because of her extraordinarily strong construction, she stayed afloat long after any other warship in existence would have been at the bottom. More torpedoes were needed to give the *coup de grace,* and at about 10:30 A. M. the cruiser *Dorsetshire* was ordered to close in and sink the German ship. The *Dorsetshire* steamed into position and launched—torpedoes. At 11:01 A. M. her work was done. The *Bismarck* settled down, water poured through the many holes beneath her water-line, and her long lean hull, smoking funnels and monumental fire-control tower sank beneath the heaving waters of the Atlantic.

The long pursuit was over. The most powerful battleship in the world had been destroyed. The *Hood* had been avenged.

Index

This is a place, person and ship index, not a subject index. Names of continents and countries that appear with great frequency are not included. For instance, America, France, England, Great Britain, Ireland, Portugal, Spain, United States are not in this index. Names of ships are in italics.

335

Index

Index

Index

Index

Index

Index

Index

343

Index